American Communities:
Between the Popular and the Political

Edited by
Lukas Etter and Julia Straub

SPELL
Swiss Papers in
English Language and Literature

Edited by
The Swiss Association of University Teachers of English
(SAUTE)

General Editor: Lukas Erne

Volume 35

American Communities:
Between the Popular and the Political

Edited by
Lukas Etter and Julia Straub

Bibliografische Information der Deutschen Nationalbibliothek

Die Deutsche Nationalbibliothek verzeichnet diese Publikation in der Deutschen Nationalbibliografie;
detaillierte bibliografische Daten sind im Internet über http://dnb.dnb.de abrufbar.

Publiziert mit Unterstützung der Schweizerischen Akademie der Geistes- und Sozialwissenschaften.

© 2017 · Narr Francke Attempto Verlag GmbH + Co. KG
Dischingerweg 5 · D-72070 Tübingen

Das Werk einschließlich aller seiner Teile ist urheberrechtlich geschützt. Jede Verwertung
außerhalb der engen Grenzen des Urheberrechtsgesetzes ist ohne Zustimmung des Verlages
unzulässig und strafbar. Das gilt insbesondere für Vervielfältigungen, Übersetzungen, Mikroverfilmungen und die Einspeicherung und Verarbeitung in elektronischen Systemen.
Gedruckt auf säurefreiem und alterungsbeständigem Werkdruckpapier.

Internet: www.narr.de
E-Mail: info@narr.de

Printed in Germany

Umschlagabbildung und Einbandgestaltung: Martin Heusser, Zürich
Illustration: © Lukas Etter

ISSN 0940-0478
ISBN 978-3-8233-8151-8

Table of Contents

Introduction	11
Eva-Sabine Zehelein (Frankfurt am Main) Community as Commodity: Of Rotary Dream Homes and Gated Geritopias as Collective Attempts to Lead a Private Life	19
Sofie Behluli (Oxford) Bonding in Bonden: A Post-Postmodernist Female Community in Siri Hustvedt's *The Summer Without Men*	43
A. Elisabeth Reichel (Basel) and Philipp Schweighauser (Basel) Folk Communities in Translation: Salvage Primitivism and Edward Sapir's French-Canadian Folk Songs	61
Pierre-Héli Monot (Munich) The One, the Many, and the Few: A Philological Problem and its Political Form	85
Dustin Breitenwischer (Freiburg im Breisgau) Creativity, Self, and Communal Being in Emerson	103
Agnieszka Soltysik Monnet (Lausanne) From Brook Farm to Burning Man: Alternative Communities in the United States	123
Christian Arnsperger (Lausanne) Communities of Reinhabitation: Bioregionalism, Biogeography, and the Contemporary North American Reflection on Sustainability	145
Roxane Hughes (Lausanne) The Common Community Made Uncommon in Brian Sousa's *Almost Gone*	165

Philipp Reisner (Duesseldorf)
Contemporary Anglo-American Drama of Exile   187

Sabin Jeanmaire (Zurich)
Timothy Findley's Community of Responsible Readers
in *Headhunter*   205

Thomas Nehrlich (Bern) and Joanna Nowotny (Zurich)
"We're not fighting for *the people* anymore – We're just *fighting*."
US-American Superhero Comics Between Criticisms of
Community and Critical Communities   223

Notes on Contributors   243

Index of Names   247

Acknowledgements

The editors of this volume would like to express their heartfelt thanks to the following individuals and institutions whose support made the SANAS 2016 Biennial Conference possible – and thus also this publication: Our conference co-organizer Ryan Kopaitich, the SANAS Board, especially Philipp Schweighauser and Ridvan Askin, Gabriele Rippl, Thomas Claviez, and our student assistants and graduate students Rahel Braunschweig, Leona Goop, Yannick Steiner, Thomas Kobel, Lobsang Gammeter, and Sarah Erard. We would like to thank Virginia Richter for her welcome speech as Dean of the Faculty of Humanities, and Miranda Joseph and Frank Kelleter for accepting our invitation to Bern and delivering an intellectually stimulating and concise keynote lecture each; both of these lectures were already scheduled for publication before we started working on the present volume.

As for financial and institutional support, we are much obliged to the US Embassy in Bern, the Swiss Academy of Humanities and the Social Sciences (SAGW), the *Mittelbauvereinigung der Universität Bern* (MVUB), and the English Department of the University of Bern. While working on this collection, we received prominent help and guidance from Lukas Erne, Martin Heusser, and Keith Hewlett, for which we are grateful. Our special thanks go to Christina Maria Koch, Michael Kühni, Carla Nyffeler, and Paulina Petracenko. Finally, our sincere appreciation is due to the anonymous Peer Reviewers, all of whom did diligent and competent work in a truly competitive time frame.

General Editor's Preface

SPELL (Swiss Papers in English Language and Literature) is a publication of SAUTE, the Swiss Association of University Teachers of English. Established in 1984, it first appeared every second year, was published annually from 1994 to 2008, and now appears three times every two years. Every second year, SPELL publishes a selection of papers given at the biennial symposia organized by SAUTE. Non-symposium volumes usually have as their starting point papers given at other conferences organized by members of SAUTE, in particular conferences of SANAS, the Swiss Association for North American Studies and SAMEMES, the Swiss Association of Medieval and Early Modern English Studies. However, other proposals are also welcome. Decisions concerning topics and editors are made by the Annual General Meeting of SAUTE two years before the year of publication.

Volumes of SPELL contain carefully selected and edited papers devoted to a topic of literary, linguistic and – broadly – cultural interest. All contributions are original and are subjected to external evaluation by means of a full peer review process. Contributions are usually by participants at the conferences mentioned, but volume editors are free to solicit further contributions. Papers published in SPELL are documented in the *MLA International Bibliography*. SPELL is published with the financial support of the Swiss Academy of Humanities and Social Sciences.

Information on all aspects of SPELL, including volumes planned for the future, is available from the General Editor, Professor Lukas Erne, Département de langue et littérature anglaises, Faculté des Lettres, Université de Genève, CH-1211 Genève 4, Switzerland, e-mail: lukas.erne@unige.ch. Information about past volumes of SPELL and about SAUTE, in particular about how to become a member of the association, can be obtained from the SAUTE website at http://www.saute.ch.

Lukas Erne

Introduction

The analysis of community has become an important research topic in the Humanities, literary studies being one of the key disciplines to engage with it in particularly productive ways (see Goldstein; Miller; Blume, Leitgeb and Rössner; Claviez). In late 2016, when the Biennial Conference of the Swiss Association for North American Studies (SANAS) took place, issues of globalization and migration pressed hard on public awareness in many countries around the globe. In the current political climate borders are being challenged or re-drawn, which makes both an everyday understanding of "community" particularly fragile and its academic theorizations all the more important. Given the acute political relevance of the topic of community and the apparent volatility of its meanings, it is necessary to take time and create spaces for contemplation. How can theories of community be usefully applied to various forms of cultural production? How do notions of "communitas" affect representations as well as critiques of society and social developments?

In the realm of popular media and culture – performances and strategies of media orchestration which by no means are exclusive to the United States – one ought to remain alert to the United States' long history of "community" both as a notion and communities in a demographic sense. Canada, too, looks back to a past where communities, their formation, co-existence, and identity politics, have always mattered. As major parts of a continent relying on immigration, both Canada and the United States have traditionally used a rhetoric of multiplicity within their nations, ever since the early days of settlement, colonization, and forced displacement.

The notion of community refers to processes of unification, of joining disparate elements, of creating a whole, but seen in their complexity, this notion is of course also related to unrulier, less homogenizing dynamics, i.e., mechanisms and processes of exclusion, marginalization, resistance, and exile. Communities can empower individuals and their voices, while also serving as reasons for war and conflict. While "community" may bear obvious positive, if not even idealistic connotations of holism, it is not an entirely inclusive concept, but also presupposes difference, otherness, subversion, or even exclusion, particularly in recent times, as Miranda Joseph's reflection on the term has shown. The arts have always been very susceptible to exactly these more vexed aspects of community. Marginalization, the social ostracizing of the individual, or the repression of entire groups have inspired creative minds at least as much as the promises of communal harmony. To a similar extent that literature and film, for example, are able to produce utopias of human bonding, they can evoke the terrors of expulsion from a community, of having to forsake one's communal identity as a member of a larger unit.

Within the discipline of American Studies, both facets of the term, its exclusive and inclusive potential, are firmly rooted in the dynamics informing revisionary approaches to literary history: Post-colonial studies, cosmopolitanism, transatlantic and transnational studies, and World Literature are just some of the approaches that over the last twenty to thirty years have produced or embedded relevant research on communities, the role of the individual within communities, and the formation of collective identities, especially in conjunction with work on difference and diversity, e.g., in the work of Homi Bhabha, Gayatri C. Spivak, and Sara Ahmed. Thus, American literature, "constantly repurposed and migratory, mutates into new forms in a global setting" (Levander 11), and as a consequence the grouping of its readers in space becomes as important as their imaginary bonds – defying spatial isolation – that Benedict Anderson had called attention to in the early 1980s and which culture theorists like Frank Kelleter have recontextualized in recent years. Rather than assuming that the nation as a whole swallows its constitutive communities, their co-existence and changing significance with regard to the individual have come to the fore. If one postulates such a thing as an "American" community to begin with, it undoubtedly has to be thought of as extending beyond, and is neither as homogeneous nor as singular as, the geographical borders allotted to it on maps. Accounts of communities today tend to be fragmented, they offer sites for resistance and they shape identity politics. Some of these narratives are familiar, others are new, and many point to the intersections between discourse and practice. Some are taken up in the contributions to the present volume, in various methodological ways, with various focal points, and without making claims of completeness. For this same reason, we left it to the authors to choose the most fitting adjective, i.e., to speak about North American, US-American/American, or Canadian and Mexican settings.

While focused on "community" in contemporary American Studies, the essays in this collection take account of developments and issues surrounding community at a moment of heightened sensitivity in many countries, certainly far beyond academia. The present collection also brings together and thereby reflects the variety of fields and approaches that have started to feed into American Studies in the past years, be it age studies, popular seriality studies, or ecocriticism. They show that more often than not, literary and other aesthetic discourses are closely entwined with other disciplines, but also bound up with emergent cultural practices as well as forms and media of popular culture, e.g., comics and TV series.

Finally, the essays explore different genres, media (e.g., literature, TV series, performance), industries (e.g., entertainment, urban planning), disciplines and discourses (e.g., literary, political, philosophical, anthropological, environmental), and practices (e.g., translation, communal living), and thus open up a somewhat panoramic view of the various levels of cultural production as well as historical contexts where "community" plays a role in current scholarship. We say "*somewhat* panoramic" with a view towards the development of the volume on the basis of a select few papers given at a specific conference; in other words, if a discussion of several topics that are equally crucial to topical notions of community (e.g., critical race, critical whiteness, critical body studies, politics of global intervention, etc.) in this volume is missing, this is due to pragmatic concerns. All contributors have, however, been willing to engage with concerns beyond their initial interest and focus, enabling a considerable breadth of topics and approaches.

The present volume begins with Eva-Sabine Zehelein's investigation into a very particular form of communal living: gated communities for privileged, mainly elderly citizens. Looking at two examples, one in the United States, the other in Canada, Zehelein shows to which extent these geritopias redefine privacy. Privacy here becomes a choice of lifestyle: The "Dream Homes" which the author studies promise individuality and the intimate privacy of "home" by beckoning, paradoxically, with the help of a branded commodity. The essay thus gives a first example of the partly contradictory implications of community and its complex relationship with individuality.

Age also plays a role in the intergenerational group of women that Siri Hustvedt's *The Summer Without Men* creates, and which Sofie Behluli discusses in her essay. Published in 2011, Hustvedt's novel counts as contemporary, for sure, but the more vexing question for Behluli is where such novels ought to be positioned with regard to postmodernism. The essay argues that the novel's representation of an all-female community reflects the torn loyalties of the post-postmodern, i.e., an affirmation of a value-based understanding of community as well as the nagging awareness of the instabilities brought about by postmodernism. Like notions of selfhood and authenticity, the claim for "community" operates with assumptions whose deconstruction it at the same time presupposes.

The third essay included in this volume, A. Elisabeth Reichel's and Philipp Schweighauser's discussion of Edward Sapir's French-Canadian folk songs, introduces a different genre, i.e., poetry; a different period, i.e., modernism; and it examines the intersection between literature and a different discipline, i.e., anthropology. The essay highlights modernism as a transnational phenomenon as well as its concomitant intercultural dimension. The authors also discuss periodical publishing as an influential platform for the success of modernism by studying works contained in *Poetry* and elsewhere. Considering aspects of translation, communication, and the folkloristic, the authors argue that the encounter between the categories of "modernist primitivism" and "salvage ethnography" resulted in a fusion – what they refer to as "salvage primitivism."

Language features prominently in Pierre-Héli Monot's contribution, which elucidates community as a "philological problem." Placing community at the heart of philological debates taking place in Europe and North America in the first half of the nineteenth century, Monot examines a transatlantic conversation between Continental hermeneutics, for example in the work of Friedrich Schleiermacher and Johann Gottfried Herder, and Transcendentalism. The nineteenth century's philological debates on community, particularism and bi-partism, intricately connected with politics of race, have shaped ensuing intellectual traditions and present-day uses of the term "community," as illustrated, for instance, by the work of Jean-Luc Nancy.

Dustin Breitenwischer's essay also focuses on nineteenth-century philosophy and aesthetic discourse by investigating the relationship between individual existence and community in the works of Ralph Waldo Emerson. With the help of a close reading of several central texts by Emerson, Breitenwischer lays bare a dense network of interconnections between creativity, utopian visions of social reform, and the crucial question of how the individual relates to the communal. In Emerson, Breitenwischer argues, the individual's place in society is experiential and processual rather than spatially rooted. Paradoxically, communal existence unfolds itself exactly in the abandonment of social relations. The self and community are thus closely entwined, but in ways that are not immediately transparent.

A famous experiment equally dating back to Emerson's time is Brook Farm, which stands at the beginning of many experiments that have sought to provide alternative models for communal life in North America. As Agnieszka Soltysik Monnet shows in her essay, religion and spirituality have, ever since the Puritans, been powerful motives to drive individuals into such alternative communities, yet they are not the only ones. A concern with environmental issues and the land has also affected the formation of intentional communities. While not always successful and indeed often romanticized in retrospect, the history of intentional communities in North America may well offer suggestions for how, on a pragmatic level, the relationship between humans and their environment can be recreated in more sustainable ways – thus the author argues.

Christian Arnsperger's contribution to the volume can be read as a companion piece to Soltysik Monnet's essay. It traces the development of bioregionalism in the United States, especially in California, in the 1960s and 1970s and beyond. Inspired by Native American practices and the idea of "inhabiting" territory that was not aligned with administrative borders, bioregionalism today refers to a practice of rethinking community as both culturally and naturally defined. The movement has always sought to avoid associations with politically dubious concepts of "soil" or homeland, Arnsperger argues. Quite the contrary: It centers around a progressive idea and may even serve as a "blueprint" for an understanding of community as biotic, and landscape as home to a variety of species.

With Roxane Hughes' piece on Brian Sousa's *Almost Gone*, a novel from 2013, the focus shifts back to literary reflections of community. Set in a Portuguese-American context, the novel depicts the challenges of communal life in relation to migration. Processes of identity formation, alienation, fragmentation of the self, and intergenerational confrontation loom large in this novel, which centers on communal existence in the face of collective dislocation and unresolved conflicts of belonging. Hughes provides a close reading of the novel's rhetoric and images with an eye toward the issue of trauma. Within the setting of the novel, she argues, community shows its ever-shifting basis and contradictory claims of (dis)connection on the individuals.

Philipp Reisner explores similar conflicts in complex and diverse social settings, but he puts the notion of exile center stage as a unifying theme that brings major contemporary plays together. His discussion of contemporary Anglophone plays by David Adjmi, Marcus Gardley, and Young Jean Lee demonstrates how religion may shape the depiction of communities. The Bible serves as a foil, adding an extra nuance of meaning to notions of "home" and "exile" that are so prominent in these plays. A theological reading of these texts, Reisner argues, enhances their philosophical concerns but also sheds light on the everyday problems and experiences which are equally fuelled by a search for answers.

Sabin Jeanmaire's essay centers on an explicitly self-reflexive text: *Headhunter* (1993), a novel by the Canadian author Thomas Findley. While other essays included in this volume exploit the utopian appeal of communities, *Headhunter* presents a dystopian vision of a psychiatric hospital in Toronto. Jeanmaire connects her observations on communities within the tense institutional setting of the hospital with a reflection on the acts of reading and story-telling and the role of the reader. She thereby alerts us to our own fragile position in a community of readers and listeners, and to how we are constantly implicated in negotiations of power.

Since the 1930s, superhero comic books have gradually become major, and exceedingly popular, forms of storytelling that invite an engagement with social and political issues. Thomas Nehrlich and Joanna Nowotny start out by tracing the development of heroism around such figures as Superman in relation to their communities, from the early twentieth century to our days. They then discuss how the conflicts depicted in contemporary superhero comic books point to deeper clashes of opposing ideologies. The representation of the relationship between superheroes and their communities as depicted in the post-9/11 United States is a mirror of social and political debates, they contend; it asks readers to diversify their conceptions of the "heroic" and to question several of the beliefs and values superheroes have classically stood for.

Lukas Etter and Julia Straub

References

Ahmed, Sara. *On Being Included: Racism and Diversity in Institutional Life.* Durham: Duke University Press, 2012.
Anderson, Benedict. *Imagined Communities: Reflections on the Origins and Spread of Nationalism.* London: Verso, 2006.
Bhabha, Homi. *The Location of Culture.* 1994. London: Routledge, 2004.
Blume, Hermann, Christoph Leitgeb, and Michael Rössner, eds. *Narrated Communities – Narrated Realities.* Leiden: Brill, 2015.
Claviez, Thomas, ed. *The Common Growl: Toward a Poetics of Precarious Community.* New York: Fordham University Press, 2016.
Goldstein, Philip. *Communities of Cultural Value.* Lanham: Lexington Books, 2001.
Joseph, Miranda. *Against the Romance of Community.* Minneapolis: University of Minnesota Press, 2002.
Kelleter, Frank, ed. *Media of Serial Narrative.* Columbus: Ohio State University Press, 2017.
Levander, Caroline F. "Introduction." *Where Is American Literature?* Malden: Wiley Blackwell, 2013. 1-31.
Miller, J. Hillis. *Communities in Fiction.* New York: Fordham University Press, 2015.
Spivak, Gayatri C. *Nationalism and the Imagination.* London: Seagull, 2010.

Community as Commodity: Of Rotary Dream Homes and Gated Geritopias as Collective Attempts to Lead a Private Life

Eva-Sabine Zehelein

This essay employs two examples – the Rotary Dream Homes (Calgary, Alberta) and the 55+ community The Villages (Orlando, Florida) – to illustrate contemporary lifestyle migration into places/spaces which cater to the desire for harmonious living in a community of the similarly minded based on an individualized lifestyle package and boxed as real estate investment. Organized as CIDs (Common Interest Housing Developments) with elaborate CC&Rs (Covenants, Conditions and Restrictions) to eliminate internal friction or conflict, these communities tend to produce an extraordinarily controlled environment potentially depriving residents of some freedoms and liberties. Chaparral Valley, Harmony and The Villages (the world's largest retirement community) exemplify the argument that in-, but at the same time exclusive mechanisms are at work in many lifestyle communities where landscape and housing as well as collective memory are created by developers and forged into a brand, a master narrative of exceptionality and lifestyle. The design of an enticing and all-encompassing comfort zone inside the perimeters contributes to segregation from "the world outside" and might be read as the revocation of the social contract in order to engage in a collective attempt to lead a private life.

Lifestyle communities as collective attempts at private, individualized and harmonious living are a remarkable concept. Usually planned, constructed, and at least in the early years governed by developers, they are often advertised as brands with master narratives of exclusivity and com-

American Communities: Between the Popular and the Political. SPELL: Swiss Papers in English Language and Literature 35. Ed. Lukas Etter and Julia Straub. Tübingen: Narr, 2017. 19-41.

fort and cater to special interest groups seeking individuality and individualized lifestyles in a reliable real estate product. This ideal of home and/as investment comes with an elaborate set of rules and regulations securing, yet also curbing your individuality and individualized lifestyle in many ways. The following will employ the examples of the (not age segregated) Rotary Dream Homes and their communities in Calgary, Alberta (Canada), as well as the notorious 55+ retirement community The Villages near Orlando, Florida (USA) in order to investigate this phenomenon.

I.

July 2013. The Calgary Stampede. In the midst of the fun fair with lots of food and games and music and people and cowboy hats and "Yeehah!" Rotary was raffling a Dream Home. And in the shadow of the iconic Saddle Dome right between a beer stand, Bratwurst, and souvenir vendors, there it was: a single family home, the Dream Home. And the Stampede visitors could tour it.[1] While queuing for nearly thirty minutes and experiencing "corporeality of movement" (Urry and Larsen 21), *vulgo*: waiting in line and shuffling forward, fully immersed in the whiffs of various fragrances, sweat, garlic, and alcohol emanating from the fellows in front and behind, I tried to grasp what I was about to engage with. In its 101st year, the 2013 Stampede attracted 1.1 million visitors (Duncan n. pag.). Founded as an "agro fair" (an agricultural exhibition), it is "The Greatest Outdoor Show on Earth" (Calgary Stampede) with the world's largest and – with more than 2 million Canadian dollars in prize money – also the most lucrative of all rodeos worldwide. Here, Calgary, today a hub for international (oil) companies, cultivates its folkloristic heritage built on cattle, where a Marlboro-style cowboy riding into the sunset can still contribute to a collective self-image, self-marketing, and self-narrative as "the Stampede City" or "Cowtown."[2] The Stampede is where the Alberta Oil Sands meet the good old cowboy of the prairies. This myth is in itself somewhat problematic, some critics claim. And the glorification of the men and women who work(ed) with cattle can turn rodeo into a creepy event reeking of testosterone

---

[1] Rotary and AVI have been raffling Dream Homes for twenty-one years (2016 Stampede Rotary Dream Home).

[2] Various sports teams are called The Stampeders, e.g., the football team (The Calgary Stampeders).

probably not experienced ever since Hemingway wrote about his admiration for the Spanish corrida. "Save the Animals"-activists and many people with a weak stomach and a different set of ethics and aesthetics have been sick over Hemingway and probably also at the Stampede – and added some gall, too: How can anyone defend this torture, this terrible treatment of animal and man, much too dangerous, uncivilized, and cruel? What machismo! What an archaic concept and performance of masculinity! How can anyone like or enjoy such a spectacle (cf. Adams; Fricker; Labchuk)?

Right at the heart of this themed site encompassed by the polyphony of multifarious discourses about capital, consumption, nostalgically enshrined heritage, collective memory, and identity construction, Rotary[3] had set up its lottery booths and the big trophy: The Dream Home. When I had finally made it through the front door, I realized that there was no way I could philander on my own and imagine living in this interior design. Visitors had to stay in line, walk along roped and undulating paths from room to room and floor to floor. And around every other corner, there were sales representatives happy to answer questions – and surveilling that no one spit on the floor, or rubbed greasy hands on white walls, or used the non-functioning lavatories. Following the prescribed path through this house-as-exhibition I was reminded of Tuan's contention that "[a]rchitectural space reveals and instructs" (114), but also of the "museumification" of culture (Macdonald 2). Huyssen has so pertinently described the museum as a "catalyst for the articulation of tradition and nation, heritage and canon" (13), now turned "a hybrid space somewhere between public fair and department store" (15). And if museums are also "global symbols through which status and community are expressed" (2) and where experiences of the individual consumer are embodied (Macdonald 7), then this was a special museum indeed. Here, culture was materialized, a modern way of seeing and comprehending the world "as if it were an exhibit" was arranged (Macdonald 7). The visitor was transformed into a more or less passive and other-directed performer instructed how to behave (no food, no beverages), where to walk and where not to take a seat. Walking through or past living and dining room, kitchen, and three bedrooms, and glimpsing at 2.5 baths she experienced a total value of 750,000 Canadian dol-

---

[3] Rotary was established in 1905 in Chicago by Paul Harris, an attorney, as a space where professionals from diverse fields can exchange ideas and experiences, and build friendships. By now, the organization has more than 1.2 million members around the globe. Service for the community is at the heart of their activities, the motto: "Service Above Self" (Rotary International).

lars (2016 Stampede Rotary Dream Home), not, though, as in a classical museum, of "things past," but of a twenty-first-century architectural phenomenon, displaying everything that was state of the art: kitchen and bathroom appliances, TV room equipment, and a fetishized built-in coffee machine. 2,330 square feet of built living space, completely furnished and decorated, were on display.[4] This house presented to the visitor a staged museal experience framed as a shrine-meets-market-driven-product,[5] with appliances and architectural features as objects of our gazes, where we were invited to perform rituals of adoration and reverence. All co-present people could launch an individual mental soul-searching: Do I like the floor plan? Do I like the appliances? Can I imagine myself living here? The individual performances of gazing were "framed by cultural styles, circulating images and texts of this and other places, as well as personal experiences and memories"; also involved were "cultural skills of daydreaming and mind travelling" (Urry and Larsen 17). I overheard some conversations: "Awesome!", "Beautiful!", "How nice! Oh, look at that patio, Jack!", "I like this big bath tub, honey, but where would I store all my clothes?", "These cabinets are really made of solid wood!", "And this is real granite here in the kitchen and bathroom!", "Look at this really gorgeous built-in coffee maker and beverage center, Charlene!" The visitors were emotionally connecting to the displayed objects, but also critically engaging with them. This architectural artefact did not just (re)present cultural identity, but created and framed it. The house was the perfect "site and testing ground for reflections on temporality and subjectivity, identity and alterity" (Huyssen 16) where people in Calgary, gathering for a special spatio-temporal moment of communal performance-experience (as theorized, e.g., by Kirshenblatt-Gimblett[6]), were paralleling their individual dreams with the one fabricated and staged here.

This Dream I could gamble for was an odd dream. It was other-created; it was someone else's idea of what my dream of a home might be. Or it was someone else's idea of what the average Canadian might consider an ideal home. The house was not an expression of anyone's

---

[4] The house-prize would come without furniture and TVs, but with all appliances.

[5] "I see the totality of the museum as a stage setting that prompts visitors to enact a performance of some kind" (Duncan in Marstine 10).

[6] "Exhibitions are fundamentally theatrical, for they are how museums perform the knowledge they create" (3).

personality or style and taste and family history à la Bachelard.⁷ It was a stage setting, a mass-produced generic ensemble, a house waiting to become a home. The Dream Home was and is also a commercial(ized) dream. It was and is not naïve and merely altruistic, but business wrapped in a wonderful narrative of dreams come true, of a better world, of benevolence and charity. The experience was premeditated and arranged and the visitor was lured to make this Dream her own and to let the gaze also glide over the advertising – a not too subtle form of product placement. Every year, all crafts donate their parts and place advertising all through the house. The concept of the house is created by the developer AVI who constructs and sells similar houses on a variety of lots around Calgary. So even if you did not win this home, you could consider buying a similar one from AVI, or maybe just the granite table top or the walnut cabinets or the built-in coffee maker. It might be safe to assume that even if some of the features may not have been everybody's cup of coffee, everybody would have accepted the prize and then, maybe, sold it. Right at the exit door there were more Rotary booths. If the product had stimulated your dreams and convinced you that it was worth your gambling money, then here was your next move: Buy lottery tickets.

Here, on the Calgary Stampede fair grounds, an epitome of twenty-first century consumer culture, where people were spending substantial sums for quick gratification – fun, food, alcohol (at 6 Canadian dollars a can), and entertainment – stood a Dream Home, "'the official story' of a particular way of thinking at a particular time for a particular group of people." This "time capsule" (Dion in Marstine 31) consisted of a house with various discursive frames: architectural artifact, museal space and commercial real estate product, potential home, as well as the first prize in a big gamble, a lottery.⁸ The Dream Home came in seven parts on a flatbed truck and would be erected on a designated lot in a suburban

---

⁷ "On whatever theoretical horizon we examine it, the house image would appear to have become the topography of our intimate being. [O]ur house is our corner of the world. [. . .] An entire past comes to dwell in a new house" (Bachelard xxxvi, 4, 5).

⁸ The concept of a lottery is to entice you to gamble, to invest small money in a promise of big gain; against the odds, with minimal chances of winning anything. Lotteries have been called a "tax on the mathematically inept" – since only those who cannot calculate the risk of losing buy lottery tickets and thus accept to support a state or institution with an amount analogous to a voluntary tax (Perez and Humphreys 936). There are claims that typically less affluent people participate in a lottery and spend disproportionate amounts of their money. This may be true. However, in the case here I argue that many other people also bought into the lottery to support a good cause. The investment is thus not so much a tax as a donation.

development named Chaparral Valley. So one did not only win the house, but also a new community. Chaparral Valley offered you, the potential winner, a community and a comfortable family home, a merchandized product usually for sale, today a great trophy. In a country which prides itself on its size, the vastness of nature and untamed wilderness, here we find tiny lots in a preconceived landscape design for sale. Your dream home had to be either in the style of a Craftsman, a Prairie, or a Colonial house as specified in the architectural guidelines provided by the developer Genstar. This design was not the result of a communal decision of inhabitants or buyers of lots, but the developer's decision and vision – after all, Genstar, as the company motto has it, "bring[s] land to life" (Genstar homepage). According to the guidelines:

> The community of Chaparral Valley will be a continuation of the early western heritage theme found throughout the successful Lake Chaparral community. The detailing used on the entry treatments, signage, amenity features and the exteriors of the homes will all borrow from the popular architectural styles of the early 20th century. By utilizing traditional architectural flair the Chaparral Valley area will also acquire the warmth and friendliness of days gone by. (Genstar, *Chaparral Valley* n. pag.)

The amalgamation of comfort through tradition and heritage, and easy identification and solidity through references to a rather unspecified (collective) past evoke an emotional package of "the good old days" of shared memories, of warmth, friendliness, and communal belonging. Chaparral Valley is a pre-planned construction effort financed, organized, and (at least in the early phases) controlled by for-profit companies. This suburban neighborhood is a commercial product with a fabricated narrative of tradition, roots, and heritage as ersatz for what is sorely lacking: tradition, roots, and heritage. What Bellah terms "community of memory" is absent here – as in all lifestyle enclaves:

> a community is a group of people who are socially interdependent, who participate together in discussion and decision making, and who share certain practices [which see] that both define the community and are nurtured by it. Such a community is not quickly formed. It almost always has a history and so is also a community of memory, defined in part by its past and its memory of its past. (Bellah et al. 333)

This trend, to sell a finished, structured/regulated real estate product and brand it as a "community," is widespread in North America, especially in the USA. Since the 1990s we have seen the significant increase of such communities generally organized as CIDs (Common Interest Housing Developments) and often considered as "private governments." This trend is most pronounced in the USA and, less, yet increasingly so, in Canada (cf. Loomis). In the USA, 68 million people lived in CIDs in 2015, which is 21.1% of the US population; 51-55% of 2015's 338,000 common-interest communities were homeowners' associations (Community Associations Institute). According to the 2009 American Housing Survey, there were 10.76 million units located in access controlled communities. Gated communities accounted for 11% of all housing.[9] In Canada, 10.3% of all dwellings in 2014 were part of a condominium development – a significant increase from 8.9% the previous year (Statistics Canada Table 203-0027).

All CIDs bring forth a community of land owners. CIDs are characterized primarily by three parameters: automatic membership in the Homeowners Association, and thus, secondly, acceptance of and adherence to a very detailed catalogue of so-called "CC&Rs" (Covenants, Conditions and Restrictions),[10] and, thirdly, common ownership of land and property. All CIDs organize and finance many municipal tasks themselves: Lawn work, pool-maintenance, snow removal, trash pickup, etc., and many services are contracted with the municipality. Instead of sliding down the slippery slope of "private *vs* public space," it has been suggested we conceptualize the nature of the CID as a club community where local public goods are provided by the HOA and financed via ownership based fees establishing exclusive use rights (Cséfalvay and

---

[9] The highest number of gated communities in the EU can be found in Poland. Warsaw alone in 2007 already had four hundred (Wyczalkowska and Janda-Debek 12). Security, cleanliness and social segregation, plus investment seem to be the motivating factors and sales pitches here (Johnsson; Polanska; Gadecki). In this context and in this form, we may rightly speak of communities of exclusion and othering. Cf. Cséfalvay and Webster: "What has been found in the European comparison is that gated communities seem to flourish in countries with a relative low level of economic development; moderate redistribution and a moderate public sector; highly centralized financing of local governments; low taxing and spending power at the local level; high social inequalities; and a high density in metropolitan areas" (306).

[10] A sample of the Chaparral Valley Restrictive Covenant specifies that "no fence or retaining wall shall be constructed on the front yards of the lots, exempt as permitted by Genstar in its sole discretion," that "no satellite dish over 18 inches in diameter, clothes line, television antenna, short wave radio antenna or any communication antennae of any size or type shall be installed, erected or be allowed to remain on any of the Lots. [N]o carport, playhouse, gazebo, shed or other storage structure shall be erected on any of the Lots" (Anon., "Restrictive Covenant" n. pag.). And this is just a minute excerpt from the real covenant a home buyer has to sign.

Webster 296[11]), therewith creating micro-territories at the intersection between market, state, and civil society (Woo and Webster 2541). In the case of gated communities, less ideologically charged also called "guarded housing units" (Glasze et al. 6), we have to add separations such as fences, walls or hill-like constructions, and always access restriction. McKenzie speaks of "American privatopia,"[12] a "hybrid of [Ebenezer] Howard's utopian ideas and American privatism" (12) and Blakely and Snyder, who have shaped the academic debate and discourse, of "Fortress America" (vii).[13]

With John Locke, man in the state of nature has the right to property, and enters into a social community in order to secure his life and property, a community which is based on the consent of all its members (think of life, liberty, and pursuit of property). The case is the reverse with the CIDs: Here the rules exist first, just as much as the physical realization, a form of ghost town, and then the concept is sold to individual people who live in this setting, according to rules which have been pre-set, and not passed by the group of residents by mutual agreement. McKenzie puts it nicely: "[A] CID is a prefabricated frame-

---

[11] The conceptual difficulties caused by terms such as "private" and "public" cannot be addressed here. Studies such as those by Webster and Glasze, in a mélange of public goods theory, economic theory of clubs, and property rights theory, argue against any simplistic understanding of "public space" à la Habermas and against the easy dichotomy between "private" and "public." Instead, they suggest various "publics" according to usage of space (Webster speaks of "public realms") and degrees of "privateness," and understand private neighborhoods – building on James Buchanan's work – as "clubs."

[12] I did my first research on this topic in 2008, right around the time when Lehman Brothers came down and the financial crisis began. For years, the real estate market had been waxing strong, also because of sub-prime mortgages and toxic financial products such as CDOs (Collateralized Debt Obligations) traded around the world. Americans had been buying and flipping homes on a large scale and on credit. Revisiting the theme in 2016, it appears to me that the CID market has recovered and prospered in the USA and Canada, and budded in Europe. For Germany, Arkadien (Potsdam), Prenzlauer Gärten (Berlin), Central Park Residence (Leipzig), and The Seven (Munich) are some random examples of forms of gated communities. Then, most academic literature came from US scholars and was about the USA. Meanwhile, a veritable proliferation of work has applied American scholarship to other parts of the world, predominantly to South East Asian and African countries. This has met with criticism. For example, C. P. Pow argues for a way to "decentre the dominance of the LA School model of urban fragmentation and its ingrained dystopian orientation" (473) and aims to "complicate the overcoded mono-logic of urban gating and segregation" (476).

[13] Vesselinov et al. speak of sites and vehicles of urban neoliberalism, a transnational gating machine that transforms cities into fortresses. See also the classics by Atkinson and Blandy (*Gated Communities*), Setha Low (*Behind the Gates*), or Bagaeen and Uduku, or more recent articles such as by Lai, Le Goix and Webster, Radetskiy et al., or Tanulku.

work for civil society in search of a population" (145). The state of nature is here closer to Genesis than Lockean philosophy; in the beginning, there was the developer, who creates a community on a piece of land – the houses, the infrastructure, the rules and regulations – and then the people are put into this setting with an "interlocking of spatial, legal and social system" (Le Goix and Webster, "Inequality" 619).[14]

The CC&Rs regulate primarily what is prohibited. They regulate the three "Ps": people, pets, and parking (Barton and Silverman 140). They transform the liberal minded into a NIMBY (Not In My Back Yard), who vehemently opts for the Banana principle (Build Nothing Anywhere Near Anything) (Duany et al. x). By necessity, one is tempted to say, these rules and regulations bear interesting fruit, which is devoured with relish by the CID critics: In Santa Ana, a retiree received a warning by her condo-association because she had kissed a friend good-bye on her own private driveway. Details of the event and the performance of the schmoozing active adults are not known (Louv A2; see also Stuart or Klein).[15] Why do at times rather bizarre conflicts such as this emerge? It seems that we witness in many areas the shift from fate communities to communities of choice. In times of conspicuous consumption, people as "consumer-voters" are often "voting with their feet" (419), as Charles Tiebout has argued. They identify their key needs and priorities, and shop for a place-centered lifestyle concept that comes with a bundle of goods and amenities (Florida 11). "Communities as commodities" or "commudities" are, in slight variation of Lewis Mumford (in Fishman x), topographical manifestations of a collective attempt to lead a private life. A dream of collective bliss based on private prop-

---

[14] CIDs in general do have political clout. Two aspects are crucial here: Over the last decades, all Republican presidential candidates and their running mates have campaigned in retirement communities such as The Villages. Secondly, all municipalities are financed to large extents by the local tax payers. A municipality thus has a vital interest in zoning regulations which encourage a certain clientele and discourage another from moving in. Only those who can actively help generate a good tax revenue and at the same time do not cause too many expenses are desirable new neighbors. Cf. for example, McKenzie; Rüb; Le Goix and Vesselinov 2134.

[15] Century Woods Estates in west LA advertises itself as "a contemporary tribute to human aspiration [. . .] created especially for individuals of supreme accomplishment." A single family home with three bedrooms can sell at 3 million dollars. Every homeowner who desires to celebrate this supreme accomplishment with a party of more than fifteen guests has to apply for permission from the residents' association (Anon., "Government by the nice" 25).

erty; an interesting paradox.[16] Zygmunt Bauman's romanticized depiction of community holds to a point and describes fairly well the fundamental dilemma at the core of all these communities: They promise a focus on the individual and its needs and freedom or autonomy, yet at the same time deprive it of sovereignty or autonomy by subjecting it to strict rules and regulations, norms and sanctions. You cannot freely decide whether, where, and what kind of patio to add to your house, or at what time to pull the trash can to the curb.[17] People subject themselves to additional restrictions to their freedom and liberty on the basis of pragmatic decision-making strategies: Stable or increasing real estate assessments, prestige, comfort, and high recreation value combined with a minimum of responsibilities and household chores in a group of similarly minded and affluent neighbors. Underneath this analytically graspable surface, however, there lurks a desire; a desire to return to the ideal of the harmonious (small town) neighborhood idyll characterized by togetherness and solidarity, of one's childhood, or maybe of a TV reality (e.g., Hayden 184). Even though today's American urbanization rate is comparable to that of Spain or France (82%[18]), the topos of the small town or home town has not lost its appeal. Connotations might be: transgenerational family roots, belonging, rural or suburban harmony (some might claim this is mutually exclusive), peace, and coziness through proximity and face-to-face contact between similarly minded and extended families. A cluster of emotions is projected onto a smallish geographical area and triggers lifestyle migration.

If we consider that the 2016 Rotary Dream Home in Calgary will be situated in "Harmony," we see that a market is, indeed, catering to a projected desire for higher quality of life. "Live in Harmony" (Live in Harmony) is more than the planned community's slogan, but a holistic human aspiration, the wish "to live, learn, work and play" (Live in Harmony), to cater to all senses and all socio-demographic groups. To build the perfect environment for people to "[re]connect with what matters most" and to find their individual "work-life balance," the developer and the team "sat at a kitchen table and got honest about the vision of what community could be" (Live in Harmony) – a city built from scratch, speaking to a perceived communal desire by merging myth,

---

[16] Dolores Hayden in *Building Suburbia* argues that the conflict between residents, builders, and developers is at the heart of suburbia's history (9).

[17] For a more detailed depiction of the protean character of CIDs cf. Zehelein 24-28.

[18] Urban population (% of total). Germany: 75%, Spain: 80%, Euro zone: 76%, Japan: 93%, France: 80% (The World Bank).

imagination, landscape, and architectural design, sketched out and constructed by a profit-oriented and market-focused company, couched in the folksy, down-to-earth, rustic image of the gathering around the kitchen table. What D. Stanley Eitzen once called "the atrophy of social life" finds here its potential antidote – rethinking urban design, bringing people together, investing in infrastructure to facilitate communal activities (15). But this is a planned community, a vision of a self-enclosed gathering of similarly minded who escape to this space for (individually defined) self-fulfillment and a new life, where recreation, rediscovery of the self and of one's desires are possible in the context of transgenerational communal living. Harmony is strongly branded[19] as a modern lifestyle community-product aspiring for holistic planning and sustainability, spreading a whiff of the New Urbanist smart-growth vision formulated for example by Andrés Duany and Elizabeth Plater-Zyberk as a walkable town accompanied by the battle cry: "Neighborhoods or nothing!" (243), of Jane Jacobs with her call for density and diversity to make a community work, or even of David Owen's tripartite credo: live smaller, live closer, drive less (46-48). The center is envisioned as a "bustling European village" (Live in Harmony), pedestrian friendly, with quaint mom-and-pops, and transgenerational gathering places, surrounded by a lake, a golf course, and beautiful landscape; close to Calgary's downtown, yet a bucolic peaceful retreat.[20] Tuan was right: "[I]dentity of place is achieved by dramatizing the aspirations, needs, and functional rhythms of personal and group life" (178). And in Harmony, the target residents will perform an ideal of individualized serene living with a rich variety of amenities and face-to-face contact, in (alleged) communal togetherness.

Although the concept "community" carries a deceptive quality of harmony and homogeneity which, in fact, rarely exists, and although the effectivity of the invocation of community is often "conservative, disciplining, and exclusionary" (Joseph xviii) – here there is a vision and narrative of just this looking for buyers and performers. Eager for internal

---

[19] "The significance of developer brand indicates a preference for living among like people, with brand being a surrogate for income and preference for exclusivity and quality" (Woo and Webster 2550). Cf. Kerr and Oliver.

[20] The fact that Harmony will be situated in the immediate vicinity of Springbank Airport, Alberta's second busiest airport, might make us wonder a little about the "Live in Harmony" theme. Springbank is a 24-hour, busy, and growing airport for smaller aircraft (Code A and Code B planes), with more than 150,000 aircraft movements in 2015 (Springbank Airport).

harmony and cohesion, these communal efforts automatically fall prone to measures of exclusion and potential discrimination:

> [R]esidents and developers manipulate what is perceived as a positive value and employ it to exclude and identify others, often with negative and even racist consequences. [. . .] Further, these 'purified communities' redefine community as an intensely private realm, and in doing so, reinforce the boundaries of social acceptability and group acceptance in narrow, and discriminatory ways. (Low, "A multi-disciplinary framework" 198-99)

II.

Harmony's most prominent and successful predecessors in collective lifestyle-oriented living are retirement or "active adult communities" for "Silverliners" or "Golden Agers," people aged "55 or better." And if we consider a number of trends, then the constant proliferation of 55+ communities is not the least surprising: "geriatrification" of Western societies, diversification of lifestyles, decrease of transgenerational geographical family togetherness, a high average degree of health and wealth.[21] The 78 million Baby Boomers, born between 1946 and 1964, have had an impact on society that started with their childhood and continues through their transition into retirement. For the real estate business, a huge market has opened up since the late 1980s which has been catered to by the construction of retirement communities. The pioneer in this segment on a large and professional scale was Del Webb with Sun City in Arizona. In 1960 Sun City opened its gates; by 1977 it was the seventh largest city in Arizona with 40,000 residents. Webb then built an additional settlement, Sun City West, for another 30,000 retirees. Today, Sun City, Sun City West, and Sun City Grand are home to nearly 80,000 people (American FactFinder).

The pensioners' general preferences are predictable: nice warm weather, low taxes, excellent health care and medical services, good infrastructure (connections to airports and Interstates), stable or increasing real estate prices as well as a low maintenance lifestyle. Add to this comfort zones of recreation (often golf), entertainment, distraction, harmony, and occasionally visions of eternal youth (cf. e.g. Bekhet et al.;

---

[21] In 2015, some 83 million Americans were "55 and better" – 27.5% of a population of 321.4 million (US Census Bureau).

Crisp et al.; Graham and Tuffin).[22] These soft factors are extremely powerful and feed into the emotionally charged concept and performed practice of community.

A fascinating contemporary example is the world's biggest retirement community, the gated geritopia (Blechman) The Villages – "Florida's Friendliest Hometown" near Orlando (The Villages). In 2016, The Villages was again America's fastest growing retirement community with a population of 110,000; by now, it is the size of Manhattan and has more golf cars than New York has taxis (Olorunnipa). The Villages is, like all other new developments, without a usable past, the members cannot re-member in a process of collective memory; the past is constructed by the creator/developer/owner in language and brick as a biographical narrative in the attempt to forge roots and identification. Centrally located, we find the large water basin styled as Ponce de León's fountain of youth, because, according to local legend, León came through this very area during his famous quest. León's fate falls prey to selective memory or an early form of Alzheimer's. The mantra repeated all over in the promotional videos and materials are variations of one theme: rejuvenation in the Golden Years. You can be anyone you want to be. You can reinvent yourself. You stay young, healthy, energetic, fun-loving, and sex-loving[23] etc. No one anywhere mentions issues such as health plans and treatment facilities, strollers, hearing aids, incontinence, blood pressure-related issues such as cardiac arrests or strokes, diabetes, dementia, or, for that matter, death. Instead, "everything you could possibly want, need, or dream of doing in your retirement years, is just a golf car ride away" (The Villages). There is fun, sun, and entertainment galore (Rüb), in a garden Eden regained, in *"the* place to live" (The Villages promotional DVD, 2008). Active Adults go to great pains for a special and exclusive lifestyle, which also incorporates at times negations of age and aging, and attempts to deny one's mortality. What happens here is the perversion of centripetal forces, the creation of ho-

---

[22] The National Association of Home Builders (NAHB) and the MetLife Mature Market Institute (MMI) jointly completed a major research project that closely examined the 55+ population – many Boomers as well as older age cohorts – and their preferences in homes and communities, as well as the housing industry's response to consumer demand. The first part of the research, *Housing for the 55+ Market: Trends and Insights on Boomers and Beyond,* was released in April 2009, the second, *55+ Housing: Builders, Buyers, and Beyond,* in September 2009. One of the most comprehensive reports dedicated to this market segment, the research included analysis of data from the most recent American Housing Surveys (AHS) from the US Census Bureau.

[23] A number of reports over the years have stated that the degree of STDs (sexually transmitted diseases) has risen decisively among the elderly. Cf. e.g. McCormack.

mogeneity which simultaneously excludes life "out there." You can choose a limited number of homes, and one of the pitch selling arguments is, of course: "We guarantee that your home will be surrounded by a product line just like yours" (The Villages promotional DVD, 2008). 98% of the population identify as white, and social status comes via the preselective tool of real estate prices. One indicator is the omnipresent golf car which can easily cost some 15,000 US dollars (used!) (The Villages News). The Villages is quasi autonomous, provides all services and amenities and thus minimizes the inhabitants' contact to the outside world. Most of the trips a senior makes are within The Villages, and all can be made with the golf car (Yoffe). All this taken together seems to create an enticing comfort zone, so constitutive of the common definition of the ideal community, leveling difference to prevent friction and to create harmony, friendliness, and peaceful neighborhoods, yet bordering on an eerie Stepford-meets-Little-Boxes-meets-Disneyland stereo-type.

The Villages is furthermore a company town and family operated with a highly complex organizational structure; the Morse family owns the local newspaper, radio station, and TV channel, and holds a controlling interest in Citizens First Bank. The holding company "is the landlord of more than 4.5 million square feet of commercial real estate, including dozens of restaurants and retailers"; and they sell homes, too (Olorunnipa). Andrew Blechman has summarized it very succinctly: "You name it; they probably own it" (111). Visitors receive a pass with a bar code with a "best before" date which functions like a visa; it determines the maximum number of days you are allowed to stay on the premises: thirty days per year (The Villages n. pag.). Age segregation is real. One chops off one's roots and revokes the trans-generational contract. This contract is substituted by highly regulated life with common interest groups to celebrate the Golden Years individually, fueled by the silent hope that the Golden Years might be Golden Decades. Life is in the *hic et nunc. Carpe diem*. 55+ communities are thus a discursive lifestyle practice of ex- as well as inclusion based on enclaves of real estate property, drawing disciplining lines as well as discriminatory borders.

III.

It remains to be seen whether this growth of geritopias will continue on this scale. The Baby Boomer cohort is very diverse in itself, and so is its retirement experience. Some recent analyses show a trend towards lifestyle or retirement communities in Costa Rica (Guanacaste), Guatemala, and Ecuador (Cuenca) – a new form of transnational mobility and agency, a form of geographic arbitrage where people sell their labor in high-cost labor countries and then buy labor power, goods, and services in low-cost labor countries (Hayes; Van Noorloos and Steel). However, lifestyle migration is not a phenomenon restricted to snowbirds or empty-nesters. The general idea to shop for a lifestyle, and to express oneself via belonging to an ex- and inclusive "commudity," has not abated. There is a future for Harmony.

All CID communities, whether age segregated, themed, or not, are first and foremost investment projects and lifestyle products. They are created/constructed by developers, architects, and builders, and sold to consumers. The sales pitch is a combination of exclusive assets such as leisure, golf, and other amenities. These are priced into the real estate as premiums. Thus they cater to a particular segment of a buyers' market – comparable income/affluence, similar leisure activities – and create or predetermine at least a thin veneer of homogeneity and communal interest. Nonetheless and indisputably, internal difference and friction often exist despite all efforts to curtail them via elaborate CC&Rs. These found an alternative world whose rules and regulations tend to be more restrictive than any encountered in life "outside": "We have a generation in this country that doesn't know you should be able to paint your house any color you want" (Louv in McKenzie 144). CIDs are topographic manifestations of strategic alliances bundling a number of interests many individuals have; they are thus not only a constant process, but also a number of communities/shared relationships in one. Community in this case is very space/place centered, a place onto which – with Bauman[24] – a cluster of emotions and fantasies, dreams and desires is projected, boxed as a real estate product often with an amenities package that comes at an extra premium; a "commudity."

During the summer of 2013, Calgary had been hit by a terrible flood of the Bow River and its tributaries. The Stampede grounds were de-

---

[24] "In short, 'community' stands for the kind of world which is not, regrettably, available to us – but which we would dearly wish to inhabit and which we hope to repossess" (Bauman 3).

stroyed, the Saddle Dome was flooded. The damage turned out to be so severe that a demolition of the entire site was deliberated. But The Stampede took place and ran under the appropriate battle cry: "Hell or High Water." 2.4 million Canadian dollars were donated to the Canadian Red Cross Alberta Flood Fund through the sale of some 150,000 T-Shirts with just this slogan (Toneguzzi). Considering how seriously the city of Calgary and its inhabitants were affected by the flood, the idea of a brand new Dream Home acquired even more allure and the dream aspect of it transformed from a lifetime achievement ideal or simply a nice-to-have to one of socio-economic survival. Many insurance companies denied payments to people who had settled in flood endangered areas. Many did not even have insurance – either due to lack of personal funds or due to insurers' abjuration of coverage for properties built in the Bow River valley (Nelson; The Canadian Press). In this context, the 2013 Dream Home could, indeed, be the symbol for a new start, a fresh opportunity, the prospect to move out of destruction, destitution, and homelessness into a new life. It could be more than just a real estate flip or a cashed-in prize. If community might indeed be located in the "contingent practices of everyday involvements in which reason and emotion are not so easily separated" (Brydon in Brydon and Coleman 252), then the Dream Home might be hope and prospects for a better future where a house can be converted into a home and a commudity might, indeed, become, through processes of constant (re)negotiations, if not a community, then at least a pleasant neighborhood.

References

2016 Stampede Rotary Dream Home. www.stampede.homes-byavi.com/2016/about-us/past-dreamhomes/#!. Accessed 15 December 2016.

Adams, Christopher. "Every Summer, There's a Chance the Calgary Stampede Chuck Wagon Races Will End Tragically." *National Observer,* 15 July 2016. <www.nationalobserver.com/2016/07/15/news/every-summer-theres-chance-calgary-stampedes-chuckwagen-races-will-end-tragically>. Accessed 15 December 2016.

Anderson, Benedict. *Imagined Communities: Reflections on the Origin and Spread of Nationalism. Revised Edition.* London: Verso, 2016.

Anon. "Government By the Nice, For the Nice." *Economist* 324.7769 (1992): 25-26.

———. "Restrictive Covenant as to Use of Land: Chaparral Valley Phase 1." 2 November 2007. <normore.com/RC%20Valley%20Pahse%-2001.pdf>. Accessed 15 December 2016.

Atkinson, Rowland and Sarah Blandy, eds. *Gated Communities.* London: Routledge, 2006.

Bachelard, Gaston. *The Poetics of Space.* 1958. Boston: Beacon Press, 1994.

Bagaeen, Samer and Ola Uduku, eds. *Gated Communities: Social Sustainability in Contemporary and Historical Gated Developments.* London: Earthscan, 2010.

Barton, Stephen E. and Carol J. Silverman, eds. *Common Interest Communities: Private Governments and the Public Interest.* Berkeley: Institute of Governmental Studies Press, 1994.

Bauman, Zygmunt. *Community: Seeking Safety in an Insecure World.* Cambridge: Polity Press, 2001.

Bekhet, Abir K., Jaclene Zauszniewski and Wagdy E. Nakhla. "Reasons for Relocation to Retirement Communities. A Qualitative Study." *Western Journal of Nursing Research* 31.4 (2009): 462-79.

Bellah, Robert N., Richard Madsen, William M. Sullivan, Ann Swidler and Steven M. Tipton. *Habits of the Heart: Individualism and Commitment in American Life.* New York: Harper and Row, 1986.

Blakely, Edward J. and Mary Gail Snyder. *Fortress America: Gated Communities in the United States.* Washington: Brookings Institution, 1997.

Blechman, Andrew D. *Leisureville: Adventures in America's Retirement Utopias.* New York: Atlantic Monthly Press, 2008.

Brydon, Diana and William D. Coleman, eds. *Renegotiating Community: Interdisciplinary Perspectives, Global Contexts.* Vancouver: University of British Columbia Press, 2008.

———. "Why Community Matters." *Renegotiating Community: Interdisciplinary Perspectives, Global Contexts*. Ed. Diana Brydon and William D. Coleman. Vancouver: University of British Columbia Press, 2008. 246-59.

Buchanan, James M. "An Economic Theory of Clubs." *Economica* 29 (1965): 371-84.

Calgary Stampede. <www.calgarystampede.com>. Accessed 15 December 2016.

Community Associations Institute (CAI). <https://www.caionline.org/LearningCenter/Pages/default.aspx>. Accessed 15 December 2016.

Crisp, Dimitry, Tim D. Windsor, Kaarin J. Anstey and Peter Butterworth. "What are Older Adults Seeking? Factors Encouraging or Discouraging Retirement Village Living." *Australasian Journal on Ageing* 32.3 (2013): 163-70.

Cséfalvay, Zoltán and Chris Webster. "Gates or No Gates? A Cross-European Enquiry into the Driving Forces behind Gated Communities." *Regional Studies* 46.3 (2012): 293-308.

Dicks, Bella. *Culture on Display*. New York: McGraw-Hill Education, 2007.

Duany, Andrés and Elizabeth Plater-Zyberk. "The Second Coming of the American Small Town." *Wilson Quarterly* 16.1 (1992): 19-49.

———, Elizabeth Plater-Zyberk and Jeff Speck. *Suburban Nation: The Rise of Sprawl and the Decline of the American Dream*. New York: North Point Press, 2000.

Duncan, Zoey. "Graphic: Calgary Stampede Attendance for 2013." *Calgary Herald*, 10 July 2013. <http://calgaryherald.com/news/localnews/calgary-stampede-attendance-lagging-somewhat-in-2013>. Accessed on 15 December 2016.

Eitzen, D. Stanley. "The Atrophy of Social Life." *Society* 9-10 (2004): 12-16.

Fisher, Adrian T., Christopher C. Sonn and Brian J. Bishop, eds. *Psychological Sense of Community: Research, Applications and Implications*. New York: Kluwer/Plenum Publishers, 2002.

Fishman, Robert. *Bourgeois Utopias: The Rise and Fall of Suburbia*. New York: Basic Books, 1987.

Florida, Richard. *Who's Your City? How the Creative Economy is Making Where to Live the Most Important Decision of Your Life*. New York: Basic Books, 2008.

Fricker, Peter. "Calgary Stampede: CBC Needs To Stop Giving Animal Cruelty Airtime." *The Huffington Post*, 12 July 2016. <www.huffingtonpost

.ca/peter/fricker/Calgary-stampede-cbc-cruelty_b_10944814.html>. Accessed 15 December 2016.

Gadecki, Jacek. "The Wild West: The Reality of Everyday Social Relations in Gated Communities in Poland." *Cities* 35 (2013): 174-80.

Genstar. *Chaparral Valley. Architectural Guidelines.* August 2007.

——. Genstar homepage. <https://www.genstar.com>. Accessed 15 December 2016.

Glasze, Georg. "Some Reflections on the Economic and Political Organisation of Private Neighborhoods." *Housing Studies* 20.2 (2005): 221-33.

——, Chris Webster and Klaus Frantz, eds. *Private Cities: Global and Local Perspectives.* New York: Routledge, 2006.

Graham, Vicki and Keith Tuffin. "Retirement Villages: Companionship, Privacy and Security." *Australasian Journal on Ageing* 23.4 (2004): 184-88.

Hayden, Dolores. *Building Suburbia: Green Fields and Urban Growth, 1820-2000.* New York: Vintage, 2003.

Hayes, Matthew. "'We Gained a Lot Over What We Would Have Had': The Geographic Arbitrage of North American Lifestyle Migrants to Cuenca, Ecuador." *Journal of Ethnic and Migration Studies* 40.12 (2014): 1953-1971.

Herbrechter, Stefan and Michael Higgins, eds. *Returning (to) Communities: Theory, Culture and Political Practice of the Communal.* Amsterdam: Rodopi, 2006.

Huyssen, Andreas. "Escape from Amnesia: The Museum as Mass Medium." *Twilight Memories: Marking Time in a Culture of Amnesia.* Ed. Andreas Huyssen. New York: Routledge, 1995. 13-35.

Jacobs, Jane. *The Death and Life of Great American Cities.* 1961. New York: Vintage Books, 1992.

Johnsson, Peter. "Gated Communities: Poland Holds the European Record in Housing for the Distrustful." *Baltic Worlds* 3-4 (2012): 26-32.

Joseph, Miranda. *Against the Romance of Community.* Minneapolis: University of Minnesota Press, 2002.

Kerr, Greg and Jessica Oliver. "Rethinking Place Identities." *Rethinking Place Branding: Comprehensive Brand Development for Cities and Regions.* Ed. Mihalis Kavaratzis, Gary Warnaby and Gregory J. Ashworth. Cham: Springer International Publishing Switzerland, 2015. 61-72.

Kirshenblatt-Gimblett, Barbara. *Destination Culture: Tourism, Museums, and Heritage.* Berkeley: University of California Press, 1998.

Klein, Karen E. "Code Blues: Rules that Govern the Life in Homeowners' Associations Are Being Challenged in Court by Angry Owners." *L.A. Times* (5 March 1995): K.1.

Labchuk, Camille. "Calgary Stampede: Torturing Cows and Horses is Wrong, Outdated and Illegal." *The Globe and Mail*, 7 July 2016. <http://www.theglobeandmail.com/opinion/calgary-stampede-torturing-cows-and-horses-is-wrong-outdated-and-illegal/article30788-704/>. Accessed 15 December 2016.

Lai, Lawrence W. C. "'Stone Walls Do Not a Prison Make, Nor Iron Bars a Cage': The Institutional and Communitarian Possibilities of Gated Communities." *Land Use Policy* 54 (2016): 378-85.

Le Goix, Renaud and Elena Vesselinov. "Gated Communities and House Prices: Suburban Change in Southern California, 1980-2008." *International Journal of Urban and Regional Research* 37.6 (2013): 2129-51.

―――― and Chris Webster. "Inequality Shaping Processes and Gated Communities in US Western Metropolitan Areas." *Urban Studies* 52.4 (2015): 619-38.

Live in Harmony. <www.liveinharmony.ca>. Accessed 15 December 2016.

Loomis, Jeff. *Privatizing Community: The Growth of Private Residence Associations*. Federation of Calgary Communities, 2006.

Louv, Richard. "Homeowner Group a Dubious New Ruler." *San Diego Union Tribune* (27 July 1994): A2.

Low, Setha. *Behind the Gates: Life, Security, and the Pursuit of Happiness in Fortress America*. New York: Routledge, 2003.

―――― . "A Multi-disciplinary Framework for the Study of Private Housing Schemes: Integrating Anthropological, Psychological and Political Levels of Theory and Analysis." *GeoJournal* 77.2 (2012): 185-201.

Macdonald, Sharon and Gordon Fyfe, eds. *Theorizing Museums. Representing Identity and Diversity in a Changing World*. Oxford: Blackwell, 1996.

―――― . "Theorizing Museums: an Introduction." *Theorizing Museums. Representing Identity and Diversity in a Changing World*. Ed. Sharon Macdonald and Gordon Fyfe. Oxford: Blackwell, 1996. 1-18.

Marstine, Janet, ed. *New Museum Theory and Practice*. Malden: Blackwell, 2006.

Maxey, Daisy. "Many Boomers Fearful of Retirement Expenses." *The Wall Street Journal* (18 November 2008): D7.

McCormack, Simon. "The Villages Retirement Community Exposed After Couple Allegedly Had Sex in Public." *Huffington Post*, 17 June 2014. <www.huffingtonpost.com/2014/06/17/the-villages-florida-_n_5504154.html>. Accessed 15 December 2016.

McKenzie, Evan. *Privatopia: Homeowner Associations and the Rise of Residential Private Government.* New Haven: Yale University Press, 1994.

McWatters, Mason R. *Residential Tourism: (De)constructing Paradise.* Bristol: Channel View Publ., 2009.

MetLife. *Housing for the 55+ Market: Trends and Insights on Boomers and Beyond.* New York: Metropolitan Life Insurance Co., 2009.

———. *55+ Housing: Builders, Buyers, and Beyond.* New York: Metropolitan Life Insurance Co., 2009.

Nelson, Jacqueline. "Alberta Flood Insurers Forced to Respond to Angry 'Name and Shame' Public Backlash." *The Globe and Mail*, 16 July 2013. <http://www.theglobeandmail.com/report-on-business/insurers-seek-to-quell-pr-headache-after-alberta-floods/article13241484>. Accessed 15 December 2016.

Olorunnipa, Toluse. "Fastest-Growing Metro Area in the U.S. Has No Crime Or Kids." *Bloomberg*, 27 June 2014. <https://www.bloomberg.com/news/articles/2014-06-27/fastest-growing-metro-area-in-u-s-has-no-crime-or-kids>. Accessed 15 December 2016.

Ong, Ai-Hwa. *Flexible Citizenship: The Cultural Logics of Transnationality.* Durham: Duke University Press, 1999, 2006.

———. *Neoliberalism as Exception: Mutations in Citizenship and Sovereignty.* Durham: Duke University Press, 2006.

O'Reilly, Karen. *International Migration and Social Theory.* London: Palgrave, 2012.

Owen, David. *Green Metropolis: Why Living Smaller, Living Closer and Driving Less Are the Keys to Sustainability.* New York: Riverhead Books, 2009.

Perez, Levi and Brad Humphreys. "The 'Who and Why' of Lottery: Empirical Highlights from the Seminal Economic Literature." *Journal of Economic Surveys* 27.5 (2013): 915-40.

"Poland: Entrenched in Luxury." *Deutsche Welle*, 23 March 2016. <http://dw.com/p/1llWa>. Accessed 15 December 2016.

Polanska, Dominika Vergara. "Gated Housing as a Reflection of Public-Private Divide: on the Popularity of Gated Communities in Poland." *Polish Sociological Review* 1.1 (2013): 87-102.

Pow, C. P. "Urban Dystopia and Epistemologies of Hope." *Progress in Human Geography* 39.4 (2015): 464-85.

Putnam, Robert D. *Bowling Alone: The Collapse and Revival of American Community.* New York: Simon and Schuster, 2000.

Radetskiy, Evgeny L., Ronald W. Spahr and Mark A. Sunderman. "Gated Community Premiums and Amenity Differentials in Residential Subdivisions." *Journal of Real Estate Research* 37.3 (2015): 405-38.

Rotary International. <www.rotary.org>. Accessed 15 December 2016.

Rüb, Matthias. "Gott, steh Florida bei!" *Frankfurter Allgemeine Sonntagszeitung* (28 October 2012): 11.

Sassen, Saskia. "When the Center No Longer Holds: Cities as Frontier Zones." *Cities* 34 (2013): 67-70.

Spocter, Manfred. "Non-metropolitan Gated Retirement Communities in the Western Cape." *Urban Forum* 27 (2016): 211-28.

Springbank Airport. <www.ybw.ca>. Accessed 15 December 2016.

Statistics Canada. "Table 203-0027 – Survey of Household Spending (SHS), Dwelling Characteristics and Household Equipment at Time of Interview, Canada, Regions and Provinces, Annual." CANSIM (last modified 2016). <www5.statcan.gc.ca>. Accessed 15 December 2016.

Stuart, Barbara. "Cat Fight Over Condo Rights; How Far Can Condo Restrictions Go?" *Recorder* (8 June 1994): 1.

Tanulku, Basak. "Gated Communities: Ideal Packages or Processual Spaces of Conflict?" *Housing Studies* 28.7 (2013): 937-59.

The Canadian Press. "Alberta Flood Victims Mostly out of Luck with Insurance." *Cbcnews*, 21 June 2013. <http://www.cbc.ca/business/alberta-flood-victims-mostly-out-of-luck-with-insurance-1.136-3664>. Accessed 15 December 2016.

The Stampeders. <www.stampeders.com>. Accessed 15 December 2016.

The Villages. <www.thevillagesflorida.com>. Accessed 15 December 2016.

The Villages News. <www.villages-news.com/villagesclassifieds/ads/2014-ford-shelby-mustang-gt500-ezgo-rxv-golf-car>. Accessed 15 December 2016.

The Villages promotional DVD, 2008.

The World Bank. "Urban Population (% of Total)." *United Nations, World Urbanization Prospects*. <Data.worldbank.org/indicator/SP.URB.TOTL.IN.ZS>. Accessed 15 December 2016.

Tiebout, Charles M. "A Pure Theory of Local Expenditures." *Journal of Political Economy* 64.5 (1956): 416-24.

Tönnies, Ferdinand. *Community and Society*. Trans. Margaret Hollis. Ed. Jose Harris. 1887. Cambridge: Cambridge University Press, 2001.

Toneguzzi, Mario. "Calgary Stampede Went forward 'Come Hell or High Water'." *Calgary Herald*, 16 June 2014. <http://www .calgaryherald .com/sports/calgary+stampede+went+forward+come+hell+high +water/9943273/story.html>. Accessed 15 December 2106.

Tuan, Yi-Fu. *Space and Place: The Perspective of Experience*. Minneapolis: University of Minnesota Press, 1977.

Urry, John and Jonas Larsen. *The Tourist Gaze 3.0*. Los Angeles: Sage, 2011.

US Census Bureau. "2015 American Community Survey S0101." <https://factfinder.census.gov/faces/tableservices/jsf/pages/productview.xhtml?src=bkmk>. Accessed 15 December 2016.

Van Noorloos, Femke and Griet Steel. "Lifestyle Migration and Socio-spatial Segregation in the Urban(izing) Landscapes of Cuenca (Ecuador) and Guanacaste (Costa Rica)." *Habitat International* 54 (2016): 50-57.

Vesselinov, Elena, Matthew Cazessus and William Falk. "Gated Communities and Spatial Inequality." *Journal of Urban Affairs* 29.2 (2007): 109-27.

Webster, Chris J. "Property Rights and the Public Realm: Gates, Green Belts, and Gemeinschaft." *Environment and Planning B: Planning and Design* 29.3 (2002): 397-412.

Woo, Yoonseuk and Chris Webster. "Co-evolution of Gated Communities and Local Public Goods." *Urban Studies* 51.12 (2014): 2539-54.

Wyczalkowska, Maria and Bozena Janda-Debek. "Residential Environment Quality and Neighborhood Attachment in Open and Gated Communities." *Polish Journal of Applied Psychology* 13.4 (2015): 9-24.

Yoffe, Emily. "Slow Ride, Take It Easy." *Slate*, 24 February 2011. <www.slate.com/articles/life/silver_lining/2011/02/slow_ride_take_it_easy.html>. Accessed 15 December 2016.

Zehelein, Eva-Sabine. "'Whatever Senior Living Choice or Lifestyle Option You Desire, You're Sure to Find It': 55+, Age Segregation and the American Social Landscape." *"Forever Young?" The Changing Images of America*. Ed. Philip Coleman and Stephen Mattherson. Heidelberg: Winter, 2012. 21-41.

Bonding in Bonden: A Post-Postmodernist Female Community in Siri Hustvedt's *The Summer Without Men*

Sofie Behluli

Some critics have declared postmodernism to be over and are speaking of "post-postmodernism," a new era generally associated with a "turn to the human" (Timmer) and notions such as coherence, unity, and community. Nicoline Timmer has identified these new trends in literature and fleshed out a list of characteristics of the post-postmodern novel, for example community, empathy, sameness, inclusiveness, storytelling, and a mock-dialogue with the reader. Taking this theory on post-postmodernism and the importance of community as a backdrop, this article analyzes the way in which a transgenerational female community is established and critiqued in Siri Hustvedt's novel *The Summer Without Men*. By singling out Timmer's features of post-postmodernism that appear in the novel, and focusing particularly on four community-establishing and -maintaining elements (gender, mother-daughter relationships, bodily contact, and storytelling), it will be shown that Hustvedt's community follows a typically post-postmodern yes/but logic: Yes, *The Summer Without Men* presents us with a seemingly idyllic transgenerational female community, but it always also questions and problematizes its ontologically unstable basis.

1. Introduction

A Woman Looking at Men Looking at Women is the title of Siri Hustvedt's newest essay collection, which sets out to bridge the gulf between the natural and the social sciences. Arguing that "all human knowledge is partial" and that "no one is untouched by the community of thinkers or researchers in which she or he lives" (xii), Hustvedt pleads for more interdisciplinarity and a critical engagement with the arbitrary boundaries "between concepts such as art and science, truth and fiction, feeling and perception" (Anonymous, *Publishers Weekly* review). As much as her essays are engaged with the deconstruction of binary oppositions, already the title sets up a crucial distinction between men and women and highlights a dichotomy that haunts all of Hustvedt's work, for instance also *The Summer Without Men*. This is a classical example of the problem that poststructuralists and deconstructionists have long struggled with, namely the inability to create a language *ex nihilo* without producing new dichotomies. Hence, even though Hustvedt does subscribe to a fundamental distinction between the sexes (and the disciplines, for that matter), she is *forced* to work with a vocabulary predicated upon binary modes of thinking.

That Hustvedt is anything but a naïve writer or a supporter of clear-cut gender dichotomies can be seen throughout her fictional work, for example in her earliest novel *The Blindfold*, where the protagonist Iris starts to cross-dress as a man, or in her latest novel *The Blazing World*, where the protagonist and artist Harriet creates three male disguises to boost her career. In both novels femaleness is experienced as a societal burden that can be escaped behind a male mask, at least temporarily. In *The Summer Without Men*, published as the fifth fictional work by the Norwegian-American novelist and essayist,[1] Hustvedt picks up on the male-female dichotomy and employs the opposite of a strategy of evasion: confrontation. While attempting to exclude the male half of *mankind*, Hustvedt's novel shifts the focus onto women and their in-group relations. The array of women presented in *The Summer Without Men* ranges from a three-year-old toddler to a one-hundred-and-two-year-old pensioner, the spectrum being interspersed with teenagers, adolescents, young adults, and middle-aged women. They are daughters, mothers, grandmothers, sisters, teachers, and friends to each other and are thus tightly linked into a transgenerational female community. Apart from their gender, the critical elements of mother-daughter relationships,

---

[1] There are few secondary sources on this literary text since, so far, the emerging scholarly interest in Hustvedt has focused mostly on her 2003 novel *What I Loved* and on the autobiographical analysis of her mental illness *The Shaking Woman*. Indeed, apart from the three monographs by Christine Marks, Corinna Sophie Reipen, and Johanna Hartmann, which all focus on the visuality and relational identity-construction in Hustvedt's work, only one recently published edited volume by Hartmann, Marks, and Zapf can be mentioned as a lengthy study on Hustvedt's border-crossing work.

bodily contact and storytelling are emphasized as community-forming and community-sustaining factors.

The *Oxford English Dictionary* defines "community" as "a group of people distinguished by shared circumstances of nationality, race, religion, sexuality, etc.; *esp.* such a group living within a larger society from which it is distinct" (*OED* 5.a.), the "etc." presumably pointing to other significant traits such as gender. The *OED* definition also includes the aspect of "shar[ing] the same interests, pursuits, or occupation, esp. when distinct from those of the society in which they live" (*OED* 5.b.). These shared interests, pursuits, and occupations in *The Summer Without Men* include, for example, the negotiation of the Self as a woman and hegemonically constituted Other in relation to men; the wish to subvert these patriarchic power relations in creative ways; and the occupation and role in society of being a mother, a daughter, a sister, a wife, and a friend. Thomas Claviez would call this conception of "community" "colored by romantic nostalgia for homogeneity, closeness, and sameness" ("Toward a Poetics" 3), a community which hopelessly strives to secure internal stability while preventing the intrusion of external threats. However idyllic and flawed this conception of "community" might be, it is still applicable to Hustvedt's novel. In the end, the female community in *The Summer Without Men* swings back and forth between a blissful/unitarian and a more critical/fragmented understanding, allowing for the complexities of this notion to shine through.

The Summer Without Men is, in fact, a typical example of the recently emerged yes/but logic, which Irmtraud Huber and others view as a fundamental characteristic of the so-called "post-postmodernism." This term is often used to label the alleged new epoch (e.g., by Nealon) that is both a break with and an extension of postmodernism (similar to the complex relationship between modernism and postmodernism). To put it in Linda Hutcheon's words: "[T]he postmodern moment has passed, even if its discursive strategies and its ideological critique continue to live on" (181). Postmodernism is by no means dead but has been followed by a form of cultural production that incorporates its ideas, hence the term "post-postmodernism." Arguing similarly, Josh Toth and Neil Brooks claim that postmodernism "became terminally ill sometime in the late-eighties [with Samuel Beckett's death or the fall of the Berlin wall in 1989] and early-nineties [as perhaps best indicated by Jacques Derrida's 'ethical turn'], [and that] it was buried once and for all in the rubble of the World Trade Center" on 9/11" (3). While Toth and Brooks believe that postmodernism failed because of its inherent contradiction – proclaiming the impossibility of positive truths and master narratives and at the same time attempting to become just that (7) –, other scholars and cultural critics see the reasons for postmodernism's downfall in its inability to keep up with today's pressing socio-political issues, e.g., religious terrorism, mass migration, climate change, and a global rise of the right wing. With reference to Frederic Jameson's influential essay "The Antinomies of Postmodernity," Peter Boxall even goes as far as claiming that postmodern thought has become "empty, static, constant" (15), unable to capture a rapidly changing temporality and to truly take the material conditions around us into account.

In the wake of postmodernism a new era seems to have dawned, that of post-postmodernism – or so at least some literary and cultural critics argue.[2] As Ihab Hassan stated in his article "Beyond Postmodernism: Toward an Aesthetic of Trust," this era and its aesthetics are primarily concerned with "new relations between selves and others, margins and centers, fragments and wholes – indeed new relations between selves and selves, margins and margins, centers and centers" (6).[3] Put differently, it is a fresh – yet old – approach to the unresolved issues that were discussed during postmodernism. Thus, post-postmodernism, which supposedly covers everything from politics and cultural production to academic discourses, is associated with an apparent "*re*turn to ethics, religio[n] and realism" (Toth and Brooks 4; cf. also Claviez, "neo-realism") and a more general return to coherence and meaning. Moreover, concepts of the body and the senses, materiality, empathy, sincerity, trust, and community, have all experienced a revival. The concept of "community" – a distinct research field that has been thriving ever since the early 1980s thanks to Jean-Luc Nancy, George Bataille, Maurice Blanchot, and Étienne Balibar –, is a conspicuously reoccurring feature in these theories of post-postmodernism, even if it is only visible on the periphery.[4]

The theory of Nicoline Timmer, which she presents in *Do You Feel it Too? The Post-postmodern Syndrome in American Fiction at the Turn of the Millennium*, is one such example. Arguing that the post-postmodern syndrome can be summarized as a "turn to the human" (51), Timmer

---

[2] "Post-postmodernism" (e.g., Nealon) is the term that has asserted itself against other labels such as "liquid modernity" (Bauman), "digimodernism" (Kirby 2009), "metamodernism" (Vermeulen and van den Akker), "altermodern" (Bourriaud), and "performatism" (Eshelman), to name just a few.

[3] Cf. also Hickman, in which the period of post-postmodernism is associated with a similarly hands-on attitude as in Ihab Hassan's article.

[4] According to Jean-Luc Nancy "the word *community* was unknown to the discourse of thought" before the early 1980s (20).

shows how it is detectable in the writing of a new generation of authors, who now emphasize the material conditions, feelings, and intersubjective connections over pure thought and isolated selves.[5] In the appendix of this monograph, Timmer has compiled a list of nineteen characteristics of the post-postmodern novel, which reflect this "turn to the human" in more detail (359-61). Six of them need to be highlighted here in particular, since they are conspicuous features in Hustvedt's *The Summer Without Men*. First, Timmer mentions a "desire for some form of community" or a "'structural need for a we'" (359). This is linked, second, to an emphasis on "'sameness' (instead of the fetishism with 'difference' in postmodern texts and theories)" (359) and, third, the "striv[ing] for 'inclusiveness'" rather than exclusiveness (359). A fourth characteristic, which is crucial for the coherence of narratives and the construction of the self, is the "sharing [of] stories as a way to 'identify with others' (and to allow others to identify themselves with you)" (359). This is connected, fifth, to "a direct appeal to the reader or narratee, a 'you'" (359). And sixth, Timmer argues that "the post-postmodern novel hinges on creating empathy (between characters, between narrators and characters, [. . .] between fictional figures and the flesh and blood 'real' reader)" (360-61). The six features stressed here – that is: community, sameness, inclusiveness, storytelling, a mock-dialogue with the reader, and empathy – can all be observed in Hustvedt's *The Summer Without Men* as defining characteristics.[6]

Needless to say, Timmer's suggestions and the idea of post-postmodernism itself are highly contested.[7] The tendency to divide history into periods and to ascribe certain traits to its cultural production has always been problematic. Regardless of the doubts over the end of the self-proclaimed "end of history" (cf. Fukuyama), one can still observe a conscious effort in today's literary production to overcome the endless play of signification, the loss of meaning and truth, the destabilization of the self, and the credo of *jouissance* in favor of pragmatic action and community-oriented thinking (cf. Huber). Noteworthy examples

---

[5] Similar to Timmer, Peter Boxall argues that the twenty-first century novel is engaged with a new way of understanding "the relationship between the *material conditions* of the contemporary culture and the narrative form within which such conditions come to expression" (17; my emphasis).

[6] Cf. Gabriele Rippl,"The Rich Zones", where she also draws on Timmer's theory to explain Siri Hustvedt's (genre-blurring) practices.

[7] Given that we are already critically discussing post-postmodernism and identifying its features, Danuta Fjellestad and Maria Engberg even suggest that this new era, too, might already be over (in paragraph 30, n. pag.).

include Jonathan Franzen's *The Corrections*, Jeffrey Eugenides' *The Marriage Plot*, David Mitchell's *Cloud Atlas*, A. S. Byatt's *The Biographer's Tale*, and finally also Hustvedt's *The Summer Without Men*. Theories of postmodernism are explicitly brought up in Hustvedt's book, in order to be modified and/or overcome in a second step. Among the plethora of intertextual references to philosophy, neurobiology, psychoanalysis, and art in the novel, Hustvedt also emphatically comments on Jacques Derrida, Jean-François Lyotard, and Roland Barthes. By showing awareness for these thinkers and their ideas and by intentionally deviating from them, *The Summer Without Men* positions itself as a work of art which goes beyond postmodernism. Similar to what Caroline Rosenthal says about Hustvedt's 2003 novel *What I Loved*, *The Summer Without Men* can be viewed as a post-postmodern novel "that returns to a more realistic form of representation, albeit with a postmodern awareness of the fragility and ambiguity of concepts like the self, the body, space, or representation" (63-64). It remains to show how the coherent yet unstable transgenerational community in Hustvedt's novel can be approached with new theories of post-postmodernism, which follow a yes/but logic – in other words, which attempt to reconcile critical thinking and pragmatic life decisions.

2. Analysis

The Summer Without Men, which the author herself called a "comedy" ("Story" 16), is a retrospective narration by the autodiegetic narrator Mia Fredricksen, who experiences a mental breakdown after Boris Izcovic, her husband of 30 years, leaves her for a much younger French woman, referred to only as the "Pause" (*Summer* 2). The "Pause" has crucial implications for the community in *The Summer Without Men*: She/it represents an interruption to a male-female community – enabling the protagonist to find a female-female community in Minnesota – but not a total break with it. Once the "Pause" is over, the male-female community is resumed. In order to deal with the blow of having been abandoned and to recover from her "Brief Psychotic Disorder" (*Summer* 1), Mia leaves New York City for the summer and goes back to her hometown Bonden, Minnesota. The name of this fictional town already suggests the "bonds" and "bonding processes" that are necessary for and characteristic of a community. Once in Bonden, the 55-year-old poet and scholar reconnects with her mother and four other women from a home for the aged, a group of 90- to 100-year-old widows whom Mia fondly calls the "Swans." Mia also gets a glimpse into the lives of seven pubescent girls, to whom she teaches a poetry class. Apart from old ladies and teenage girls, the age spectrum of the female characters encompasses toddlers, young adults, and other middle-aged women – hence the notion of a *transgenerational* female community. Over the course of the summer, Mia recovers from her breakdown and redefines her identity, one that is detached from her partner, Boris.[8] She does it with the support of this varied group of women, and, to her surprise, experiences a pleasant summer within a mostly female community. In reflecting upon her own condition, Mia asserts that "[i]nsanity is the state of profound self-absorption" (*Summer* 8). In recovering, however, self-absorption gives way to an awareness of community which is, as will be seen, established and maintained primarily through four critical elements: gender, mother-daughter relationships, bodily contact, and storytelling. The novel's strong emphasis on community and these last three elements in particular are clear indicators of what Timmer describes as a "turn to the human," i.e., the post-postmodern syndrome.

The title *The Summer Without Men* suggests that gender is the main distinctive feature for Hustvedt's community. However, this seemingly complete exclusion of the male sex is questionable since, first, the word "men" appears prominently in the title and, second, the word "without" includes the word "with" in it. Put differently, the title of this novel encapsulates both the presence and absence of men. For the most part of the summer in 2009,[9] during which time the story unfolds, the male characters are either dead or physically and/or emotionally absent. The most conspicuous absence in Mia's life – and her narration – is her husband, Boris. His voice is sometimes rendered through e-mails, in which he tries to woo back his wife, but he is never actually physically present. Another male persona only present in the digital world is Mr. Nobody. He appears as but a voice, hailing Mia (and the reader) from the digital sphere. Because his e-mails go from mean provocations to more positive forms of communication in the course of the story, their development being concurrent with Mia's healing process, Carmen Birkle argues

---

[8] Identity and self are important themes in *The Summer Without Men*, as Mia herself says when she plays around with her name: "Mia. I rescrambled it. I am. I wrote it over and over in my notebook. I am. I am Mia" (37). Anna Thiemann has interpreted this negotiation of the (female) self through the story of recovery as a "subversive retelling of [Charlotte Perkins Gilman's 'The Yellow Wallpaper']" (320).

[9] In addition to the ambivalence of the title discussed above, the definite article in front of "*Summer*" suggests a limited time period for the physical absence of men and the constellation of a predominantly female community.

that he "comes across as a second voice within [Mia]" who verbalizes her opinion of herself (214). This is also why Birkle interprets him as the personification of Mia's id (216). It's no surprise then that Mia eventually wonders "if Mr. Nobody couldn't just as well be Mrs. Nobody" (206), which would mean that one of the strongest male voices in the novel could in fact be female, too. Indeed, the ambiguous figure of Mr. Nobody – as marginal in the story as he is – reveals cracks in that seemingly homogenous female community. Yes, it is a female community and the role of gender is crucial for the formation and maintenance of it, but men are not as neatly excluded as it appears. To the contrary, their ambivalent position between presence and absence is a powerful driving force behind the female community in *The Summer Without Men*.

Apart from these ambiguities, the community around Mia is predominantly female and straddles all ages from the 3-year-old Flora to the 102-year-old Georgiana. These characters give a microcosmic version of females in all life stages, that is, being an infant, a teenager, a young woman in her 20s, a mother of adolescents, a menopausal woman, or a woman in old age. Through her role as a narrator, Mia, being 55-years-old and thus more or less in the center of the age range, is the one who brings all these different women together, both literally and symbolically. She is the node on which the transgenerational female community in this novel hinges. Moreover, her bitter, mocking, and sarcastic tone (e.g., "The magic of authority, money, penises" [*Summer* 8]), her inclusive and coercive gestures toward the reader (e.g., "Even you, Dear Reader, can easily be persuaded that [. . .]" [*Summer* 77-78]), combined with a rather male-excluding title and a book cover design that is more likely to appeal to women,[10] make it rather probable that the implied reader is female, too.

It would be wrong, however, to interpret this intentional dominance of women in and around the novel as an idyllic state, as an unreflected version of a perfect community. To the contrary, Hustvedt uses this focus on women to discuss poststructuralist identity politics. In line with Butler's contestation of gender difference, Mia claims: "It is not that there is no difference between men and women; it is how much difference that difference makes, and how we choose to frame it" (*Summer* 152). Aside from Mia, who mounts a critique of gender inequality by listing the relatively absurd reasons for male dominance throughout his-

---

[10] The original 2011 Sceptre editions feature a) a yellow cover with the illustration of a fragmented woman leaping through the title of the novel and b) a somewhat romantic photograph of a prostrate woman reading on top of a wardrobe in a forest.

tory (e.g., *Summer* 146-53), the 94-year-old Abigail represents a subtler form of subversion and rebellion. Her embroideries, "secret amusements" that depict masturbating and raging women (*Summer* 39-43, 190), represent "female rage at society, at being relegated and reduced to housework and sexuality" (Birkle 214; cf. also Thiemann 321). Conveniently enough, these secret pleasures are rendered through ekphrasis, an Ancient mode of writing that is known to problematize power relations in a creative way, as argued for example by David Kennedy or Gabriele Rippl ("Postcolonial Ekphrasis"). Even in the non-ekphrastic passages Hustvedt manages to show how our perception influences and constructs reality, especially when it comes to gender.[11] Perception creates difference and this, in turn, contorts perception again. The transgenerational female community in *The Summer Without Men* has come together not only by choice (Mia chooses to leave New York) but also because its members are the perceived Other in a patriarchical society. It is an assembly of those denied access to the larger (male) community. In this respect, the unity and coherence of this female community is both reinforced and subverted. This particular yes/but logic reveals that *The Summer Without Men* goes beyond the postmodern paradigm.

Though the concept of gender is socially constructed, sex is a slightly different matter, classically exemplified by the ability to give birth. The women are linked to each other through this ability in general, and through the resulting mother-daughter relationships in particular. These mother-daughter relationships can be either genealogical blood relations, as in the case of Mia, her mother Laura, and her daughter Daisy, or non-genealogical, symbolical relations, as in the case of Abigail and Mia or Mia and Lola, where the former woman acts as a "foster mother" to the latter, respectively. Motherhood, as an overarching theme in the novel, creates spaces for expressions of empathy between characters, which is in turn one of the traits of post-postmodern literature, as defined by Timmer. Despite certain conflicts, these women deeply care for each other and form a tight community of love, trust, and empathy. Mothers are associated with feelings of security, shelter, and love and presented as near-mythical creatures. Mia, for example, says that her "mother was a place for [her] as well as a person" (*Summer* 13), thereby evoking the symbolism of space and (physical) origin. Indeed, the turn to the human is expressed as a turn to the origin of every single human: the mother.

---

[11] At one point Mia states that "[p]erception is never passive. We are not only receivers of the world; we also actively produce it" (*Summer* 77). Cf. also Böger.

Moreover, mothers are also ideal examples for Hustvedt's emphasis on relational identity-formations as proposed by Maurice Merleau-Ponty,[12] and the "recognition of the self-other entanglement, that is, the intersubjectivity without which human beings would not be human" (Birkle 212). As Christine Marks argues: "One reason why women have always held a special position with regard to the boundaries of the self is their ability to become two in one during pregnancy. [. . .] Mother and child are indistinguishably connected, which results in an insoluble enigma of interconnected subjectivities" (138). Hence, choosing mothers and daughters as the focus of her novel is an ideal way for Hustvedt to make her point about intersubjective formations of identity and also community. That this interconnectedness does not end with birth can be shown in the following passage when Mia recounts the birth of her daughter Daisy:

> there is the sudden slide of her body from mine, me/she, two in one; and between my open legs I see a red, slimy foreigner, with a little bit of black hair, my daughter. I remember nothing of the umbilical cord, do I? Nothing of the cutting. (*Summer* 211)

The actual cutting of the umbilical cord is omitted to highlight this continuing bond between mother and daughter. The women and girls in *The Summer Without Men*, who are all mothers and/or daughters, are inextricably linked to, and their identities are shaped by, each other.

These close bonds between mothers and daughters, whether they are genealogical or not, are not only dependent on corporality, but also expressed through it. The looks and touches that these women exchange sustain the bodily connection after mother and child cease to share the same body. There is no need to go into detail on the function of "looking," since most publications mentioned above have dealt with this aspect in Hustvedt's work (cf. Marks; Reipen; Hartmann). In short, "looking" is not only a way to create these intersubjective identities but also, according to Astrid Böger, to "allow[ ] for an extraordinarily rich spectrum of embodied visual experiences challenging readers to 'enter into the picture'" (292). In *The Summer Without Men*, this stance towards the connection between perception and identity formation, this "find[ing] ourselves in the faces of others" (37), as Mia puts it, basically boils down

---

[12] Hustvedt herself counts Merleau-Ponty among the most fundamental thinkers informing her work (*A Woman Looking* xix). Even her fictional character Mia is strongly influenced by his ideas (cf. *Summer* 71).

to the following utterance: "I want you to *see* me, see Mia. *Esse est percipi*. I am" (81). To be is to be perceived.

This embodied experience is furthermore highlighted through touch, between the characters but also between Mia and the implied reader. There is an abundance of passages where women simply touch each other to express empathy, support, and love (cf. *Summer* 30-31, 55, 96, 157-59, 204, 210), as in the following instance when Mia is about to say goodbye to Abigail: "Then, lifting my hands to her lips, she [Abigail] kissed them, turned her head to one side, and pressed her cheek hard against the skin of my knuckles" (*Summer* 80). Another notable instance of bodily contact occurs in the following scene, right after the thirteen-year-old Alice confesses to Mia and her mother how the other girls from the poetry class bullied her:

> Ellen had managed to coax her big girl onto her lap. Mother and daughter were enfolded in the beanbag chair [. . .]. Alice buried her head in her mother's neck [. . . while] Ellen's hand was moving up and down her daughter's back, slowly and rhythmically. (*Summer* 128)

This is a remarkable scene because, among all the generations within Mia's female community, the teenage girls constitute the group within which bodily contact practically never occurs. This can be explained by the fact that these girls are in the most pivotal phase of identity construction in their lives, and that their unstable selves are also more difficult to be brought into corporal, intersubjective relations with others. Moreover, the missing bodily contact between the girls is a clear indicator of the disharmony in and instability of their community.[13] As soon as these tensions are resolved at the end of the novel, Mia immediately recounts a scene in which the girls hug her (*Summer* 202). Thus, bodily contact is crucial in Hustvedt's novel when it comes to establishing and maintaining a tight community.

While postmodernist literature often focuses on the failure of communication and the insurmountable solitude that comes with it, Hustvedt tries to show that our bodies are the bridges to each other, moreover, that our selves can only be constructed in relation to one another.

---

[13] This group of seven teenage girls, who are at a critical, identity-negotiation, transitory phase from being children to becoming young women, is dominated by tensions, jealousy, and mind games. Eventually, one of the girls, Alice, ends up being bullied by the other six, most probably as an attempt to stabilize their fragile community by selecting an outcast through which their own group can be asserted. This clique unity crumbles as soon as it comes to distributing the blame for the bullying.

This idea is so far-reaching that it even crosses the ontological border between fiction and reality, or, put differently, this community-formation through bodily contact goes as far as to include the implied (female) reader.[14] Throughout the novel, Mia directly addresses this implied reader, a practice which at first only appears to be a colloquial, oral style of narrating, for example when she says "I was afraid of her, you see" (*Summer* 2). This soon turns into a direct dialogue with a "you" (*Summer* 87) or even "you, Dear Reader" (*Summer* 34, 77). The narrative is also littered with little asides, which refer back to something Mia has already said and which function as insider jokes, creating an intimate relationship between her and the reader (cf. *Summer* 108, 119, 123, 134-35, 143, 148, 173-74, etc.). One could even say that these direct addresses and sometimes bitterly ironic asides coerce the reader into agreeing or sympathizing with Mia, creating a strong feeling of complicity between her and this implied reader. Moreover, these instances integrate the reader in Mia's female community, as Mia treats the reader with as much trust and empathy, seeking a similar form of bodily contact as with her mother, daughter, or female friends. The following passage illustrates this point perfectly:

> But before I get to that, I want to tell you, Gentle Person out there, that if you are here with me now, on the page, I mean, if you have come to this paragraph, if you have not given up and sent me, Mia, [. . .] then I want to reach out for you and take your face in both my hands and cover you with kisses, kisses on your cheeks and chin and all over your forehead and one on the bridge of your (variously shaped) nose, because I am yours, all yours. (*Summer* 105)

Mia figuratively "reaches out" of the pages,[15] transgresses the boundaries of fiction, touches the reader's face, and showers her with kisses – a gesture of affection that occurs multiple times among the female characters, too. Fittingly, this passage can be found at the exact middle of the novel, a clear formal sign of the centrality of bodily contact for community formation. Along with the corporal aspect for communal bonds, this passage also highlights the fact that Mia is telling a story to the reader, as indicated for example by the temporal marker "before I get to

---

[14] This metafictional strategy could also be interpreted as a postmodern one. This goes to show again that postmodernism continues to persist, albeit in different shapes which can be called post-postmodern.

[15] Hustvedt herself sees writing as a symbolical reaching out to the reader, as a "reach toward another person" (*Living* xiii).

that." Mia recounts what happened to her during the summer of 2009 in Bonden and emphasizes the difficulties of storytelling. One time she asks the reader "How to tell it?" (*Summer* 134) because of the incommensurable simultaneity of life and linearity of a story; or differently put: "It is impossible to divine a story while you are living it; it is shapeless; an inchoate procession of words and things, and let us be frank: We *never* recover what was" (*Summer* 38). Mia also refers to her own life as "[t]his story of Mia and Boris" (*Summer* 99) and compares it to the stories of one of the most famous literary storytellers, Scheherazade from *Arabian Nights* (*Summer* 99). Despite the challenges of storytelling – problems, which seem to be countered by four simple illustrations that recount Mia's journey visually –,[16] Mia concludes: "there are NO RULES in art" and "[t]he enchantment is in the feeling and in the telling; that is all" (*Summer* 181).

Indeed, difficulties of storytelling are irrelevant since it fulfills its community-strengthening function anyway. The transgenerational female community in Hustvedt's novel depends on the stories the women tell each other; whether that is to give advice on relationship problems that the storyteller is familiar with (*Summer* 29-31); to pass on secrets about one's own past, thereby emphasizing trust and empathy (*Summer* 191-92); or simply to pass the time and bond with each other even more (*Summer* 86). These stories are only so effective in building and strengthening the community because of one crucial factor: repetition. These women can only empathize with each other so much because they have heard, seen, and lived these universal stories before. Each story is merely a repetition of a previously told one and each act of listening to these stories mirrors previous such cases. Here we can observe the "sharing [of] stories as a way to 'identify with others,'" as Timmer puts it (359), and furthermore a typically post-postmodern creation of coherence – both in Mia's story and in the more general experience of being a woman.

---

[16] *The Summer Without Men* includes four illustrations, presumably drawn by Mia to express her emotional state. These four illustrations always occur after a decisive moment in the narration: after her mental breakdown (*Summer* 6); after bonding with Lola (*Summer* 70); after the first signs of Boris' regret (*Summer* 115); and finally, after Mia feels in control over her (love) life again (*Summer* 207). While the first image depicts a woman within a box reaching helplessly towards the sky, the last one shows a smiling woman floating outside of that box. They visualize Mia's emotional and mental progress towards health.

Storytelling also comes into play when Mia's poetry class has to work through a bullying incident by writing down what happened from the various perspectives:

> The trick was, we would have to agree, more or less, on the content. [. . .] The story they all took home on Friday was not true; it was a version they could all live with, very much like national histories that blur and hide and distort the movements of people and events in order to preserve an idea. (*Summer* 183-201)

By imagining themselves in the body of someone else, the girls finally come to a consensus and find closure. Mia's statement that the story they created "was not true" hints at the poststructuralist underpinnings of the novel. As Ihab Hassan argues, however, the truth that was debunked in the period from Nietzsche to Derrida was an "absolute, transcendent, or foundational" one (6), not however a pragmatic truth which "rests on personal, social, cognitive trust" (7). This Habermasian and post-postmodern idea of truth being that which has been pragmatically established through rational consensus, is clearly at play in *The Summer Without Men*. Mia and her poetry girls construct a satisfying story by putting themselves into the shoes of each other, which yet again demonstrates Hustvedt's understanding of an intersubjectively created identity and community. Just like storytelling itself, Hustvedt's female community is constructed – in spite of the naturalness being evoked through mother-daughter relationships – and far from coherent.

3. Conclusion

The growing interest in ideas of "community" since the 1980s seems to go hand in hand with the wake of postmodernism and its radical critique of a coherent, unified self. In spite of a worldwide resurgence of nationalism and the tendency toward nation-based insularity, the wish for a type of community has asserted itself. In fact, major theoretical concerns are intentionally pushed to the background in favor of a more pragmatic approach. Some theorists have called this trend "post-postmodernism" and have argued that it is characterized by a return to realism, coherence, meaning, empathy, and especially community, while the discursive strategies of postmodernism still live on.

Following Nicoline Timmer's theory on the characteristics of the post-postmodern novel – community, sameness, inclusiveness, storytelling, a mock-dialogue with the reader, empathy, and a general turn to the human –, it can be argued that Siri Hustvedt's *The Summer Without Men* is such a novel. The intensity with which (a transgenerational female) community is established and critiqued here – primarily through the key features of gender, mother-daughter relationships, bodily contact, and storytelling – is symptomatic of the balancing act that post-postmodernism attempts to manage. To use the yes/but logic of post-postmodernism: Yes, *The Summer Without Men* presents us with a seemingly idyllic transgenerational female community, but it always also questions and problematizes its ontologically unstable basis. Given the extremely destabilized notion of "self" that postmodernism has left us with, it seems that any conception of "community" today has to live with one or the other inconsistency. In a way, both the contemporary obsession with community and this so-called post-postmodernism express a yearning for that which seems forever lost.

References

Anonymous. Review of *A Woman Looking at Men Looking at Women: Essays on Art, Sex, and the Mind*, by Siri Hustvedt. *Publishers Weekly* 26 September 2016. http://www.publishersweekly.com/978-1-5011-4109-6. Accessed 29 December 2016.

Bauman, Zygmunt. *Liquid Modernity*. Cambridge: Polity, 2000.

Birkle, Carmen. "'No Self is an Island': Doctor-Patient Relationships in Siri Hustvedt's Work." *Zones of Focused Ambiguity in Siri Hustvedt's Works: Interdisciplinary Essays*. Ed. Johanna Hartmann, Christine Marks and Hubert Zapf. Anglia Book Series 52. Berlin and Boston: DeGruyter, 2016. 193-223.

Böger, Astrid. "'I Look and Sometimes I See': The Art of Perception in Siri Hustvedt's Novels." *Zones of Focused Ambiguity in Siri Hustvedt's Works: Interdisciplinary Essays*. Ed. Johanna Hartmann, Christine Marks and Hubert Zapf. Anglia Book Series 52. Berlin and Boston: DeGruyter, 2016. 281-93.

Bourriaud, Nicolas. "Altermodern." *Altermodern: Tate Triennial*. Ed. Nicolas Bourriaud. London: Tate Publishing, 2009. 11-24.

Boxall, Peter. *Twenty-First Century Fiction: A Critical Introduction*. Cambridge: Cambridge University Press, 2013.

Byatt, A. S. *The Biographer's Tale*. London: Chatto and Windus, 2000.

Claviez, Thomas. "Introduction: Neo-Realism and How to 'Make It New'." *Amerikastudien/American Studies* 49.1 (2004): 5-18.

———. "Introduction: Toward a Poetics of Community." *The Common Growl: Toward a Poetics of Precarious Community*. Ed. Thomas Claviez. New York: Fordham University Press, 2016. 1-13.

"community, n." *OED Online*. Oxford University Press. http://www.oed.com/view/Entry/37337?redirectedFrom =-community#eid. Accessed 31 October 2016.

Eshelman, Raoul. *Performatism, or the End of Postmodernism*. Aurora: Davies Group, 2008.

Eugenides, Jeffrey. *The Marriage Plot*. New York: Picador, 2011.

Fjellestad, Danuta and Maria Engberg. "Toward a Concept of Post-Postmodernism or Lady Gaga's Reconfigurations of Madonna." *Reconstruction* 12.4 (2013): n. pag. <http://reconstruction.eserver.org/Issues/124/Fjellestad-Engberg.shtml.>. Accessed 20 May 16.

Franzen, Jonathan. *The Corrections*. London: Fourth Estate, 2001.

Fukuyama, Francis. *The End of History and the Last Man*. New York: The Free Press, 1992.

Hartmann, Johanna. *Literary Visuality in Siri Hustvedt's Works: Phenomenological Perspectives*. text und theorie. Würzburg: Königshausen und Neumann, 2016.

———, Christine Marks and Hubert Zapf, eds. *Zones of Focused Ambiguity in Siri Hustvedt's Works: Interdisciplinary Essays*. Anglia Book Series 52. Berlin and Boston: DeGruyter, 2016.

Hassan, Ihab. "Beyond Postmodernism: Toward an Aesthetic of Trust." *angelaki* 8.1 (2003): 3-11.

Hickman, Larry A. *Pragmatism as Post-postmodernism: Lessons from John Dewey*. New York: Fordham University Press, 2007.

Huber, Irmtraud. *Literature After Postmodernism: Reconstructive Fantasies*. Basingstoke: Palgrave Macmillan, 2014.

Hustvedt, Siri. *The Blindfold*. London: Sceptre, 1992.

———. *What I Loved*. London: Sceptre, 2003.

———. *The Shaking Woman or A History of My Nerves*. New York: Picador, 2009.

———. *The Summer Without Men*. London: Sceptre, 2011.

———. *Living, Thinking, Looking*. London: Sceptre, 2012.

———. *The Blazing World*. London: Sceptre, 2014.

———. *A Woman Looking at Men Looking at Women: Essays on Art, Sex, and the Mind*. New York: Simon and Schuster, 2016.

———. "Why One Story and Not Another?" *Zones of Focused Ambiguity in Siri Hustvedt's Works: Interdisciplinary Essays*. Ed. Johanna Hartmann, Christine Marks and Hubert Zapf. Anglia Book Series 52. Berlin and Boston: DeGruyter, 2016. 11-25.

Hutcheon, Linda. *The Politics of Postmodernism*. 2nd ed. Abingdon: Routledge, 2002.

Jameson, Frederic. "The Antinomies of Postmodernity." *The Cultural Turn: Selected Writings on the Postmodern, 1983-1998*. London: Verso, 1998. 50-72.

Kennedy, David. *The Ekphrastic Encounter in Contemporary British Poetry and Elsewhere*. Farnham: Ashgate, 2012.

Kirby, Alan. *Digimodernism: How New Technologies Dismantle the Postmodern and Reconfigure our Culture*. New York and London: continuum, 2009.

Marks, Christine. *"I Am Because You Are": Relationality in the Works of Siri Hustvedt*. Heidelberg: Winter, 2014.

Mitchell, David. *Cloud Atlas*. London: Sceptre, 2004.

Nancy, Jean-Luc. "The Confronted Community." Trans. Jason Kemp Winfree. *The Obsessions of George Bataille: Community and Communication*. Ed. Andrew J. Mitchell and Jason Kemp Winfree. New York: Suny Press, 2009. 19-30.

Nealon, Jeffrey T. *Post-Postmodernism, or, The Cultural Logic of Just-in-Time Capitalism*. Stanford: Stanford University Press, 2012.

Reipen, Corinna Sophie. *Visuality in the Works of Siri Hustvedt*. Frankfurt: Peter Lang, 2014.

Rippl, Gabriele. "Postcolonial Ekphrasis in the Contemporary Anglophone Indian Novel." *Handbook of Intermediality: Literature – Image – Sound – Music*. Ed. Gabriele Rippl. DeGruyter Handbook Series 1. Berlin and Boston: DeGruyter, 2015. 128-55.

———. "The Rich Zones of Genre Borderlands: Siri Hustvedt's Art of Mingling." *Zones of Focused Ambiguity in Siri Hustvedt's Works: Interdisciplinary Essays*. Ed. Johanna Hartmann, Christine Marks and Hubert Zapf. Anglia Book Series 52. Berlin and Boston: DeGruyter, 2016. 27-38.

Rosenthal, Caroline. "'A carnival in hell': Representations of New York City in Siri Hustvedt's Novels." *Zones of Focused Ambiguity in Siri Hustvedt's Works: Interdisciplinary Essays*. Ed. Johanna Hartmann, Christine Marks and Hubert Zapf. Anglia Book Series 52. Berlin and Boston: DeGruyter, 2016. 51-65.

Thiemann, Anna. "Portraits of the (Post-)Feminist Artist: Female Authorship and Authority in Siri Hustvedt's Fiction." *Zones of Focused Ambiguity in Siri Hustvedt's Works: Interdisciplinary Essays*. Ed. Johanna Hartmann, Christine Marks and Hubert Zapf. Anglia Book Series 52. Berlin and Boston: DeGruyter, 2016. 311-25.

Timmer, Nicoline. *Do You Feel it Too? The Post-postmodern Syndrome in American Fiction at the Turn of the Millennium*. Amsterdam: Rodopi, 2010.

Toth, Josh and Neil Brooks. "Introduction: A Wake and Renewed." *The Mourning After: Attending the Wake of Postmodernism*. Ed. Neil Brooks and Josh Toth. Amsterdam: Rodopi, 2007. 1-13.

Vermeulen, Timotheus and Robin van den Akker. "Notes on Metamodernism." *Journal of Aesthetics and Culture* 2 (2010): 1-14.

Folk Communities in Translation: Salvage Primitivism and Edward Sapir's French-Canadian Folk Songs

A. Elisabeth Reichel and Philipp Schweighauser

This essay zooms in on a less known aspect of major Boasian anthropologist Edward Sapir's work: His publication of French-Canadian folk songs in the July 1920 issue of *Poetry*, one of the flagship little magazines where modernist poetry flourished. A review of *Poetry* issues of the first three decades of the twentieth century shows that the magazine's inclusion of these songs is by no means an exception: The magazine's editors display a sustained interest in the cultural productions of "folk" communities, from lyrical imitations of Native American songs and prayers in the magazine's "aboriginal issue" of February 1917 to Cowboy songs and translations of New Mexican folk songs in the August 1920 issue. Sapir's translations of Québécois folk songs for *Poetry* and for *Folk Songs of French Canada* (1925), a volume he co-authored with Marius Barbeau, testify to what we call "salvage primitivism," the convergence of modernist primitivism and salvage ethnography's urge to preserve for posterity cultures deemed on the verge of extinction. A careful analysis of Sapir's theory and practice of translation reveals that his related publications of folk songs in *Poetry* and *Folk Songs of French Canada* deliver on the prospect of salvage to differing extents and with diverging results.

When poets and literary scholars think of *Poetry* magazine, they think first and foremost of its pivotal role in the modernist revolution. At Ezra Pound's urging, T. S. Eliot's "The Lovesong of J. Alfred Prufrock" was published there; as were Pound's own "In a Station of the Metro" and many of his cantos. *Poetry* also published a great number of additional poems that have become fixtures in the modernist canon, among them H. D.'s "The Pool," "Hymen," and "Halcyon"; Wallace Stevens's "Anecdote of the Jar" and "Sunday Morning"; William Carlos Williams's "The Shadow"; Amy Lowell's "The Day that Was that Day!"; and Robert Frost's "Snow."[1] Much of this work was iconoclastic in form and some of it daring in content, prompting angry reactions among the magazine's readers, to which its editor Harriet Monroe responded with comments that bore titles such as "The Enemies We Have Made" (May 1914) and "A Word to the Carping Critic" (November 1917). Yet browsing the magazine's early-twentieth-century issues, now freely available in its complete online archive, one is struck by their inclusion of a wide variety of poetic forms, only some of which can justly be called experimental in a modernist vein. In this essay we focus on another surprise that the early issues of *Poetry* magazine hold in store: their generous inclusion of what was variously called "folk-songs" or "folk-poetry" then. The two surprises are related as the modernist search for new forms often takes a detour through supposedly simpler modes of expression. In the well-documented phenomenon of modernist primitivism – from Gauguin's Tahiti paintings to T. S. Eliot's essay "War-Paint and Feathers" – this engagement is driven by a desire to rejuvenate one's own, Western art and culture through an engagement with artifacts and cultural practices that are perceived as fresher, more authentic, and less corrupted by processes of civilization and modernization.[2] This essay probes what we call "salvage primitivism": the convergence of modernist primitivism and salvage ethnography's urge to

---

[1] This essay grows out of the Swiss National Science Foundation research project "Of Cultural, Poetic, and Medial Alterity: The Scholarship, Poetry, Photographs, and Films of Edward Sapir, Ruth Fulton Benedict, and Margaret Mead." We wholeheartedly thank the participants in the project-related workshop "Anthropology, Literature, the Senses: Questions of Cultural, Poetic, and Medial Alterity," which took place at the University of Basel on 25-26 November 2016, for much valuable feedback on an early version of this essay, in particular our colleagues in the project (Gabriele Rippl, Walter Leimgruber, Silvy Chakkalakal) and our invited guests: David Howes, Regina Bendix, Richard Rath, and Sieglinde Lemke. We owe special thanks to Alexandra Grasso for diligently formatting and proofreading our essay.

[2] Frances S. Connelly aptly captures primitivism's double temporal trajectory when she notes its "urge toward deliberate regression combined with an even more compelling desire for rejuvenation" (35). For good accounts of modernist primitivism, see Flam and Deutch; Torgovnick; Gess; and Lemke.

preserve for posterity cultures deemed on the verge of extinction.[3] With its well-known role in the promotion of modernist poetry and its less-explored interest in ethnographic materials, *Poetry* magazine proves a particularly rewarding test case for our exploration of this convergence. In what follows, we first zoom in on major Boasian anthropologist Edward Sapir's contributions to the magazine and then examine this body of work in the context of its author's own theoretical writing on literary translation,[4] in order to provide, finally, a comprehensive assessment of Sapir as a "salvage primitivist." One of our main findings is that, judged by Sapir's own theory of translation, his renditions of Québécois folk songs in the July 1920 issue of *Poetry* and in his and Marius Barbeau's *Folk Songs of French Canada* (1925) deliver on the promise of salvage to differing extents and with diverging effects.

---

[3] In Jacob W. Gruber's words in the 1970 essay that introduced the concept of "salvage ethnography": "Though the idea of the corrupting influences of civilization was not a new one – it is, in fact, a continuing theme in Western culture – the idea that such alterations were the necessary price of an indefinite progress was a particular product of nineteenth-century optimism. In the face of the inevitable and necessary changes, in the face of an almost infinite variety of man whose details were essential to a definition of man, the obligation of both scientist and humanist was clear: he must collect and preserve the information and the products of human activity and genius so rapidly being destroyed" (1293). Gruber identifies British anthropologist James Cowles Prichard's alarmist 1839 intervention before the British Association for the Advancement of Science as a foundational moment in this specific branch of ethnographic thought and practice and traces its translation into Boasian anthropology. For a classic critique of salvage anthropology, see James Clifford's "On Ethnographic Allegory," his contribution to his and Marcus's *Writing Culture: The Poetics and Politics of Ethnography*. For a more recent, media-conscious account, see Brian Hochman's *Savage Preservation: The Ethnographic Origins of Modern Media Technology*.

[4] During the 1920s and 1930s, Sapir was also a regular contributor of critical essays to little magazines. While our focus here lies with his chapter "Language and Literature" from *Language* (1921) and the monograph *Folk Songs of French Canada* (Barbeau and Sapir 1925), Sapir's writings on literature and music offer further vantage points through which his renditions of folk songs can be profitably approached. Sapir's article "Percy Grainger and Primitive Music" (1916), for instance, discusses the views of composer Percy Grainger regarding the merit of the study of folkloric music. "The Twilight of Rhyme" (1917), "The Heuristic Value of Rhyme" (1920), and "The Musical Foundations of Verse" (1921), to name just a few other examples, form by contrast an intervention in modernist debates over the value of free verse. Siding with Amy Lowell, Sapir conceives in "The Musical Foundations of Verse" of a form of verse whose rhythm is not defined by patterns of rhyme but by the regular time intervals that characterize classical music. Tellingly, he uses his poem "To Debussy: '*La Cathédrale Engloutie*'" to illustrate this concept of modern poetry ("Musical Foundations" 937-38), whereas the folklore translations that he published in *Poetry* and *Folk Songs of French Canada* employ regular rhyme patterns.

Poetry's July 1920 issue begins with a brief introductory poem by Sapir titled "French-Canadian Folk-Songs." The poem is followed by Sapir's translations into English of four of the eponymous songs: "The Prince of Orange," "The King of Spain's Daughter and the Diver," "White as the Snow," and "The Dumb Shepherdess."[5] Immediately following Sapir's translations of Québécois songs, we find another translation, the poet and literary scholar Albert Edmund Trombly's rendition of "Three Children" from "the Old French." Later in the same issue, at the end of its poetry selection, we encounter Sapir's three-page "Note on French-Canadian Folk-Songs." Why this conspicuous presence of "folk songs" in an issue of one of the little magazines where U.S. modernism began? One might think that its editor's decision to publish Sapir's songs is an oddity in one of the major vehicles for experimental modernist poetry. But this is not so, for at least three reasons.

First, the editorial staff of *Poetry* awarded Sapir an honorable mention for this work ("Announcement" 109), thus granting his songs a special status as particularly representative of one kind of literature that the magazine seeks to promote. Further, far from being a rare guest of honor, Sapir contributed regularly to *Poetry*. Between 1919 and 1931, he published no less than twenty-three of his own poems in its pages, sometimes single ones, sometimes groups of poems under headings such as "Foam-Waves" (January 1926) and "Feathered Songs" (July 1927). These twenty-three poems represent only a small selection of Sapir's literary work: During his lifetime, and in parallel to his prolific career as a major voice in U.S. linguistics and cultural anthropology, he produced a substantial oeuvre of over 500 published and unpublished poems. In fact, Sapir was not the only early-twentieth-century anthropologist to write verse. Often under her pen name Anne Singleton, Ruth Fulton Benedict also wrote over 130 poems, thirteen of which were published in *Poetry* in its 1928 and 1930 issues. Margaret Mead, probably

---

[5] In his "Note on French-Canadian Folk-Songs," Sapir defers to his collaborator Marius Barbeau's judgment as he classifies these four songs: "*The Dumb Shepherdess* is a religious *complainte*, and is known in the lower St. Lawrence region, both north and south shores. *The King of Spain's Daughter* is a work ballad, especially used as a paddling song, and is based on versions from Temiscouata and Gaspé counties. *The Prince of Orange* is another paddling song, collected at Tadousac, one of the oldest French settlements in Canada, on the lower St. Lawrence. *White as the Snow* is a good example of the genuine ballad; it is one of the best known folk-songs of Quebec, having been recorded in no less than twelve versions" (212-13).

the best-known Boasian anthropologist, wrote over 220 poems, though most of them remain unpublished.[6]

We already hinted at the third reason why the inclusion of Sapir's French-Canadian folk songs in the July 1920 issue of *Poetry* is less of an oddity than may appear at first sight. The magazine's early publication history testifies to a sustained interest in making available the cultural productions of communities then commonly referred to as "folk."[7] Most famously, the magazine's so-called "aboriginal issue" of February 1917 contains lyrical imitations of Native American songs and prayers by four North American poets: Frank S. Gordon, Alice Corbin Henderson, Mary Austin, and Constance Lindsay Skinner. In her editorial comment, Harriet Monroe notes that this work is "[v]ivid [. . .] in its suggestion of racial feeling and rhythm," adding on a more sombre note that

---

[6] Previous research has mostly neglected this large corpus of poetry written by three of the most influential twentieth-century American anthropologists, with the exception of the intentionalist, author-centered readings put forward by biographers (Banner; Bateson; Caffrey; Darnell; Howard; Lapsley; Mead; Modell). While the latter tend to reduce the poems to an outlet of personal expression and conduit for private thoughts, Richard Handler's and A. Elisabeth Reichel's articles on Sapir and Philipp Schweighauser's and Karin Roffman's writings on Benedict offer analyses which consider the diverse academic and artistic contexts in which this corpus is enmeshed.

[7] Handler notes that the notion of the "folk society" has been "seductive" to European and North American thinkers "since the eighteenth century at least," featuring prominently, for instance, in nineteenth-century sociological theory and such dichotomies as Marx's antithesis between town and country, Maine's status and contract, Tönnies's *Gemeinschaft* and *Gesellschaft*, and Durkheim's mechanical and organic solidarity (*Nationalism* 63). In the context of ethnographic studies of French Canada, Horace Miner was the first to systematically apply the concept, in the specific sense that Robert Redfield had defined it (*Nationalism* 63-65). The debate among Canadian scholars on the utility of this model followed with a delay of two decades, as part of a current of historical revisionism after World War II. The controversy is a prime example, Handler argues, of "how well sociological models of the folk society match nationalistic visions of a rural Quebec out of which the nation has been born" (*Nationalism* 66). See also Handler, "In Search of the Folk Society."

For a critical analysis of the emergence of "folk" discourse in the late eighteenth and early nineteenth centuries which pays particular attention to the categories of folk song and folk music, see Gelbart. Filene starts from its eighteenth- and nineteenth-century origins to make sense of twentieth-century folk music revivalism.

While different in scope and focus, we share with these and many other recent scholars a sensitivity to the politically charged and highly problematic history of categories qualified by the term "folk." To be sure, social constructions marked as "folk" have always been discursively aligned with "the 'savages'" and "'primitives'" to some extent to serve as "foils to modern civilized Europeans" (Gelbart 12).

> the danger is that the tribes, in the process of so-called civilization, will lose all trace of it; that their beautiful primitive poetry will perish among the ruins of obliterated states. [. . .] The phonograph is a valuable aid to these modern investigators. (Monroe, Sandburg, and Corbin 251-53)

In his editorial comment, Carl Sandburg jokingly suggests that "[s]uspicion arises definitely that the Red and his children committed direct plagiarism on the modern imagists and vorticists" (255).

Further examples abound. In the November 1918 issue, Alice Corbin Henderson, one of *Poetry*'s two associate editors and a contributor to its "aboriginal issue," reviews *The Path on the Rainbow*, an anthology of Native American songs and chants edited by George W. Cronyn. Corbin, who would publish an anthology of indigenous New Mexican poetry herself in the following year and publish selections of these in the August 1920 issue of *Poetry*, applauds the volume's preservation of "authentic Indian poems," noting that the study of Native American poetry requires more than the ethnographer's scientific expertise: "it has remained, and still remains, for the artist and poet to interpret adequately many phases of Indian expression" (Corbin, "Review" 41). Having dismissed talk about "the vanishing race" – the very talk that Monroe engages in in her editorial note on the "aboriginal issue" – and having expressed her dislike of the "far-distant-sounding word 'aboriginal'," Corbin turns Sandburg's joking comparison between Native American and modernist poetry into an utterly serious statement: "Stephen Crane would have qualified as an Indian poet, and in the *Mid-American Chants* of Sherwood Anderson," which were also published in *Poetry*, "one finds almost precisely the mood of the songs accompanying the green corn dances of the pueblo Indians" (42). Like Monroe, Corbin is after authenticity, too: She notes the songs' "pristine freshness" (45) and judges them to be "the most consummate, primal art" (46).

As a final example of *Poetry* editors' predilection for "folk cultures," consider the issue immediately following the July 1920 issue that published Sapir's French-Canadian folk songs. Here we find Cowboy songs, dialect poems of the Western U.S., and Corbin's translations of New Mexican folk songs. In her essay on these songs and poems entitled "The Folk Poetry of these States," Corbin distinguishes between two types of folk poetry: first, the "instinctive," "unconscious," "naive," "primitive," and "unsophisticated" productions of the people themselves; second, the reworking of this material by more refined minds, e.g., James Russell Lowell, John Hay, Bret Harte, Joel Chandler Harris, Paul Laurence Dunbar, and Vachel Lindsay. Corbin identifies several types of American folk poetry of non-European stock, among them "the Negro dialect poems of Thomas Nelson Page or Joel Chandler Harris," which refine the songs and spirituals of "the primitive negro poet" (Corbin, "Folk Poetry" 266); the "primitive poetry of the American Indian" (267); and the "Spanish folk-songs of the Southwest" (269) that Corbin herself is particularly interested in.[8]

What unites all of these folklore contributions to *Poetry* magazine is first and foremost a sustained interest in the cultural productions of folk communities that are imagined to be more primal, more pristine, and more authentic. In this sense, Sapir's folk songs do fit very well into one of the flagship magazines of the modernist movement, since they tie in perfectly with modernist primitivism in its various guises (from Tristan Tzara's "Negro Songs" to Picasso's tribal masks in *Les Demoiselles d'Avignon*). What becomes clearer here than elsewhere is how closely aligned modernist primitivism is with salvage ethnography's desire to preserve the customs and artifacts of communities that are assumed to vanish in the face of inexorable progress.

Moreover, in particular Corbin's contributions highlight the extent to which salvage primitivism is a nationalist project. While *Poetry* did publish a number of folk songs from outside of North America – the "Old Folk Songs of Ukraina" in the April 1919 issue are an example – it focused mainly on native songs, claiming them as part of an American national heritage. In Corbin's words,

> The soil has to be turned over; we have to examine our roots to know what they are. [. . .] [S]tudents of folk-songs have placed a greater emphasis on the survivals of traditional English ballads in our remote mountain regions than on the more truly native and indigenous material that is all around us, which has been overlooked simply because of its more obvious familiarity and its lack of literary ancestry. ("Folk Songs" 269-70)

For students of American culture, this patriotic enlistment of domestic ethnic and minority communities rings familiar, from the personification of America as a half-naked Native American woman in the famous anti-British cartoon "The able doctor, or, America swallowing the bitter draught" (1774) to the nationalist origins of transnationalism in Randolph Bourne, for whom internal diversity is a sign of external strength, and beyond.

---

[8] Corbin's words of praise are especially troublesome in regard to Page, the most prominent representative of the Southern plantation romance.

While Sapir's contribution to the study of folklore aligns him less readily with such nationalist projects, the career trajectory of his Canadian collaborator Marius Barbeau, with whom he co-authored *Folk Songs of French Canada* (1925), testifies to the nationalist underpinnings of the late-nineteenth- and early-twentieth-century folklore vogue in which salvage primitivists were caught up. An immensely prolific researcher and popularizer of French-Canadian folk traditions, Barbeau is widely considered the founder of folklore studies in Canada.[9] As Richard Handler has compellingly shown in *Nationalism and the Politics of Culture in Quebec*, the movement of folklorists that Barbeau spearheaded was rooted in an idealized vision of French Canada as an isolated, rural folk society, which was taken to be the authentic essence out of which the present nation had been born (63-75). This romantic nationalist conception of Quebec is apparent in Barbeau's journalistic piece "The Fisher-Folk of Northern Gaspé," which was published in the *Quebec Daily Telegraph* in 1923. It opens with these words:

> Isolated and forsaken as they are, on lonely shores, between the boundless waters of the St. Lawrence and the wild *Chikchoc* mountains, the fisher-folk of Northern Gaspé need not be pitied by their sympathetic visitors. [. . .] [T]heir simple life, reminiscent of the past and in close association with nature, brings them many compensations. They suffer less than we do from the evils that sprang out of Pandora's box. And if, as in the ancient tale, a King were again to send his heirs in search of happiness, the lucky third son would find it in a humble Gaspesian loghouse, sheltered far from the hustling crowds, while his elders might fail to detect it in the palaces of the rich and mighty. (2)

Barbeau goes on to interlace snippets of Sapir's translations of French-Canadian songs to illustrate the "delight on returning to the realm of nature," "from the summits [. . .] to the starting point of all human endeavors and creations" (2). Sapir's translation of the song "Three Poisoned Roses," for instance, appears as an "irresponsibly genial" "little ballad," which "quickened notions of courtly glory and frivolity in naïve imaginations" (3).

Despite obvious differences in genre and medium of publication, Sapir's introductory poem in the July 1920 edition of *Poetry* magazine

---

[9] For his significance to both Canadian anthropology and a popular appreciation of French-Canadian folklore, see especially the publications of Barbeau scholar Andrew Nurse. Nurse claims that "Barbeau was arguably the most prominent anthropologist in Canadian History" ("But Now" 436) and "may certainly have been the best known" ("But Now" 466 n11).

strikes a very similar tone. In "French-Canadian Folk-Songs," Sapir notes that the songs he wishes to make heard come from "the past" (l. 1) and calls them "little flowers" (l. 8) that have "tiny roots" (l. 3) and sing a "tiny song" (l. 5), thus indicating their fragility. To the attentive listener, though, these songs offer something precious: "We shall weave him a tiny wreath / For the strange today" (l. 16-17). The meaning of these two final lines of the poem is ambiguous. In the most straightforward reading, "strange" is the adjectival modifier of "today," suggesting that "today," that is, present, modern life, is "strange." This reading is the most probable one because it easily fits the first two lines of the poem's second stanza, "We are weaving tiny roots / In the strange today" (l. 6-7). In another reading of the poem's final line, however, "today" refers to the moment at which the songs impact the listener and "the strange" are the recipients of the songs' gift. A third reading finds that, in singing, the songs weave a "tiny wreath" (l. 16) dedicated to their own strange selves that is then offered to an other. In that case the songs *themselves*, or the community they sing from, are "strange." In all three readings, the poem highlights the distance between the listener and the songs and attributes redemptive power to those songs. Only by turning "[f]rom the highway" (l. 15), the poem's spatial metaphor for modernity, can the songs be heard. These "tiny song[s]" (l. 5), these "little flowers" (l. 8), then, either promise to redeem the strangeness of the present or they themselves offer the gift of strangeness. Salvage ethnography's moral imperative – pithily summarized by Gruber as "the savage is disappearing; preserve what you can; posterity will hold you accountable" (1295) – once more meets modernist primitivism's desire for enstrangement and rejuvenation.

Interestingly though, Sapir's companion essay "Note on French-Canadian Folk-Songs" strikes a notably different chord. While it does begin with an assertion of the pristine quality of Québécois culture, which is said to preserve pre-modern French culture because it is unaffected by "[t]he great current of modern civilization" (211), there is no alarmist warning against its impending disappearance. Neither does Sapir wax lyrical about its authenticity. Instead, he acknowledges the extensive research on French-Canadian folk culture done by Barbeau, whom he calls "incomparably its greatest authority" (211). Sapir also comments on how the original folk songs were recorded by phonograph and writing, where the songs were collected, what types of songs there are, and which of these types his selections for *Poetry* magazine belong to. The essay ends with a brief general discussion of some issues of translation that we will return to below. In this "Note," then, Sapir wears three different masks: first, that of the poet who can appreciate the quality of these folk songs; second, that of the translator who opts for a literal rather than a lyrical rendition of his material; and third, that of the anthropologist who studies a folk community's artifacts and practices. But Sapir's anthropologist and translator personae are clearly foregrounded here.

That this is so becomes even clearer when we compare Sapir's "Note" to his and Barbeau's joint book *Folk Songs of French Canada*, a collection of French-Canadian folk songs that includes the four translations that Sapir published in *Poetry* plus 37 additional ones. The tone of this volume is markedly different from that of Sapir's note in *Poetry* magazine. In their introduction to the volume as a whole and their brief explanatory notes before each song, Barbeau and Sapir tap deep into nostalgic discourses about the impending disappearance of a primal, authentic culture under the pressures of modern civilization. "Folk songs were once part of the everyday life of French America" (xiii). On this regretful note begins their introduction. The volume ends with an assertion of the songs' vibrant pastness that is reminiscent of Barbeau's "The Fisher-Folk of Northern Gaspé":

> [t]he best claim to recognition of the French folk songs of America undoubtedly rests in their comparative antiquity. Sheltered in woodland recesses, far from the political commotions of the Old World, they have preserved much of their sparkling, archaic flavor. (Barbeau and Sapir xxii)

In Barbeau and Sapir's understanding, these songs are understood as an antidote to a modernity that is painted as equally spiritless and desiccated as Eliot's in *The Waste Land*. Here is how this sounds in the introductory note before "The King of Spain's Daughter":

> In the leisurely days of old, folk songs and tales provided a favorite entertainment for all, high or low, on land and on the sea, under the open sky and by the fireside in the long winter evenings. [. . .] Ever since man was banned from Eden, work has remained a punishment, a dire law to the many. And the penalty for the sin of Adam has not grown lighter with the lapse of millennia. In a past epoch work was only an incident in life and starvation a too-often recurring accident. Work was the mere provider of necessities, by no means banishing enjoyment out of life, yet, slight as it might be, it was made more attractive by a spontaneous concentration, an artistic refinement unfamiliar to the present generation. Work songs of all kinds sustained the rhythm of the hand in toil, while the mind escaped on the wing of fancy to the enchanted realm of wonderland. Now that labor is sullen under its crushing, mechanical burden, now that profit and luxury

have become the very essence of human endeavor, an ominous silence has invaded the workshop. (Barbeau and Sapir 100)

Passages such as this one abound; they are suffused with a profound sense of nostalgia that is spatial as well as temporal and in this instance even assumes Biblical proportions, taking, in the final sentences quoted here, the form of a jeremiad or, indeed, that of a Marxist account of alienation.

In marked contrast, in his "Note on French-Canadian Folk-Songs" in the July 1920 issue of *Poetry*, Sapir projects the persona of the distanced, objective observer. Why does this poet-anthropologist adopt this particular stance in an essay for one of his era's major poetry magazines? The answer, we believe, is this: There is no need for Sapir to extol the beauty and authenticity of folk songs here because, for early-twentieth-century readers of *Poetry* magazine, this goes without saying. Others' interpretations and translations of folk songs, others' essays on folk songs, and others' reviews of collections of folk songs provide the framework within which the cultural value of this material is self-evident. Thus, Sapir can adopt the stance of scientific observer to confirm the authenticity of these songs without having to indulge in the same pathos. Sapir's contributions to the July 1920 issue of *Poetry* magazine are thus firmly embedded in the nexus between salvage ethnography and modernist primitivism without wearing that affiliation on their sleeves.

Yet to determine with precision Sapir's place in the discourse of salvage primitivism, we need to consider more closely the question of translation. Importantly, Sapir stands out among Boas's students as the anthropologist who continued his teacher's strong early interest in linguistics while this interest became less pronounced in Boas's later research. Thus, apart from his contributions to the emergence of a cultural pluralist and relativist paradigm in anthropology, Sapir is known today primarily for his accomplishments in linguistics, most famously as a pioneer of linguistic relativity and teacher of Benjamin Lee Whorf. In fact, the one full-length book that Sapir wrote in the course of his career is an introduction to the study of language. *Language: An Introduction to the Study of Speech* was first published in 1921 and is today considered a classic in the history of modern linguistics, foundational of its American structuralist school. The final chapter, "Language and Literature," manifests most strikingly Sapir's abiding concern for literature. Yet rather than offering a discussion of the relation between language and literature, as its title suggests, the chapter starts by cutting short this very question: "When the expression is of unusual significance, we call it literature" (236), Sapir declares laconically. After all, the book is called *Language*, not *Literature*. Anticipating objections to his shorthand, however, he adds a footnote:

> I can hardly stop to define just what kind of expression is "significant" enough to be called art or literature. Besides, I do not exactly know. We shall have to take literature for granted. (236 n.1)

With the tedious business of literariness out of the way, he is free to focus on what he is really concerned with: how to *translate* literature.

Or rather, whether to do so. For Sapir's first line of reasoning suggests that "a work of literary art can never be translated" (237); every art is limited by its medium, he presumes, maintaining a "resistance of the medium" (236). "Language," then, "is the medium of literature as marble or bronze or clay are the materials of the sculptor," and "[s]ince every language has its distinctive peculiarities, the innate formal limitations – and possibilities – of one literature are never quite the same as those of another" (237). Their effects on the art thus "cannot be carried over without loss or modification" (237). Sapir agrees with the Italian philosopher Benedetto Croce in his refutation of literary translation in the *Aesthetic* (1909 [1902]).[10] "Nevertheless," he immediately counters, "literature does get itself translated, sometimes with astonishing adequacy" (237).

To resolve this paradox, Sapir introduces another layer of language, apart from the "specifically linguistic art that is not transferable," its phonetic, morphological, and syntactic particularities:

> This brings up the question whether in the art of literature there are not intertwined two distinct kinds or levels of art – a generalized, non-linguistic art, which can be transferred without loss into an alien linguistic medium, and a specifically linguistic art that is not transferable. I believe the distinction is entirely valid, though we never get the two levels pure in practice. Literature moves in language as a medium, but that medium comprises two layers, the latent content of language – our intuitive record of experience – and the particular conformation of a given language – the specific how of our record of experience. (237-38)

---

[10] In this way, Croce reappears in the final chapter of *Language*, after being acknowledged in its preface as "one of the very few who have gained an understanding of the fundamental significance of language. He has pointed out its close relation to the problem of art. I am deeply indebted to him for this insight" (iii).

Thus, the second layer is "an intuitive basis that underlies all linguistic expression" and "is immediately fashioned out of a generalized human experience – thought and feeling – of which his [the artist's] own individual experience is a highly personalized selection" (239). Again, Sapir refers to Croce, who, in Sapir's reading of the *Aesthetic*, uses the term "intuition" to denote this level of a generalized human experience in language.

Croce's *Aesthetic: As Science of Expression and General Linguistic* is notorious for its claim that art is expression but has also attracted much scholarly attention for its conclusion that all artistic expression is language:

> Aesthetic and Linguistic [. . .] are not two different sciences, but one single science. [. . .] Whoever studies general Linguistic [. . .] studies aesthetic problems, and *vice versa. Philosophy of language and philosophy of art are the same thing.* (234)

It does not surprise, then, that Croce has been resurrected in recent decades as an important precursor of structuralist semiotics and the linguistic turn.[11] It is important to remember, though, that Croce's *Aesthetic* is grounded in an idealist metaphysics and epistemology. It

> is founded upon a view of the creation of meaning as the property of the speaking individual, rather than as the effect of differences within a closed system of signs. [. . .] Rather than Saussure's argument that meaning is produced by linguistic structure, here it resides in the individual language user. (Burke, Crowley, and Girvin 16)

Croce's idealist understanding of knowledge as created by the human mind prior to the operations of sensory perception is manifest in his assertion of the "[i]dentity of intuition and expression": "intuitive knowledge is expressive knowledge, [. . .] intuition [. . .] is distinguished [. . .] from the flux or wave of sensation [. . .], and this form, this taking possession of, is expression. To have an intuition is to express" (18-19). Interestingly, it is precisely this idealism and Croce's consequent failure to account for the formative role of tradition that Sapir takes issue with in his personal notes:

---

[11] See, for example, René Wellek's respective entry in his *History of Modern Criticism, 1750-1950* ("Benedetto Croce"; see also "Joel Elias Spingarn") and Richard Shusterman's publications on Croce ("Analytic Aesthetics"; "Deconstruction and Analysis"; "Croce on Interpretation").

> "Expression" is all very well, but what is Croce's attitude towards the obvious presence of traditional patterns? If art were altogether a matter of individual expression, should there be as close adherence to such traditional forms as we actually find? Either, then, expression is to be defined with reference to social norms, in which case it can hardly be considered as the immediate external correlate of intuition; *or* we must assert that even the most successful expression, the greatest work of art, is theoretically a failure, adulterated by conformity to ready-made types, or at least imperceptibly swayed by powerful analogies. Note that we have precisely the same problem in language. One creates in speaking [. . .], but the material of expression is given by tradition; one is at the mercy of historical limitations. But presumably Croce would grant all that as being implicitly provided for in his idea of "expression." ("Suggestive Notes" 20-21)

Clearly, Sapir's two-layered model of language in "Language and Literature" and his acknowledgement of an indebtedness to Croce in his elaborations on both these levels is based on this charitable reading of Croce's *Aesthetic* as "implicitly provid[ing]" for tradition as "the material of expression," which is "at the mercy of historical limitations."

With regard to the question of literary translation, this model entails that "[l]iterature that draws its sustenance mainly – never entirely – from [the] level [of intuition] [. . .] is translatable without too great a loss of character" (Sapir, "Language and Literature" 238). That is, when read against Sapir's own, first conception of literary translation, we find implicit in the renditions of French-Canadian songs that he published in *Poetry* the assumption that they as well – like the "Whitmans and Brownings" that Sapir cites – partake of an absolute language that is formed out of a universal "human experience" (239).

Yet while going back on the claim that literature is not translatable, Sapir still reserves the highest praise for those that cannot be translated without loss – "the Shakespeares and Heines" in his ranking: literature that presents a "completed synthesis" of the two levels of language, "of the absolute art of intuition and the innate, specialized art of the linguistic medium" (240). Heine, for instance, is able "to fit or trim the deeper intuition to the provincial accents of their daily speech," so that his audience is left "under the illusion that the universe speaks German. The material 'disappears'" (240). Despite Sapir's crabwise recognition that literature is translatable, by evoking an absolute, universal language that connects all human experience, his views firmly rest on a linguistic holism:

> Every language is itself a collective art of expression. There is concealed in it a particular set of esthetic factors – phonetic, rhythmic, symbolic, morphological – which it does not completely share with any other language. These factors may either merge their potencies with those of that unknown, absolute language to which I have referred – this is the method of Shakespeare and Heine – or they may weave a private, technical art fabric of their own, the innate art of the language intensified or sublimated. (240)

The latter method is practiced by "the Swinburnes" (240) in Sapir's classification. It is the holistic conception of language most clearly expressed in this passage that prompts Sapir's initial dismissal of literary translation and which now reappears as a devaluation of literature that gets itself translated *too easily* and in its entirety – without "resistance of the medium" (236).

Sapir's holistic conception of language, and of a literary work bound by a specific language as its medium, is also symptomatic of his dual imbrication in modernist aesthetics and anthropological debates, which were connected in Sapir's time not only through their shared salvage imperative but also through an emerging structuralism. Eric Aronoff's *Composing Cultures: Modernism, American Literary Studies, and the Problem of Culture* (2013) explores this very convergence, featuring Sapir as a key figure in a network of anthropologists and literary critics who conceived of cultures, literary works, and languages as relative, internally coherent systems of meaning.[12] In "Language and Literature," this enmeshment of disciplinary affiliations is most explicit in Sapir's persistent reference to Croce's aesthetics. Aronoff assumes that Sapir was introduced to Croce's theory by Joel Spingarn, professor of comparative literature at Columbia University and co-founder of Harcourt, Brace and Company, the publishing house that first printed *Language* (Aronoff 121-22). Spingarn's reading of Croce is famously captured in his lecture *The New Criticism*, which was delivered at Columbia University on 9 March 1910, and vehemently calls for a new criticism that "clearly recognizes in every work of art an organism governed by its own law" (21).

Sapir's notion of language as an integrated whole in which "a particular set of esthetic factors" is "concealed" ("Language and Literature" 240) and which creates "the innate formal limitations – and possibilities – of one literature" (237) is further necessary to understand his "pedantic literalness" as a translator, to which he admits in the "Note" on his

---

[12] Marc Manganaro has also noted this connection between modernist aesthetics and criticism and early-twentieth-century conceptions of culture in his study *Culture, 1922: The Emergence of a Concept* (2002). Aronoff acknowledges his great debt to Manganaro.

French-Canadian songs (213). His pedantry notwithstanding, two aspects of the French originals were not carried over into his English translations: First, "[n]ot all the originals [. . .] make use of strict rhymes; assonances are often used instead" (213). Second, the songs "can hardly be adequately understood or appreciated" without the music (211), which for him forms an integral part in the meaning-making process, a part which the renditions in *Poetry* also lack. Thus the latter, while testifying to the songs' involvement in an absolute, universally human language, fail on at least two grounds to represent the second layer and necessary prerequisite for "the greatest [. . .] literary ar[t]" ("Language and Literature" 240) in Sapir's conception: the specific, coherent meaning-making system of the native language – what Sapir, in idealist fashion, also frequently calls the linguistic "genius" of a culture (*Language* 33 et passim).

By contrast, *Folk Songs of French Canada*, published five years later, presents the songs both in English translation and in French, as well as together with the music as transcribed by the authors in European musical notation.[13] Note, for example, how in "The Prince of Orange" ("Le Prince d'Orange"; Figure 1), the first song in both this anthology

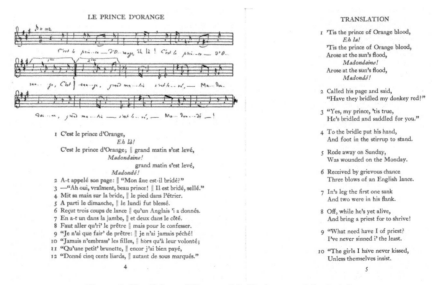

Figure 1: "Le Prince d'Orange," in Barbeau and Sapir 4-5.
Reproduced by kind permission.

---

[13] To be precise, Barbeau "is responsible [. . .] for the musical transcriptions" (xi).

and the sequence in *Poetry*, the changed arrangement allows the reader to witness the "genius" of the native language: the use of assonances instead of strict rhymes, for instance, which Sapir points out in his "Note" (the assonant "s'est levé" or "Il est bridé, sellé" instead of "blood/flood," "said/red," "true/you," and so forth). This "innate" peculiarity of French-Canadian literary language is lost in translation. In other words, as opposed to his renditions in *Poetry*, the songs presented in *Folk Songs of French Canada* appear as both translatable and untranslatable, as forming an internally coherent, self-contained whole, which may be translated but not without significant loss. In Sapir's taxonomy, they thus qualify for a place among "the Shakespeares and Heines," who offer "a completed synthesis of the absolute" and culturally specific art of language ("Language and Literature" 240).

In concluding, let us return to *Poetry* magazine and relate our reading of Sapir's French-Canadian songs against his own theory of literary translation back to the pervasive salvage imperative that we explore in the first half of the essay. To this we have added that, from the perspective of Sapir the poet, anthropologist, translator, *and* linguist, *Poetry*'s renditions must fail to a certain extent to deliver on the prospect of salvage. When presented only in English translation, a constitutive literary component, bound to the songs' source language, is lost. At the same time, it is these translations that were Sapir's greatest success in modernist literary circles: In addition to its honorable mention, *Poetry* paid Sapir 40 dollars, more than any of his other poems earned him, and *The Literary Digest* immediately published a reprint of "The King of Spain's Daughter and the Diver," "White as the Snow," and "The Dumb Shepherdess." *Folk Songs of French Canada* was also received very favorably. In a review published in the September 1926 issue of *Poetry*, Monroe grouped together four "Folk-Song Collections," including Barbeau and Sapir's anthology, testifying once more to the intricate intertwinement of modernist primitivism and salvage ethnography that we call "salvage primitivism." "Such books as these are extremely valuable records of a too-perishable past," she concludes, agreeing with fellow editor Alice Corbin that "[t]he[ir] purpose [. . .] is to preserve these old folk-songs while there is still time" (350). That the songs under review vary widely in their source language and place of origin – from French Canada to Spanish in New Mexico – matters little in this scheme, with the critical distinction being diachronic, between "a too-perishable past" and fast-moving, all-vanquishing progress toward modernity. The specifics of synchronic data, geographic as well as linguistic, must yield to the moral urgency of this salvage operation. Thus while being an avid contributor and loyal subscriber, Sapir's "pedantic literalness" ("Note" 213) and insistence on linguistic particularity ultimately also set him somewhat apart from the modernist and primitivist mainstream represented by *Poetry*. Given the political ramifications of the allochronism inherent in salvage ethnography, this is not nothing: It equips Sapir's particular brand of salvage primitivism with an attention to synchronic detail that gets in the way of the wholesale projection of spatial differences onto a temporal scale that Monroe's dominant variety involves.[14]

---

[14] The disenfranchisement of communities that follows from what Johannes Fabian has influentially termed "allochronism," that is, the denial of the coeval existence of spatially remote people by positioning them in an earlier, "savage" or "primitive" stage of human development, has been extensively studied by both historians of anthropology and scholars of primitivist literature. "[T]he mode of scientific and moral authority associated with salvage [. . .] ethnography" is not only based on the "assum[ption] that the other society is weak and 'needs' to be represented by an outsider" but also "that what matters in its life is its past, not present or future" (Clifford 113). As Hochman reminds us, "[w]riters and anthropologists championed the salvage endeavor as a scientific opportunity and a moral imperative, very often turning a blind eye to the realities of survival and change that surrounded them" (xv).

References

"Announcement of Awards." *Poetry* 17.2 (November 1920): 105-14.
Aronoff, Eric. *Composing Cultures: Modernism, American Literary Studies, and the Problem of Culture*. Charlottesville: University of Virginia Press, 2013.
Banner, Lois W. *Intertwined Lives: Margaret Mead, Ruth Benedict, and Their Circle*. New York: Knopf, 2003.
Barbeau, C. M. [Marius]. "The Fisher-Folk of Northern Gaspé." *Quebec Daily Telegraph* (Christmas Number 1923): 2-3, 9.
—— and Edward Sapir. *Folk Songs of French Canada*. New Haven: Yale University Press, 1925.
Bateson, Mary Catherine. *With a Daughter's Eye: A Memoir of Margaret Mead and Gregory Bateson*. New York: Morrow, 1984.
Bourne, Randolph S. "Trans-National America." *The Atlantic* (July 1916): 86-97.
Burke, Lucy, Tony Crowley, and Alan Girvin. "Theorising the Sign." *The Routledge Language and Cultural Theory Reader*. Ed. Lucy Burke, Tony Crowley, and Alan Girvin. London: Routledge, 2000.
Caffrey, Margaret M. *Ruth Benedict: Stranger in this Land*. Austin: University of Texas Press, 1989.
Clifford, James. "On Ethnographic Allegory." *Writing Culture: The Poetics and Politics of Ethnography*. Ed. James Clifford and George Marcus. Berkeley: University of California Press, 1986. 98-121.
Connelly, Frances S. *The Sleep of Reason: Primitivism in Modern European Art and Aesthetics 1725-1907*. University Park: Pennsylvania State University Press, 1995.
Corbin Henderson, Alice. "The Folk Poetry of These States." *Poetry* 16.5 (August 1920): 264-73.
——. Review of *The Path on the Rainbow: An Anthology of Songs and Chants from the Indians of North America*. Edited by George W. Cronyn, with an introduction by Mary Austin. *Poetry* 14.1 (April 1919): 41-47.
Croce, Benedetto. *Aesthetic: As Science of Expression and General Linguistic*. 1902. London: Macmillan, 1909.
Darnell, Regna. *Edward Sapir: Linguist, Anthropologist, Humanist*. Berkeley: University of California Press, 1990.
Eliot, T. S. "War-Paint and Feathers." *Primitivism and Twentieth Century Art: A Documentary History*. Ed. Jack Flam with Miriam Deutch. Berkeley: University of California Press, 2003. 121-23.
Fabian, Johannes. *Time and the Other: How Anthropology Makes Its Object*. 1983. New York: Columbia University Press, 2014.

Filene, Benjamin. *Romancing the Folk: Public Memory and American Roots Music.* Chapel Hill: University of North Carolina Press, 2000.

Flam, Jack D., and Miriam Deutch, eds. *Primitivism and Twentieth-Century Art: A Documentary History.* Berkeley: University of California Press, 2003.

Gelbart, Matthew. *The Invention of "Folk Music" and "Art Music": Emerging Categories from Ossian to Wagner.* Cambridge: Cambridge University Press, 2007.

Gess, Nicola. *Primitives Denken: Wilde, Kinder und Wahnsinnige in der literarischen Moderne (Müller, Musil, Benn, Benjamin).* Munich: Fink, 2013.

Gruber, Jacob W. "Ethnographic Salvage and the Shaping of Anthropology." *American Anthropologist* 72.6 (1970): 1289-99.

Handler, Richard. "Anti-Romantic Romanticism: Edward Sapir and the Critique of American Individualism." *Critics Against Culture: Anthropological Observers of Mass Society.* Madison: University of Wisconsin Press, 2005. 73-95.

———. "The Dainty and the Hungry Man: Literature and Anthropology in the Work of Edward Sapir." *Edward Sapir: Critical Assessments of Leading Linguists.* London: Routledge, 2007. 289-311.

———. "In Search of the Folk Society: Nationalism and Folklore Studies in Quebec." *Culture* 3.1 (1983): 103-14.

———. "Introduction to Sections Four and Five: Edward Sapir's Aesthetic and Cultural Criticism." *Culture.* Ed. Regna Darnell, Richard Handler, and Judith T. Irvine. Berlin: Mouton de Gruyter, 1999. 731-47.

———. *Nationalism and the Politics of Culture in Quebec.* Madison: University of Wisconsin Press, 1988.

———. "Sapir's Poetic Experience." *American Anthropologist* 86.2 (1984): 416-17.

———. "Vigorous Male and Aspiring Female: Poetry, Personality, and Culture in Edward Sapir and Ruth Benedict." *Critics Against Culture: Anthropological Observers of Mass Society.* Madison: University of Wisconsin Press, 2005. 96-122.

Hochman, Brian. *Savage Preservation: The Ethnographic Origins of Modern Media Technology.* Minneapolis: University of Minnesota Press, 2014.

Howard, Jane. *Margaret Mead: A Life.* London: Harvill Press, 1984.

Lapsley, Hilary. *Margaret Mead and Ruth Benedict: The Kinship of Women.* Amherst: University of Massachusetts Press, 1999.

Lemke, Sieglinde. *Primitivist Modernism: Black Culture and the Origins of Transatlantic Modernism.* Oxford: Oxford University Press, 1998.

Manganaro, Marc. *Culture, 1922: The Emergence of a Concept*. Princeton: Princeton University Press, 2002.

Mead, Margaret. *An Anthropologist at Work: Writings of Ruth Benedict*. Boston: Houghton Mifflin, 1959.

Modell, Judith. *Ruth Benedict: Patterns of a Life*. London: Chatto and Windus, 1984.

Monroe, Harriet. "Folk-Song Collections." Review of *Folk-Songs of the South*, edited by John Harrington Cox; *Folk Songs of French Canada* by Marius Barbeau and Edward Sapir; *Ballads and Songs of the Shanty Boy*, collected and edited by Franz Rickaby; and *Spanish Folk Songs of New Mexico*, collected by Mary R. Van Stone. *Poetry* 28.6 (September 1926): 348-50.

———. "Tradition." *Poetry* 2.2 (May 1913): 67-68.

———, Carl Sandburg, and Alice Corbin Henderson. "Aboriginal Poetry." *Poetry* 9.5 (February 1917): 251-56.

Nurse, Andrew. "The Best Field for Tourist Sale of Books: Marius Barbeau, the Macmillan Company, and Folklore Publication in the 1930s." *Papers of the Bibliographical Society of Canada* 36.1 (1997): 7-30.

———. "'But Now Things Have Changed': Marius Barbeau and the Politics of Amerindian Identity." *Ethnohistory* 48.3 (2001): 433-72.

———. "Marius Barbeau and the Methodology of Salvage Anthropology in Canada, 1911-51." *Historicizing Canadian Anthropology*. Ed. Julia Harrison and Regna Darnell. Vancouver: University of British Columbia Press, 2006. 52-64.

———. "Tradition and Modernity: The Cultural Work of Marius Barbeau." Ph.D. dissertation. Kingston: Queen's University, 1997.

———, Lynda Jessup, and Gordon Smith, eds. *Around and About Barbeau: Modeling Twentieth-Century Culture*. Gatineau: Museum of Civilization, 2008.

"Poetry." *Archive: Poetry Magazine Since 1912*. Poetry Foundation. 2017. <https://www.poetryfoundation.org/poetrymagazine/archive>.

Reichel, A. Elisabeth. "Sonophilia / Sonophobia: Sonic Others in the Poetry of Edward Sapir." *Literature, Ethics, Morality: American Studies Perspectives*. SPELL: Swiss Papers in English Language and Literature 32. Ed. Ridvan Askin and Philipp Schweighauser. Tübingen: Narr, 2015. 215-29.

Roffman, Karin. *From the Modernist Annex: American Women Writers in Museums and Libraries*. Tuscaloosa: University of Alabama Press, 2010.

Sapir, Edward. "The Dumb Shepherdess." *Poetry* 16.4 (July 1920): 183-85. Reprinted in *Literary Digest* 66.4 (1920): 36.

———. "French-Canadian Folk-Songs." *Poetry* 16.4 (July 1920): 175-76.

———. "The Heuristic Value of Rhyme." 1920. *Selected Writings of Edward Sapir: In Language, Culture and Personality*. Berkeley: University of California Press, 1973. 496-99.

———. "The King of Spain's Daughter and the Diver." *Poetry* 16.4 (July 1920): 179-82. Reprinted in *Literary Digest* 66.4 (1920): 36.

———. "Language and Literature." *Language*. Edward Sapir.

———. *Language: An Introduction to the Study of Speech*. New York: Harcourt, Brace and Company, 1921.

———. "The Musical Foundations of Verse." 1921. *Culture*. Ed. Regna Darnell, Judith T. Irvine, and Richard Handler. Berlin: Mouton de Gruyter, 1999. 930-44.

———. "Percy Grainger and Primitive Music." 1916. *Culture*. Ed. Regna Darnell, Judith T. Irvine, and Richard Handler. Berlin: Mouton de Gruyter, 1999. 869-75.

———. "Note on French-Canadian Folk-Songs." *Poetry* 16.4 (July 1920): 210-13.

———. "The Prince of Orange." *Poetry* 16.4 (July 1920): 176-79.

———. "Suggestive Notes." MS. Edward Sapir Papers, American Philosophical Society, Philadelphia, Pennsylvania.

———. "To Debussy: 'La Cathédrale Engloutie'." *Dream and Gibes*. Edward Sapir. Boston: Gorham, 1917.

———. "The Twilight of Rhyme." 1917. *Culture*. Ed. Regna Darnell, Judith T. Irvine, and Richard Handler. Berlin: Mouton de Gruyter, 1999. 886-90.

———. "White as the Snow." *Poetry* 16.4 (July 1920): 182-83. Reprinted in *Literary Digest* 66.4 (1920): 36.

Schweighauser, Philipp. "An Anthropologist at Work: Ruth Benedict's Poetry." *American Poetry: Whitman to the Present*. SPELL: Swiss Papers in English Language and Literature 18. Ed. Robert Rehder and Patrick Vincent. Tübingen: Narr, 2006. 113-25.

Shusterman, Richard. "Analytic Aesthetics, Literary Theory, and Deconstruction." *Monist* 69.1 (1986): 22-38.

———. "Croce on Interpretation: Deconstruction and Pragmatism." *New Literary Theory* 20.1 (1988): 199-216.

———. "Deconstruction and Analysis: Confrontation and Convergence." *British Journal of Aesthetics* 26.4 (1986): 311-27.

Spingarn, Joel. *The New Criticism: A Lecture*. New York: Columbia University Press, 1911.

Torgovnick, Marianna. *Gone Primitive: Savage Intellects, Modern Lives*. Chicago: University of Chicago Press, 1990.

Trombly, Albert Edmund. "Three Children." *Poetry* 16.4 (July 1920): 186-87.

Wellek, René. "Benedetto Croce (1866-1952)." *French, Italian, and Spanish Criticism, 1900-1950*. New Haven: Yale University Press, 1992. *A History of Modernism Criticism, 1750-1950*. Vol. 8. 187-223.

———. "Joel Elias Spingarn." *American Criticism, 1900-1950*. *A History of Modernism Criticism, 1750-1950*. Vol. 6. 61-63. London: Jonathan Cape, 1986.

The One, the Many, and the Few: A Philological Problem and its Political Form

Pierre-Héli Monot

Beginning with a brief reading of Kant's *Metaphysics of Morals* and its indeterminate conception of "partial" logical and political formations, this essay outlines, historically as well as theoretically, the constitution of the concept of "community" as a classical philological problem. The essay describes the advent of a general theory of interpretation in the Romantic era, as well as the conflation of the anti-Semitic discourses prevalent in Jena Romanticism with the generalization of interpretive doctrines from 1830 onwards. The hermeneutic doctrines of Friedrich Schleiermacher and Johann Gottfried Herder, as read by the American Transcendentalists and Ralph Waldo Emerson in particular, came to shape a major segment of the modern American philological field: Reinvested as poetic and metapoetic discourses, these hermeneutic doctrines invariably reproduced the equivocations of the concept of "community" and its counterpart in term logic, the "particular." The essay concludes with a brief reading of the later European reception of this chapter of Euro-American intellectual history and with a discussion of the classic model of "community" in recent philosophical formalism, Jean-Luc Nancy's *The Inoperative Community*.

I. Introduction

In *The Metaphysics of Morals* (1797), Kant establishes a number of parallelisms between the classical tripartition of political regimes (democracy, aristocracy and "autocracy," i.e., monarchy), the tripartition of state powers (sovereign authority, executive authority, and legislative authority) and the tripartition of practical syllogisms:

> These [three state powers or forms of sovereignty] are like the three propositions in a practical syllogism: the major premise, which contains the *law* of that will; the minor premise, which contains the *command* to behave in accordance with the law, that is, the principle of subsumption under the law; and the conclusion, which contains the *verdict* (sentence), what is laid down as right in the case at hand. (Kant, *Metaphysics* [§ 45] 90-91)

Kant goes on to suggest, as Jean-Claude Milner has noted, that the classical tripartite model of possible political regimes (democracy, aristocracy, and "autocracy") can be rephrased as a political transposition of the central categories of classical Aristotelian term logic, at least in its secular *versio vulgata* articulating *universal, particular,* and *singular* terms, and this despite the fact that Kant does not explicitly refer to Aristotle in this context:

> Now, the relation of this physical person ["the sovereign"] to the people's will can be thought of in three different ways: either that *one* in the state has command over all; or that *several,* equal among themselves, are united in command over all the others; or that *all* together have command over each and so over themselves as well. In other words, *the form of a state* is either *autocratic, aristocratic* or *democratic.* (Kant, *Metaphysics* [§ 51] 110-11)

Milner has forcibly argued that this "logico-political parallelism"[1] made the transposition of the *dictum de omni et nullo* from syllogistic logic to political discourse possible, naturalizing the articulation of the *omnes* (all) to the *unus* (one) as a logical relation, rather than revealing its inadequacy as a frame within which political legitimacy may be conquered (Milner 30-31). I would like to suggest that this transposition also deprived the classical Enlightenment political organon of the means of dealing with political formations that belong, or claim to belong, to the median, or *particular* (as opposed to the *universal* or *singular*) order in Aristotelian term logic. The two logico-political series one/few/many and one/some /all and their parallel suspension of the particular justly prompted Marx to identify the "Jewish Question" in post-revolutionary, that is "Christian" Europe, as a *structural* one (47).[2]

Yet the English translation of Kant's *Metaphysik der Sitten,* as quoted above, is somewhat misleading in its terse description of the qualities that constitute particular logico-political terms. The "several" (the

---

[1] My translation of Milner's original "parallélisme logico-politique." Milner also comments upon both excerpts from Kant's *Metaphysics of Morals* (Milner 32).

[2] "The formulation of a question is its solution. Criticism of the Jewish question provides the answer to the Jewish question" (Marx 3).

"einige" or "few") are "equal among themselves" in English, yet "einander gleich" in German.³ In the original, their coalition also *predates* their "Vereinigung," or unification. The original contains the suggestion, at no point further elucidated, that a relation of resemblance between the "einige" precedes their political coalition as the "aristoi" or, in the "altered form" of aristocracy, as *hoi oligoi* (Kant, *Metaphysik* [§ 52] 462). The English translation, on the other hand, suggests that this semblance is effectuated by the political system only. The German text binds the few on the grounds of a preexisting *similitude*, the English text with a contingent *equality*.

In what follows, I will argue that logico-political ambiguities of this kind prompted the Jena Romantics and the American Transcendentalists to reject the possibility of the "particular" in their hermeneutic, poetic, and political doctrines. I will briefly retrace the advent of the ideology of logico-political *bi*partition in Schleiermacher's general hermeneutics, and outline its crucial influence on the development of the romantic literary field in the United States. The argument I wish to make unfolds on two planes: While logico-political *bi*partition originated in the anti-Semitic discourses of Jena Romanticism, it developed into a full-fledged poetic system that enabled the circulation of *racial* markers among those who participated in the literary field of American Romanticism. I will argue that this logico-political heritage proved decisive for the constitution of intellectual and literary history as academic disciplines, and has deprived current discussions around the notion of "community" of much of its historical content and political significance.

2. Sects and Sections

Tocqueville's analysis of Democratic Man in the United States takes the Romantic contraction of Kant's tripartite logico-political model into a bipartite one for granted: "[Each citizen] has only very particular and very clear ideas, or very general and very vague notions; the intermediate space is empty" (154; my translation). Tocqueville perceives bipartition, or the experience of politics as the intimate commerce of the One with the Many and of the Many with the One, as the state of affairs of democratic society. This, of course, illustrates Tocqueville's somewhat self-

---

³ "[E]ntweder daß einer im Staate über alle, oder daß einige, die einander gleich sind, vereinigt, über alle andere, oder daß alle zusammen über einen jeden, mithin auch über sich selbst gebieten" (Kant, *Metaphysik* 461).

sacrificial posture quite well, and serves as a reminder to the reader of *Democracy in America* that the demise of aristocratic particularism is predicated upon the advent of a democratic society, an advent that Tocqueville considers to be unavoidable.

Tocqueville's analysis was both prescient in its identification of the rejection of the particular as a central feature of *democracy as a political regime*, and belated in its identification of its origins as a central feature of *democratic culture*. The educated New England class and the dominant social and cultural order it represented had long discovered bipartite logic to be at the core of the "German thought" which Emerson revered for its articulation of philosophical sophistication and racial prestige, and which legitimized the Romantic claim to belong to what Emerson identified as the "Teutonic race," giving further credence to their claims as "lords, true lords, land-lords, who understand the land and its uses and the applicabilities of men" (Emerson, *Essays* 224). A generation of young New England scholars (the fabled "Harvard-Göttingen Men"[4]) studied in Germany and facilitated the transfer of Romantic knowledge practices between Germany and the United States.

On the cusp of Romanticism's institutional breakthrough in Europe, Friedrich Schlegel's *Athenäums-Fragmente* (1798) and, barely a year later, Schleiermacher's *On Religion: Speeches to its Cultured Despisers* (1799) established the modalities of the evacuation of partial communities from the conditions of possibility of Romantic aesthetics, Romantic politics, and Romantic religious sentiment. Schlegel embraced "totality" and "the common" as the poles that demarcate the realm of Romantic poetics, while Schleiermacher supplied an apophatic, negative definition of "totality"[5] of Romanticism:

---

[4] Notably, Emerson's brother William studied in Göttingen from 1823 onwards (Hurth 8-22).

[5] Schlegel, in Jonathan Skolnik's translation: "Romantic poetry is a progressive universal poetry. Its destiny is not merely to reunite all of the different genres and to put poetry in touch with philosophy and rhetoric. Romantic poetry wants to and should combine and fuse poetry and prose, genius and criticism, art poetry and nature poetry. It should make poetry lively and sociable, and make life and society poetic. It should poeticize wit and fill all of art's forms with sound material of every kind to form the human soul, to animate it with flights of humor. Romantic poetry embraces everything that is purely poetic, from the greatest art systems, which contain within them still more systems, all the way down to the sigh, the kiss that a poeticizing child breathes out in an artless song" (Schlegel 37-38).

Of one form [of religion] only I should speak, for Judaism is long since dead. Those who yet wear its livery are only sitting lamenting beside the imperishable mummy, bewailing its departure and its sad legacy. Yet I could still wish to say a word on this type of religion. My reason is not that it was the forerunner of Christianity. I hate that kind of historical reference. Each religion has in itself its own eternal necessity, and its beginning is original. (Schleiermacher, *Religion* 238)

Much anecdotal history has been circulated about how Jewish salonnières, notably Henriette Herz, contributed to the intellectual socialization of the often-provincial young men who constituted the early Romantic constellations in Jena and Berlin. While it is true, if anecdotal, that Schleiermacher maintained personal ties with Jews throughout his life, and regularly corresponded with Dorothea Veit, daughter of Moses Mendelssohn and wife of Friedrich Schlegel, these ritualized biographical narratives have arguably overshadowed the structural function of anti-Semitism in the progressive institutionalization of Romantic hermeneutics in the literary and academic fields of the mid-nineteenth century. On account of the amount of evidence for the provisional historical culmination of anti-Semitic sentiment in German Romanticism, we can offer a supplementary *teleological* explanation of the function of such sordid passages in Schleiermacher's early work, focusing on what these proscriptions made possible both for the elaboration of a general theory of interpretation and for the dissemination of hermeneutics as a dominant cultural paradigm in the United States of the mid-nineteenth century, progressively constituting what Roger Lundin has called a hegemonic American "culture of interpretation"[6] that predicated cultural participation upon interpretive competences.

The passage from *On Religion* quoted above arguably prefigures, albeit negatively, the intersubjective, or "divinatory" interpretive modes Schleiermacher elaborates in his later technical writings on hermeneutics. The postulated suspension of all anthropological, linguistic, cultural, and ideological differences that alienate the interpretive subject from his or her interpretive object, in other words the generalizations and universalizations that purportedly legitimize *unmediated* insights into textual or anthropological material, are made conditional upon the same kind of logico-political parallelisms described above with respect to Kant. On its logical side, "das Jüdische" runs against the bipartite structure of hermeneutic circularity, which articulates a language with a specific text, a

---

[6] See also Lundin's astute reading of Schleiermacher's early works in light of his later development of a systematic hermeneutic theory (67-75).

paradigm with an exemplar, a syntactic rule with a specific sentence structure, or the One with the Many. On its political side, the "particular" (as opposed, again, to the universal and the singular), understood as a hypothesized cypher for "das Jüdische," denotes communitarian social formations that persist alongside political bipartition or, in a more scriptural version of the same, alongside the US-American national motto *E Pluribus Unum* – "Out of the Many, One."[7] Here again, Schleiermacher explicitly conflates political arguments and logical expositions so as to undermine the legitimacy of supplementary, partial formations:

> If the character of any special religion is found in a definite quantity of perceptions and feelings, some subjective and objective connection, binding exactly these elements together and excluding all others, must be assumed. This false notion agrees well enough with the way of comparing religious conceptions that is common but is not agreeable to the spirit of religion. A whole of this type would not be what we seek to give religion in its whole compass a determinate shape. It would not be a whole, but an arbitrary section of the whole; it would not be a religion, it would be a sect. (Schleiermacher, *Religion* 220)

Teleologically, religious "sects" and logical "sections on the whole" are strictly synonymous. Within the context of the institutionalization of hermeneutics as a general political and cultural paradigm, they correlate as two versions of the same interdiction. Teleologically, "Jews," as logical "sections of the whole" and as a religious "sect," run counter to an epistemic and cultural doctrine that declares "meaning" to be generally problematic,[8] and problematic meaning to be one that must be apprehended, interpreted, and decomposed through the application of hermeneutic methods only. In other words, Schleiermacher institutes a technocratic approach to textuality and meaning that, if it posits "understanding" as its horizon and ultimate justification, nevertheless exclusively predicates "understanding" upon its *production*, rather than its *recognition*; here, the rather subtle fault line of Kant's *Metaphysics of Morals* reveals its productivity. Anthropologically, and negatively, the "Jew" is construed as the member of a partial religious and political formation for which meaning must not be essentially problematic; put another

---

[7] See W. C. Harris's excellent discussion of Emerson's "The Lord's Supper" (25-30).

[8] Along with the circular articulation of the *grammatical* and *divinatory* methods of interpretation, Schleiermacher's insistence that "misunderstanding" arises naturally in the course of interpretation is crucial here: *"The more strict practice [of interpretation] assumes that misunderstanding results as a matter of course and that understanding must be desired and sought at every point"* (*Hermeneutics* 22).

way, Schleiermacher declares the "Jew" to be the sole figure that can eschew the total investment of the logico-political field by technical interpretation, and to whom, conversely, access to both singularity and universality is denied. As such, its claims to legitimacy and cultural participation must be repealed.

The Romantic Interpreter and the Democratic Citizen share a common trait and a common faculty: Both have been granted singularity, and both may attain a form of logico-political assimilation, or dissolution, in the totality of the One. We can thus rephrase Schleiermacher's reading of Kant's "einander gleich sein" as a *nur einander gleich werden dürfen*. The Culture of Interpretation initiated by Schleiermacher protects its proprietorship on similitude – a similitude that can only be performed through hermeneutic exertions, and that cannot preexist its becoming legitimate by the demonstration of methodical, hermeneutic abilities.

3. A Cold Reading of Emerson

This bipartite logic came to define the emerging American literary field of the 1840s as well as, a century later, a national philological discipline that was purportedly attuned to the specific cultural traits of its source material.

Emerson's "The American Scholar" served as the blueprint for the dissemination of this logic and for the delegitimization of communal or particular claims across the literary field. Ostensibly a critique of the scholarly assiduity that purportedly characterized "German thought," "The American Scholar" nevertheless presupposes exacting scholastic dispositions. Emerson's discourse on power, social segmentation, and the originary "Unity" of man stages the reciprocations and prevarications of the One and the Many he had learned to wield through his reading of Schleiermacher's early work:

> The fable implies, that the individual, to possess himself, must sometimes return from his own labor to embrace all the other laborers. But unfortunately, this original unit, this fountain of power, has been so distributed to multitudes, has been so minutely subdivided and peddled out, that it is spilled into drops, and cannot be gathered. (Emerson, *Essays* 54)

The competent reader nevertheless finds that the great unification of the One with the Many and of the "*divided* or social state" (69) with Man is not to be achieved through the withdrawal from social (or *divisive*) institutions, but rather through the competent exertion of readerly abilities – here, Emerson is being self-reflexive: "This writing is blood-warm. Man is surprised to find that things near are not less beautiful and wondrous than things remote. The near explains the far. The drop is a small ocean" (Emerson, *Essays* 69).

If Emerson claims to have left the "abstractions of the scholar" (*Essays* 69) behind, the "fountain of power" of originary totality has nevertheless spurted, source-like, ocean-sized drops; Emerson makes legible the transcendental "trifles" that bristle "with the polarity that ranges [them] instantly on an eternal law" (69). Arguably, the style of poetic utterance developed by Emerson in "The American Scholar" could be described as a collection of Barnum Statements, in that Emerson's aphorisms manage to convey the impression of representing a national "singularity" precisely by virtue of their generality. Yet intellectual history suggests a somewhat less benign intent behind Emerson's weaving together of micro- and macrocosmic discourses in the essay.[9]

Let us briefly add another layer to the historicization of the early suspension of the partial order in American poetics. Johann Gottfried Herder's writings on hermeneutics, which Emerson demonstrably read during his formative years as a Unitarian minister, put forth an elaborate doctrine of hermeneutic indeterminacy that layers several performative intentions, such as the location of authorial intentionality, the clarification of the meaning of ambiguous or incomplete texts, and, most importantly, the production and attribution of racial characteristics and markers to the practitioners of this hermeneutic theory.[10] Herder's recurrent metaphor for processes of interpretation, the "cultivation of a jungle," commingles the concrete historical reality of plantation slavery and the anti-Semitic sentiments prevalent in early Romanticism, Jews being described as "parasitic weed" (*Ideen* 702; my translation) feeding off the wilderness of literary texts that are not "their own." Intent on turning the textual "jungle" of unmediated texts into the pleasant "palm-grove" of philologically mediated *Werke*, interpreters must however submit to a crucial, imperative hermeneutic principle, put forth in the form of a fictional dialogue between two philologists:

---

[9] See also Bluford Adams' discussion of Emerson's treatment of Barnum in his notebooks (20-30).

[10] The following discussion of Herder repeats, albeit with notable discursive changes, an argument I have made in a recently published monograph (Monot 154-63).

> *Euthyphron:* The language [of ancient Hebrew poetry] abounds in roots [. . .], and our commentators, who rather dig too deep than too superficially, have uncovered enough of them. They never know when to quit, and if possible would lay bare all the roots and fibres of every tree, even where one would like to see only their flowers and fruits.
>
> *Alciphron:* These are the negroes, I suppose, upon your palm plantation.
>
> *Euthyphron:* They are necessary and useful people. We must treat them with mildness, for even when they do too much, they nevertheless do it with a good intention. (Herder, *Geist* 666; my translation)

Adequate interpretive work, like adequate agricultural work, rests on the philological or agricultural laborer's ability to circumvent certain unspecified yet specifically unproductive labor steps. When he is unable, unwilling, or unfit to avoid unnecessary hermeneutic toil, the interpreter becomes, in Herder's wording, "ein Schwarzer," that is, a figuration of the philological interpreter whose hermeneutic dispositions are also the least Romantic ones (Herder, *Geist* 666). With Herder, Romantic reading thus becomes an *auto-anthropometric* instrument enabling interpreters to produce and authenticate their own Romanticism, linguistic maturity, and whiteness. James Marsh's highly influential 1833 translation of Herder's *Spirit of Hebrew Poetry* suggests the possibility of a more essentialist take on the production of racial markers in the process of textual interpretation:

> *Alciphron:* These are the *slaves* I suppose upon your plantation of palms.
>
> *Euthiphron:* A very necessary and useful *race*. We must treat them with mildness, for even, when they do too much, they do it with a good intention. (Herder, *Spirit* 36; my emphasis)

Herder's theory of interpretation legitimizes the attribution of racial markers ("negroes") and the dissemination of a genteel humanism ("people"); Marsh's translation and transculturation of Herder harshly privileges the racialization, or naturalization of slavery ("a very useful race"), while blurring the specific racial discourse on Blackness that Herder explicitly refers to (Marsh: "These are the *slaves* I suppose [. . .]"). This, I believe, made it possible for Emerson to encrypt the promise of racial and technocratic superiority of American Romanticism's defining metalinguistic text. In what is perhaps the most frequently commented upon passage in the American Romantic corpus, Emerson elaborates on the Boehmian and Swedenborgian theory of signatures, while reinvesting Herder's metahermeneutic doctrine, as a kind of racial contraband, in *Nature*'s metapoetic commentary:

> Every word which is used to express a moral or intellectual fact, if traced to its root, is found to be borrowed from some material appearance. *Right* means *straight*; *wrong* means *twisted*, *Spirit* primarily means *wind*; *transgression*, the crossing of a *line*; *supercilious*, the *raising of the eyebrow*. [. . .] Most of the process by which this transformation is made, is hidden from us in the remote time when language was framed; but the same tendency may be daily observed in children. Children and savages use only nouns or names of things, which they convert into verbs, and apply to analogous mental acts. (Emerson, *Essays* 21)

Laboring in Emerson's metaphorical and metonymical wilderness, a reader whose philological dispositions were those of a Herderian "negro" or a Marshian "slave" would quickly identify the paradoxical valence of "root" as both etymological metaphor and exemplar of organic growth. In this passage, "root" serves as the covert intersection of biology and etymology; the "transformation" of material appearances into words is *both* a natural process and a cultural procedure, causing Emerson's ambiguous metalinguistic and programmatic exposition to collapse. Following Herder in his prompting of "knowledgeable renunciation" as a hermeneutic attitude, Emerson also follows Herder in the circulation and attribution of racial markers during the process of interpretation, instituting metalinguistic awareness as a form of racial autoanthropometry. Again, participation in the romantic readership that was emerging in the Boston area around 1840 was predicated upon the reader's willing surrender of all his or her "particular" hermeneutic dispositions, notably those which might have made a critique of Emersonian linguistics possible. Correlatively, American Romanticism, at least in its shrewd Emersonian incarnation, promised a type of racial assimilation *through* reading that casually dispensed with constitutional provisions and neglected to disclose the terms of the *philological contract* that binds the interpreter with the *omnes* of white, that is, "transparent"[11] Romanticism.

---

[11] I am of course referring to the political content of Emerson's great color-blind trope in *Nature*, the "transparent eye-ball" (Emerson, *Essays* 10).

4. "Community" as a Philological Fable: Two Theses

In what follows, I propose to sever some of the ties that bind academic commentary to the Romantic configuration described above. The two theses that follow attempt to revoke the philological contract that predicates critical legitimacy upon the perpetuation of political bipartition.

a) The hermeneutic rationalities of the Euro-American nineteenth century rejected "the particular" as an interpretive and political position. Simultaneously, the appearance of an institutional discourse on hermeneutic method instituted a technocratic regime in the philological field that correlated interpretive competence with racial belonging. In his early notes on scientific racism, Emerson outlined the core belief of this new regime: "The negro is imitative, secondary; in short, reactionary merely in his successes; and there is no organization with him in mental and moral spheres" (Cabot 430). Within barely two decades, Emerson's Transcendentalist doctrine and its manifest racial contents made its way back to Europe, and disclosed the anti-Semitic origins of its structural forms anew. In a number of essays in comparative religion, Ernest Renan, in his function as the dignitary of bourgeois humanism during the Second French Empire,[12] duly presents a particularly sordid kind of *circulus in probando*, in which Schleiermacher's *On Religion* comes to act as the demonstration of the superior technical abilities of Christian hermeneuts:

> The Hebrew people, like all Semitic peoples, do not know what a method of thought is. The idea that truth comes forth out of effort, from a succession of hypotheses and conclusions – such as we see at work among the Indo-European peoples who produced philosophy and science – was unknown among the Hebrews. (qtd. in Graetz 218)

> The East has never produced anything as good as we have. What is Jewish about our Germanic and Celtic Christianity, about St. Francis of Assisi [. . .], Schleiermacher, Channing? Are you comparing those flowers open to the romantic and delightful wind of our seas and mountains to your Esthers and Mordechais? (qtd. in Graetz 218)

The inclusion of Unitarian theologian William Ellery Channing in Renan's canon of methodically inclined, *hence* non-Semitic thinkers is, I think, of some importance, for it shows that the process of seculariza-

---

[12] Edward Said is particularly astute in his reading of Renan's position in the philological field of the Second Empire (133-46).

tion initiated by Schleiermacher's development of a general theory of interpretation was conceived of as a transatlantic process as early as 1860, i.e., during Emerson's lifetime (Jaffe 56-59; Monot 272-74). The recognition of the American literary field by European secular humanists rested, as I would like to argue, on the successful demonstration by American public intellectuals (an anachronistic yet convenient term) that the logico-political structures of European Romanticism had been solidly implemented in the United States. If, as Renan claims, "the Jews handed over the Hebraic Bible to European science," thus sealing their fate as a people with "nothing essential left to do" (239),[13] I would nevertheless like to stress that Renan's historical discourse is thoroughly geared towards the reformulation of "European" as a *global* category that is ethnically informed, yet one that manages to obscure this ethnic content through the foregrounding of technical, interpretive dispositions.

Hence, the globalization of general hermeneutic practices triggered off a double movement that, in my reading, has become constitutive of modern, post-Romantic philology. On the one hand, the implicit addressees of literary texts became universalized, or generalized as the *omnes* of universal discourse, and the appropriate understanding of literary texts became motivated with the promise of the attribution of a generalized, unmarked ethnic identity. On the other hand, and correlatively, philological practice became the backdrop against which institutional interpreters could freely inscribe their exegetical virtuosity as a natural competence; in this respect, it is worth noting that the ritual opposition of Deconstruction and Gadamerian philosophical hermeneutics seems to falter when we consider the emblematic value of their respective claims that their interpretive or deconstructive dispositions do not constitute "a method" (Derrida 273).[14] Emptied of its specific historical content as *aristoi*, sect or section, the "particular" order, now under the guidance of benevolent *maîtres penseurs*, could again function within the bipartite logico-political structure of a purportedly democratic philology, while delivering the gratifications – narcissistic and otherwise – of those intellectual dispositions that purportedly *cannot be taught*; thus, Derrida

---

[13] This passage is not quoted in Graetz's otherwise extensive treatment of Renan's anti-Semitism. My translation of: "Depuis Jésus-Christ, les juifs, selon moi, n'ont servi qu'à conserver un livre. Du jour où ils ont transmis la Bible hébraïque à la science européenne, [. . .], ils n'ont plus rien eu d'essentiel à faire" (Renan 239).

[14] "Deconstruction is not a method and cannot be transformed into one" (Derrida, "Letter" 273); see also Gadamer 27.

could claim somewhat ingenuously: "no deconstruction without democracy, no democracy without deconstruction" (Derrida, *Politics* 105).[15]

b) Recent discussions of "community" in the philological humanities have canonized rather formalist historical narratives that deconstruct (and hence construe, *ante* deconstructive gesture) the advent of the "modern individual" as the result of the dissolution of "originary" communities. Jean-Luc Nancy's much discussed account of this process in *The Inoperative Community* is characteristic of this formalist strain:

> The first task in understanding what is at stake here consists in focusing on the horizon *behind* us. This means questioning the breakdown in community that supposedly engendered the modern era. The consciousness of this ordeal belongs to Rousseau, who figured a *society* that experienced or acknowledged the loss or degradation of a communitarian (and communicative) intimacy – a society producing, of necessity, the solitary figure, but one whose desire and intention was to produce the citizen of a free sovereign community. (9)

While Nancy purports to revise Rousseau's account, he nevertheless reverts to a thesis that reproduces all of the messianic-historical traits that, as he suggests, are covertly at work in Rousseau's narrative; the analysis of "the horizon *behind* us," a metaphor as archetypal for the hermeneutic tradition as Friedrich Schlegel's definition of the historian as a "rückwärts gekehrter Prophet" (Schlegel, *Fragmente* 85), produces little more than a formalist reenactment of the same:

> The genuine community of mortal beings, or death as community, establishes their impossible communion. Community therefore occupies a singular place: it assumes the impossibility of its own immanence, the impossibility of a communitarian being in the form of a subject. In a certain sense community acknowledges and inscribes – this is its peculiar gesture – the impossibility of community. A community is not a project of fusion, or in some general way a productive or operative project – nor is it a *project* at all [. . .]. (Nancy 15)

---

[15] "Saying that to keep this Greek name, democracy, is an affair of context, of rhetoric or of strategy, even of polemics, reaffirming that this name will last as long as it has to but not much longer, saying that things are speeding up remarkably in these fast times, is not necessarily giving in to the opportunism or cynicism of the antidemocrat who is not showing his cards. Completely to the contrary: one keeps this indefinite right to the question, to criticism, to deconstruction (guaranteed rights, in principle, in any democracy: no deconstruction without democracy, no democracy without deconstruction)" (Derrida, *Politics* 105).

Let me attempt to formulate an avowedly ingenuous paraphrase of the above and propose a simplification of Nancy's alternative account of "community" as the specter that haunts the imaginary of philological modernity:

1) Death is the genuine community of mortal beings.

2) Mortal beings cannot achieve community in death, because they would not be mortal anymore, but dead (suspension of the subject).

3) Consequently, the concept of "community" is, in Nancy's (rather than Aristotle's) sense of the word, "singular," because it denotes something that is "impossible" (suspension of the predicate).

4) This impossibility is "inscribed' (by whom? for whom?) in the concept of "community."

5) This anonymous inscription is nevertheless "assumed" and "acknowledged" by the concept of "community" itself as the impossibility of the "immanence" of what it denotes.

6) The concept of "community" also "assumes" and "acknowledges" the impossible immanence of what it denotes as the impossibility of its "being" as subject ("Community therefore [. . .] assumes [. . .] the impossibility of a communitarian being in the form of a subject").

7) Things that "are" cannot be "a community."

8) A dead community, made possible (that is: a dead community of "mortals") would resolve the aporias described in points 2) to 6).

9) "Community" is not a project of something in particular.

10) "Community" is not a project at all.

For the sake of the argument, I will assume that my reader will consider the above paraphrase to be rigorous, hence fair. In light of this attempted clarification, Nancy is right, of course, but for the wrong reasons. Even though points 9 and 10 serenely reverse the *dictum de omni et nullo* that served as the starting point for the present essay, and even though I readily grant that it is in the nature of neoliberal rhetoric to capitalize on the dismantling of logical axioms, I would like to suggest that, despite appearances, Nancy's account is *not* aporetic, but rather devoid of its concrete historical referent. It seems to me that the formal description of "community" presented by Nancy readily admits of a different reading, in which rigidly normative claims (points 2 and 7) give way to *constative*, that is, historically informed arguments. In the present essay, I have described how the concept of "community" was informed by the rejection of *particular* logico-political structures from the early stages of European Romanticism onwards, and how the crucial actors of the Romantic movements in Europe and in the United States conflated these particular logico-political formations with figural representation of the "Jew." It seems evident to me that the canonization, or at least the institution of formalist narratives as critical paradigms in the philological humanities, has not managed to mitigate the suspicion (possibly shared by Nancy himself [Hammerschlag 11-15; 164-95]) that these *forms* merely conceal a *name* – a name relegated, like the particular logico-political formations it was conflated with, to *non-being*.[16] Replacing these forms with a name is the price the philological humanities must pay for a non-aporetic reading of their recent theoretical tradition.

---

[16] Boyarin's critique of Nancy is even more direct, and worth quoting at length: "Nancy would doubtless be horrified at the suggestion that his rhetoric is complicit in perpetuating the annihilation of the Jew, yet it seems clear that this is one potential accomplishment of his further allegorization of Blanchot. *That which the Jew represented before 'he' was annihilated is that which 'we' must let come, must let write itself.* The word 'henceforth' indeed implies that the secret of freedom from myth has passed from the Jews to a community which does not exist, which is only imaginable in and by theory. The secret becomes potentially available to all who await a second coming of this sacrificed Jew. I insist: This plausible yet 'uncharitable' reading cannot be stretched to an accusation of anti-Judaism. On the contrary, it is clear that Nancy and thinkers like him are committed to a sympathetic philosophical comprehension of the existence and annihilation of the Jews. My claim is rather that within the thought of philosophers such as Nancy lies a blindness to the particularity of Jewish difference which is itself part of a relentless penchant for allegorizing all 'difference' into a monovocal discourse" (Boyarin 223-24).

References

Adams, Bluford. *E Pluribus Barnum: The Great Showman and the Making of U.S. Popular Culture*. Minneapolis: The University of Minnesota Press, 1997.

Boyarin, Daniel. *A Radical Jew: Paul and the Politics of Identity*. Berkeley: University of California Press, 1994.

Cabot, James Elliot. *A Memoir of Ralph Waldo Emerson*. Vol. 2. Cambridge: The Riverside Press, 1887.

Derrida, Jacques. "Letter to a Japanese Friend." *A Derrida Reader: Between the Blinds*. Ed. Peggy Kamuf. New York: Columbia University Press, 1991. 269-76.

———. *The Politics of Friendship*. London: Verso, 2005.

Emerson, Ralph Waldo. *Essays and Lectures*. Ed. Joel Porte. New York: Literary Classics of the United States, 1983.

Gadamer, Hans-Georg. *Wahrheit und Methode: Grundzüge einer philosophischen Hermeneutik. Gesammelte Werke*. Vol. 1. Tübingen: Mohr Siebeck, 2010.

Graetz, Michael. *The Jews in Nineteenth-Century France: From the French Revolution to the Alliance Israélite Universelle*. Stanford: Stanford University Press, 1996.

Hammerschlag, Sarah. *The Figural Jew: Politics and Identity in Postwar French Thought*. Chicago: The University of Chicago Press, 2010.

Harris, William Conley. *E Pluribus Unum: Nineteenth-Century American Literature and the Constitutional Paradox*. Iowa City: University of Iowa Press, 2005.

Herder, Johann Gottfried. *Ideen zur Philosophie der Geschichte der Menschheit. Werke*. Vol. 6. Ed. Martin Bollacher. Frankfurt am Main: Deutscher Klassiker Verlag, 1989.

———. *The Spirit of Hebrew Poetry*. Trans. James Marsh. Burlington: Edward Smith, 1833.

———. "Vom Geist der Ebräischen Poesie: Eine Anleitung für die Liebhaber derselben und der ältesten Geschichte des menschlichen Geistes." *Schriften zum Alten Testament. Werke*. Vol. 5. Ed. Rudolf Smend. Frankfurt am Main: Deutscher Klassiker Verlag, 1993. 661-1308.

Hurth, Elisabeth. *Between Faith and Unbelief: American Transcendentalists and the Challenge of Atheism*. Leiden: Koninklijke Brill, 2007.

Jaffe, Adrian. "Ernest Renan's Analysis of Channing." *The French Review*, 28.3 (1955): 218-23.

Kant, Immanuel. *Metaphysik der Sitten. Werkausgabe.* Vol. 8. Ed. Wilhelm Weischedel. Frankfurt am Main: Suhrkamp, 2015.

———. *The Metaphysics of Morals.* Ed. Mary Gregor. Cambridge: Cambridge University Press, 1996.

Lundin, Roger. *The Culture of Interpretation: Christian Faith and the Postmodern World.* Grand Rapids: Eerdmans, 1993.

Marx, Karl. "On the Jewish Question." *Selected Writings.* Ed. Lawrence H. Simon. Cambridge: Hackett, 1994. 1-26.

Milner, Jean-Claude. *Les penchants criminels de l'Europe démocratique.* Lagrasse: Verdier, 2003.

Monot, Pierre-Héli. *Mensch als Methode: Allgemeine Hermeneutik und partielle Demokratie. Friedrich Schleiermacher – Ralph Waldo Emerson – Frederick Douglass.* Heidelberg: Winter, 2016.

Nancy, Jean-Luc. *The Inoperative Community.* Ed. Peter Connor. Minneapolis: University of Minnesota Press, 1991.

Renan, Ernest. "L'avenir religieux des sociétés modernes." *Oeuvres Complètes.* Vol. 1. Ed. Henriette Psichari. Paris: Calman-Lévy, 1947.

Richardson, Robert D. *Emerson: The Mind on Fire.* Berkeley: University of California Press, 1995.

Said, Edward W. *Orientalism.* London: Penguin, 1977.

Schlegel, Friedrich. *"Athenäums"-Fragmente und andere Schriften.* Ed. Andreas Huyssen. Stuttgart: Reclam, 2005.

———. *Kritische Schriften.* Ed. Wolfdietrich Rasch. Munich: Carl Hanser Verlag, 1958.

Schleiermacher, Friedrich. *Hermeneutics and Criticism, and Other Writings.* Ed. Andrew Bowie. Cambridge: Cambridge University Press, 1998.

———. *On Religion: Speeches to Its Cultured Despisers.* New York: Harper, 1958.

Tocqueville, Alexis de. *De la Démocratie en Amérique.* Vol. 3. Paris: Charles Gosselin, 1840.

Creativity, Self, and Communal Being in Emerson

Dustin Breitenwischer

In an attempt to engage in the debate about Ralph Waldo Emerson's understanding of self and community, this essay seeks to explore the *ontological hermeneutics of communal being* in Emerson's philosophy. Principally opposed to all matters of social participation, institutional framing, and submission to the normative orders of a superficial individuality, Emerson's thinking nonetheless relies on a particular mode of communality and relatedness without which individual autonomy, self-understanding, and potentially "authenticating" forms of social (inter-)action are unthinkable. In fact, this essay wants to show that it is essentially in "thinking" as in an intersubjective mode of philosophizing that Emerson locates the self-affirming viability of community and creative power. The essay moves from a discussion of Emerson's critique of social reform communities such as Brook Farm via a close reading of his essays "Experience" and "Quotation and Originality" to his assumption that in order to understand the original relation of self and world we need to "treat things poetically." According to such an ontological hermeneutics of communal being, community *is* being one's self.

I. Introduction

"We think a man unable and desponding. It is only that he is misplaced. Put him with new companions, and they will find in him excellent qualities, unsuspected accomplishments, and the joy of life," Emerson states in "Social Aims" (*Letters and Social Aims* 82). To excel in one's utmost potentiality, one needs to be rightly placed:

American Communities: Between the Popular and the Political. SPELL: Swiss Papers in English Language and Literature 35. Ed. Lukas Etter and Julia Straub. Tübingen: Narr, 2017. 103-21.

> 'T is a great point in a gallery, how you hang pictures; and not less in society, how you seat your party. The circumstance of circumstance is timing and placing. When a man meets his accurate mate, society begins, and life is delicious. What happiness they give, – what ties they form! (82-83)

What may be taken as a mere call for harmony or an organicistic understanding of social formation is, in fact, an attempt to assess the complex nature of what will in the following be explored as the essential relatedness of *communal being*. "Life is delicious" when "society begins," but, as the following essay will argue, the beginning of society depends on the prereflective working of the individual's self-empowerment as always already being communal. Emerson's statement is thus exemplary for the greater objective of my essay, as he uses the image of proper placement to conflate the most paradigmatic trope of his philosophy, the self, with that of communal interconnectivity. In other words, Emerson does not put emphasis on the "delicacies" of social interaction, but rather posits a particular mutual situatedness in society. People's social being thus depends on a model of *knowing one's place*. The question Emerson herein raises is that of how one is to *think*, that is, fully grasp the essence of the conflation of self and community. Thinking, for Emerson, as will be shown, is not only philosophy's mode of being, but Emerson's mode of being in a world that is, on the one hand, prereflective of a given social embeddedness, and, on the other, a form-giving principle in the active relation of different life-worlds. After I have properly established an understanding of this thought, I will turn to Emerson's idea of creativity and his recurring vision to "treat things poetically." In short, the key issue my essay seeks to explore in its attempt to contribute to the debates abut selfhood in Emerson scholarship is thus concerned with the idea of communality in Emerson's philosophy of the self.[1] The underlying assumption is that Emerson philosophically envisions an ontological hermeneutics of the self that is essentially communal and in and of itself *unthinkable* outside a particular communal context.

So even though Emerson hardly seeks to write a theory of society, society, as will be shown, nonetheless offers him an extraordinary playspace for the ontic anchoring of his ontological premises, and it furthermore offers him a conceptual contrast foil against which he is able to formulate the philosophical positioning of the self-reliant individual as communal being. Emerson, in other words, explores community

---

[1] I want to thank Herwig Friedl for our ongoing discussion of Emerson and creativity. His comments have been extremely helpful and have shaped this essay noticeably.

against the backdrop of its social reality.² He philosophizes community as a particular mode of self-scrutiny and self-understanding that is both prior to all sociality and ultimately intertwined with it. And even though some of Emerson's written reflections – such as "Experience" and "Quotation and Originality" – will feature more prominently in my discussion, this essay attempts to explore Emerson's mode of philosophizing community by engaging in a greater dialogue with a multitude of Emersonian writings and some of those of his most important critics.³ For, after all, thinking community, in Emerson's work, is a paradigmatically philosophical task – an *Aufgabe* that is as much a *task* as it is a mode of *abandonment*.

II. "Where do we find ourselves?"

The mid nineteenth-century New England culture was marked by the emergence of countless reformist, utopian, and socialist communities such as the transcendentalist community of Brook Farm. Despite his philosophical assumption that the self cannot be thought in isolation, Emerson was outspokenly skeptical of the idea of institutionalized communities. As sympathetic as Emerson may have been at first – George Kateb notes that there once was a "brief[] flirt[] with the idea of living" in Brook Farm (175) – he determinedly refused to participate in the reformist mission.⁴ Around the time of the inauguration of Brook

---

[2] Here, I concur with Johannes Voelz who argues, if only in a footnote, that "the Emersonian self is to be conceptualized as inextricably embedded in its social surroundings" ("Dual Economy" 555 n4).

[3] In the tradition of a dominant line in Emerson scholarship – from Cavell through Friedl to Posnock – this essay seeks to think critically "through" Emerson, rather than historically "about" him.

[4] Ultimately and only after a few years of existence, Brook Farm failed as a utopian project and a pragmatic community. It stumbled over its financial instability and, maybe even more so, its overbearing desire to erect a "Modern Arcadia," as Hawthorne entitled one of the chapters in his Brook Farm satire *The Blithedale Romance*. Even so, when reading a passage from a letter Brook Farm founder George Ripley sent Emerson in 1840 against the backdrop of much of Emerson's philosophical inclinations, one can understand the intellectual and spiritual temptation on the side of Emerson. Ripley writes: "Our objects, as you know, are to ensure a more natural union between intellectual and manual labor than now exists; to combine the thinker and the worker, as far as possible, in the same individual; to guarantee the highest mental freedom by providing all with labor adapted to their tastes and talents, and securing to them the fruits of their industry; to do away with the necessity of menial services by opening the benefits of education and the profits of labor to all; and thus to prepare a society of liberal, intelligent, and

Farm, he polemically states in a letter to Thomas Carlyle that Americans are "a little wild here with numberless projects of social reform. Not a reading man but has the draft of a new community in his waistcoat pocket" (Holmes 125). In his essay "New England Reformers," Emerson explains and, at the same time, criticizes these "men's" agenda even more explicitly: "These new associations are composed of men and women of superior talents and sentiments [. . .] but remember," he alerts his readers, "that no society can ever be so large as one man. He, in his friendship, in his natural and momentary associations, doubles or multiplies himself; but in the hour in which he mortgages himself to two or ten or twenty," as in a reform community, "he dwarfs himself below the stature of one" (*Essays and Lectures* 598).

As his thinking revolves around the communal nature of the individual self, Emerson seems to suspect an essential communality that is pre-reflective of but nonetheless feasible within the dynamics of social participation. "All association must be compromise," he writes in "Friendship" (345). And every compromise is, of course, first and foremost a self-compromise. Which is not cause for Emerson to advocate mere egotism. To the contrary, as in the "Culture" chapter of *The Conduct of Life*, he notes that "the pest of society is egotists" (1015). Emerson thus rejects excesses both in self-compromise and self-involvement. Rather, the individual has to will into the daunting task to unite by isolation: "union," i.e., community, "must be inward," he tells his audience and readers in "New England Reformers" (599), and "the union is only perfect, when all the uniters are isolated." As "union must be inward" and the "uniters" "isolated," community cannot primarily be a matter of social participation and submission, but it must be understood as a mode of individual self-discrepancy – as practiced and discussed most strikingly in "Experience."

How, then, does Emerson think the isolation of the uniting self? "I know that the world I converse with in the city and in the farms, is not the world I *think*," Emerson famously writes towards the end of "Experience" (491). "I observe that difference, and shall observe it. One day, I shall know the value and law of the discrepance. But I have not found that much was gained by manipular attempts to realize the world

---

cultivated persons whose relations with each other would permit a more simple and wholesome life than can be led amidst the pressure of our competitive institutions" (Frothingham 307). Based on the ideas of transcendental philosophy and Fourierian socialism, Brook Farm was thus one of the first institutionalized collectives dedicated to the individual's creative self-expression. For a closer analysis of Brook Farm as a reform community see Agnieszka Sołtysik Monnet's essay in this volume.

of thought" (491-92). Emerson distinguishes between the world of social interaction and another world that is both product and producer of his thinking. Far from consenting to the Cartesian dichotomy of subjective mind and objective world, Emerson is as skeptical about the "world of thought" as he is sure of its existential necessity. Emerson rejects the idea of a self-sufficient, world-making mind that is confronted with a self-constructed reality purposefully at one's disposal. At the same time, the "world of thought" is a world that perpetually affirms its own worldly withdrawal. Despite his sober skepticism, Emerson draws on a discrepancy that may be accounted for as an extraordinary opening to his thinking of self and community.

This may become even clearer when we turn to the famous opening lines of "Experience," in which Emerson asks, "Where do we find ourselves?", to reply: "In a series of which we do not know the extremes, and believe that it has none" (471).[5] Against the backdrop of his aforementioned incompatibility of worlds in the passage towards the end of the essay, one may understand both the question, or, more precisely, the performative act of it being asked, and the "series" in which we are integrated, but of whose extremes (its beginning and end) we have no knowledge, as the "world of thought" as such. Or, to be more precise, as the place of philosophical thinking and hermeneutic self-inquiry, in which the self is always already confronted with its being communal (i.e., its *communal being*).[6] In *Less Legible Meanings*, Pamela Schirmeister develops an understanding of community in Emerson's "Experience" that is as complex as it is insightful for our purposes. To explain the discrepancy between the solitary self (in "Experience," we encounter a crisis-ridden self in mourning) and its other (in the sense of both an inner and an outer alterity), Schirmeister identifies the workings of a "community without a community" and of a "community without place" (145, 149), i.e., communities whose paradoxical natures allude to

---

[5] He imagines life as a series of events whose beginning and end are existentially unknown to us, curiously anticipating Heidegger's ontology of "thrownness." In this context, we should certainly not overemphasize Emerson's idea of seriality, and we should definitely not deem it teleological. "Finding ourselves" is, to use Stanley Cavell's word, "founding ourselves" ("Emerson, Coleridge, Kant" 60) – i.e., to emerge in the midst of our "extremes."

[6] "Experience" may be the moment when Emerson learned to accept that nothing is naturally one's own (and remains that way eternally) and that, equally, nothing is naturally (and eternally) other. As has all too often been noted, the death of Emerson's son Waldo and the ensuing essay "Experience" mark somewhat of a turn or, at least, a shift in Emerson's thinking from transgressive optimism to a more sober skepticism. See for example Packer; Voelz, "Dual Economy" 568-70.

the self's communal being as essentially evolving beyond the confining scope of social normativity and distinct place-boundedness (as for instance in clubs, churches, etc.). The "community without a community" and the "community without a place" are communities of self-inquiry.

"Where do we find ourselves?" is thus the philosophical premise of Emerson's understanding of true community; a community without a place that exists and evolves in the space of the ever-looming question. As the question asks both for the place where one will be and where one is, it is the perpetual affirmation that we cannot possibly determine our place in it. And to be placeless in such a manner can no longer be tied to the emphatically transgressive thinker who seeks the "call of Genius" ("Self-Reliance") to create a new world. Rather, worlds appear essentially in tension, existing in a rift of (one's) self-scrutiny. "The world of thought" is thus not the world of creative genius and its alternate sociality, but a world that is its own inquiry – and it is so only by the forcefulness of its recurrent opening. As Schirmeister aptly puts it in her elaboration on the aforementioned paradoxical communities, one of the underlying questions of this inquiry into the nature of our self-seeking ultimately is: "What kind of community could we ever achieve?" (140).[7] We, the isolated uniters, in our "masterfully self-conscious struggle against the haunting sense of 'Reality''s usual absence" (Buell 128). Schirmeister's question will, in one way or another, lead us through the rest of this essay.

III. "Relation and connection"

At this point, we must, first of all, think the community without a place along the lines of Emerson's idea of series. And to be in a series, for Emerson, is to be in an in-between space, i.e., to be positioned in a somewhat prereflective "place," as Johannes Voelz writes, "where we can watch the secret of the world in the making" (*Transcendental Resistance* 88). Put in that place we are both observers of the world's creative forces and, at the same time, fully inclined to be ourselves the concentration of these forces. To "find ourselves" is as much a passive as it is an active enterprise – an experience that unfolds "in a series of experiences" (Voelz, "Dual Economy" 571). And as such, "Where do we find ourselves?" is the appearance of *presence*, in which the inquiring self finds

---

[7] Sacvan Bercovitch refers to this as "the paradox" in Emerson between "the exaltation of the individual and the search for a perfect community" (176).

itself in an all-pervasive relation with the world; with a "community without community," a "community without a place," or, to adopt a congenial image by Heidegger, a "'now' that bends back into itself" (20).[8] In short, the self encounters itself in relations, yet unknowing of their extremes but fully immersed in their excesses.[9]

But in the turmoil of its communal placelessness – the paradox of its communal solitude – how can the self make itself understandable and simultaneously be the noticeable appearance of its understandability? Would not such noticeability be essential for even the most paradoxical form of communal interaction? For Emerson, those are questions that turn out to be their own answers. He knows that that self can only appear in relation to the multitude of its interpretative self-interrogations. In his "Worship" chapter in *The Conduct of Life*, he fittingly writes: "relation and connection are not somewhere and sometimes, but everywhere and always" (*EL* 1065). Everywhere and always are we empowered to draw connections: This dynamic marks the freedom of our (self-)interpretation. In short, to interpret oneself – to ask where to find oneself – in order to make one's self *as* self understandable is the strenuous effort of our being. (And this may be the point where Emerson's ontological hermeneutics of self appears most political, for it provokes the question of who is when and where in a position to interpret in the first place.) The self is the freedom of its interpreter – its unfolding is equiprimordial (as in the Heideggerian sense of being, in one way or another, of the same origin) with the series we always already find ourselves in. And to showcase this, to make one's self noticed, is to be one's self. In other words, to assert one's freedom of self-interpretation as being one's self is to always already be in relation to others.[10] For especially the later Emerson, as we will see shortly, understands that to be one's self is to make oneself understandable beyond oneself. Thinking

---

[8] Here, Heidegger uses an image with which one could certainly embark on a greater genealogical reading of Emerson (and his idea of the circular), Nietzsche (and his idea of "eternal recurrence"), and Heidegger (who draws on Nietzsche in his remark).

[9] Emerson stresses this mode of prereflectivity in "Intellect" where he writes: "Long prior to the age of reflection is the thinking of the mind" – a thinking, we may want to add, that is not personal or social but essentially communal. "We do not determine what we will think. We only open our senses, clear away, as we can, all obstruction from fact, and suffer the intellect to see" (*EL* 418, 419).

[10] Curiously enough, John Haugeland makes a similar point in his analysis of the communal nature of Heidegger's ontological definition of *Dasein* ("Heidegger on Being a Person"). And even though Haugeland defines the communal much in a manner of a social background, a comparative analysis of Emerson and Heidegger with regards to communal being could produce fascinating results.

this in the recurrent Emersonian image of "the circular" would, in this regard, surely not intend a mode of self-revolving constriction but one of self-extending inclusion.[11] The self, for Emerson, is essentially contextual.[12]

In his philosophical attempt to situate the self in a true community without a place, Emerson seeks to withdraw the self from the dynamics of social participation and assessment, as he unfolds that community in the (allegedly authentic) realm of philosophical thought.[13] At the same time, he senses a rift – a "discrepance" – due to which the self can only bring itself forward (*ex-press* itself) in and as part of its context. The self is thus contextual and thereby always already expressive of its context. Self and community, in this mode of self-imposed *dual countering*, do not exist in opposition but in a tension-filled relationship, thus marking the essence of Emerson's hermeneutics – and also, as Voelz has convincingly shown, the essence of Emerson's theory of recognition.[14] What Voelz notes about Emerson's self-recognition can therefore easily be applied to the latter's philosophy of communal being, in that it "describes a mode of being-in-thinking which depends on the economy of social recognition without being reducible to it" ("Dual Economy" 574).

To practice, embrace and understand this requires *distance* – and it is distance Emerson seeks. He famously calls this distance "abandonment," as he describes a mode of being in which we, as he declares in "Circles," "forget ourselves" (*EL* 414) to be all the more present (to us

---

[11] On Emerson's place in a hermeneutic history of circular imagery (between Kant and Gadamer) see Keiling.

[12] In the logic of his ontological hermeneutics, the self (as autonomous communal being) is not its ontic fact as merely "being there," but instead as a processual being constantly immersed in the dynamics of self-encounter and self-abandonment. In the words of Günter Figal's insightful interpretation of Heidegger's "being-with," the self, for Emerson, is "without reference to itself, but that which signifies the context of 'I' sentences. It is part of self-evidence [as one's understanding of oneself] to be in this context" (*Martin Heidegger* 147; my translation and comment). This is not to say that "context" is by definition communal, but it is essentially interrelated.

[13] In this regard, my analysis of Emerson's understanding of self as communal being could very well be situated within the larger framework of discourses on authenticity. It is, in fact, striking that leading introductory literature on the phenomenon of authenticity hardly ever mentions Emerson. A comparative analysis of Emerson and thinkers such as Rousseau, Heidegger, and even Sartre could be highly advantageous for the development of "thinking" authenticity. For an introduction to the philosophical discourse on authenticity see Golomb.

[14] *Dual countering* is a phenomenological term – as can be seen in the works of thinkers such as Heidegger or Wolfgang Iser (in his study *The Fictive and the Imaginary*). Its German equivalent is the extraordinarily figurative term *Gegenwendigkeit*.

and our others). This presence, as has been noted before, *is* the self – the self as "endless seeker with no Past at [her] back" (412). If we think this through, to forget oneself means to leave oneself behind, to bury oneself in a past that no longer exists, in short, to cut off a relation to one's self as other. Against this backdrop, Herwig Friedl reminds us that "human being *is* 'circular power returning into itself,'" quoting Emerson's famous phrase from "The American Scholar" (Friedl 279; emphasis by Friedl).[15] In this mode of self-abandonment, distance and presence become equiprimordial. They not only bring forth each other, but *are* mutually each other.

IV. Quotation and Originality

In this mode of self-abandonment, one is, first and foremost, *original*. In his inspiring Emerson reading, Ross Posnock refers to this mode of enabling one's originality through abandonment as an act and process of "the power of generative renunciation" that is "to serve as a compositional resource" (*Renunciation* 284). Abandonment by renunciation – by revoking one's place in the world in order to find it compositionally – "becomes the means of creative turning" (297). And creative turning, for Emerson, is to comport one's self to the world philosophically, asking where to find ourselves and, by asking (not answering), finding oneself in a web of relations. Creative turning means to understand one's self as a contingent expression of perpetual creative forces, as a paradigmatic "mode of the self's relation to itself," to use Stanley Cavell's terms ("Thinking of Emerson" 17): "Then whatever is required in possessing a self, will be required in thinking and reading and writing" (17). Following Cavell and Posnock, the self's abandoning self-relation in Emersonian thinking can thus not only be understood as a forthbringing power expressive of one's essential creative forcefulness. Rather, and at this point I would like to turn to my discussion of Emerson's "Quotation and Originality," "original power is usually accompanied with assimilating power" (*LSA* 181), for "truth is the property of no individual, but is the treasure of all men" (183).

---

[15] See Emerson, *EL* 55.

Creativity, for Emerson, is thus the working of a universal power.[16] Only through acts of creative disengagement, of "leaving," to use Branka Arsić's image – that is, aesthetic experience as a way to abandonment and self-extension – can self-reliant being overcome and "forget" itself.[17] And it is, in turn, an obscure communal power that allows the self to abstract from itself as its self. The communal must thus be understood as a mode of self-relation that is simultaneously pre-social and always already beyond sociality. It is the ultimate mode of one's originality, which is, in turn, not only a matter of aesthetic judgment, but, as we will see below, of an ontological self-positioning as "being one's self" (*LSA* 191) in originality. Creativity, for Emerson, is not the way to turn towards one's abandoned self and thereby leave and desert one's communal ties. In other words: Even though the manner in which creativity dispenses itself is by disengagement, this disengagement is the self's attempt to cope with its world creatively. "The world," Emerson writes in "The American Scholar," "– this shadow of the soul, or *other me*, lies wide around. Its attractions are the keys which unlock my thoughts and make me acquainted with myself. [. . .] [S]o far have I extended my being" (*EL* 60). Emerson frames this mode of disengaging self-extension, of refraining from oneself to more truthfully *be* oneself, even more powerfully in "The Poet," in which he draws on "a secret which every intellectual man quickly learns," namely that "beyond the energy of his possessed and conscious intellect, he is capable of a new energy (as of an intellect doubled onto itself)" (459). An intellect doubled onto itself marks the recurrence of one's self as a product of creative disengagement.[18] The recognition of this difference marks the moment in which the self is not falling into the abyss of existential solitude but instead realizes that "beside [her] privacy of power as an individual [human being], there is a great public power" (459). The creative self as

---

[16] In his speech on "The Emancipation of the Negroes in the British West Indies," Emerson, as vigorously as hardly anywhere else, turns this power into an ethical and radically political tool. He speaks of "the voice of the universe" that "pronounces Freedom": "The Power that builds this fabric of things affirms it in the heart" (32). This Power, in turn, is hardly anywhere more expressive and explicit than in acts of creation.

[17] See Arsić.

[18] Emerson thus uses an image that has become paradigmatic in the realm of hermeneutics and aesthetic theory. It may be promising to compare Emerson's understanding of abandonment-as-disengagement with such positions as Dewey's "[being] beyond ourselves to find ourselves" (195) or Gadamer's idea of "being outside oneself" (122). I have hinted at this discussion in my study *Dazwischen*.

communal being is, in existence and thinking, *committed* to its antecedent community.

Against this backdrop, an existential part of the discrepancy between quotation and originality that Emerson's essay revolves around is the observable discrepancy of worlds he discusses in "Experience." That discrepancy is one between inner and outer self, but also between, so to say, one's *inner* inner and outer self. We would "do well" in our understanding of Emerson, John Lysaker therefore argues, "to live in observance of that fact, that difference between primary experience – our temporal, moody, and occasionally ecstatic conversation [with self, world, texts] – and whatever reflective life puts into and draws out of it" (118; my comment). We are thus challenged by a discrepancy of experience that mutually concerns our being and our worldly relations, for how else are we to understand the receptive nature of our conversations, our thinking, reading, and writing?

In "Quotation and Originality," Emerson therefore notes, "one would say there is no pure originality. [. . .] By necessity, by proclivity, and by delight, we all quote" (*LSA* 170). Human action and human thought, reading literature and philosophy, the work of the imagination and of the hands, the use of speech and writing – they are all marked by one's retreat into the placeless community of tradition, culture, genius, of the common, the near, and the distant. Christopher Newfield claims that "Quotation and Originality" falls into the phase of Emerson's philosophy in which he becomes "explicitly collective" (158), so that he turns proper quotation into a cultural practice, in which, as Newfield furthermore argues, "[t]he active agent becomes personhood as a mass" (158). Yet rather than further pursuing Newfield's critique of Emersonian liberal individualism, in which he perpetually relates Emerson's ideas of the communal back to the dynamics of "market circulation" (163), I want to expand upon the alleged "collectivity" of "mass agency" and stress its function for Emerson's *philosophizing* the communal self. I believe that the turn to the collective, for Emerson, means riding the razor's edge. On the one hand, it allows him to make tradition and intellectual affinity part of the self's unfolding of creative power; on the other hand, collective action, or, as Kateb puts it, "[s]ystematic association," always bears the risk of "disfigurement, a loss of integrity" (173). And Emerson explicitly warns his readers "that men are off their centre; that multitudes of men do not live with Nature, but behold it as exiles" (*LSA* 179). They are marked "as foreigners in the world of truth"; they "quote thoughts, and thus disown them" (179).

Emerson knows that any form of communal interaction is delicate and in and of itself always in danger of being corrupted or corrupting. "Disowning" by improper (one may even say, vulgar) quotation turns society into a masquerade ball, a play of semblances and insincerities. In his Notes to the "Courage" chapter of *Society and Solitude*, he states: "People wrap themselves up in disguises, and the sincere man is hard to reach. A man is concealed in his nation, concealed in his party, concealed in his fortune, [. . .] concealed in his body at last, and it is hard to find out his pure nature and will" (431). And not only are people wrapped up, "[t]hey speak and act in each of these relations after the use and wont of these conditions" (431). They quote and imitate according to the norms and standards of their communal interaction, and their prestige and status within it. One encounters these "men" and is unable to un-conceal their authentic being. They cannot be found, for they have already suffered their communal death. As the Emerson reader knows from "Self-Reliance," "imitation is suicide" (*EL* 259).[19] In other words, if community is merely based on the strenuous and ultimately impossible efforts of its members to reveal the true self of their fellows, self-reliant being – as "the steady effort of thinking one's thoughts and thinking them through" (Kateb 31) – is nearly impossible. In the intricate relation between quotation and originality, communality must be thought differently. Emerson, I argue, attempts to do so in an ontological hermeneutics of communal being as creative being.

So Emerson asks: "And what is Originality?" – "It is being"; it is, as I have already quoted above, "being one's self" (*LSA* 191). To *be* original is to be both independent of and marked by comparison; it means to be perpetually new and, as such, essentially by oneself. But the original is not essentially contrasted by that which is not original. Rather, in Emerson's tantamount description of being and originality, originality may either be or not be, but there is no immediate "other" to it. Hence, originality does not work against the backdrop of some obscure other that is decidedly not original. And yet, by suggesting that there is such a thing as (socially and ontologically) improper quotation – i.e., imitation – Emerson nonetheless attempts to dispense (understood in the figurative mode of the German *freistellen*) originality by way of tying it to the self. The self is original because originality is being one's self. Crucially,

---

[19] In a brief passage in *Art as a Social System*, Luhmann retraces the long history of "imitation" that led into its philosophical depreciation in modernity when "originality" became the paradigm of creative action. See esp. Chapter 7.

it is only in the dynamics of this ambiguous figure that true community can emerge and exist.

This may become clearer when we return to "The Poet." Here, Emerson more emphatically presents what in "Experience" is marked by sober skepticism.[20] "Where do we find ourselves?" – "We stand before the secret of the world," "The Poet" answers, "there where Being passes into Appearance, and Unity into Variety" (*EL* 453). "Appearance" is not *mere appearance*; it is neither superficial occurrence nor occurrence of superficiality. Rather, appearance is *being present*. It is *being* that makes an issue of itself through self-extension. To "stand before the secret of the world" is thus not only related to the "series of which we do not know the extremes" (cf. "Experience") but to simultaneously being in the presence of our unknowability and, hence, the extremes as such. Let us retrace this ontological occurrence: Being, for Emerson, is originality that, as soon as we engage in the marvel of where to find ourselves, passes into appearance. And appearance is always appearance for and in front of something or another. Appearance as presence, as we have learned, is to be in a "community without a place" – a community in creative flux where abandonment appears in its modes of quotation and originality, where, to come full circle, unity of creative power (tradition, culture, etc.) passes into variety.

In this regard, we may understand quotation and originality as synonymous with the aesthetic processes of appropriation and creation.[21] This means that the abandoning self relates to itself and its context of abandonment in a manner of appropriating one's self as other, thereby bringing itself forth in an unforeseen and original way.[22] But again, Emerson is hardly treating this as a matter of private pleasure or mere individual self-excitement. Appropriation and creation as essential modes of being of quotation and originality are always already tied to one's communal and social relatedness. And this is not contradicted but, in fact, underlined by the fact that "there remains the indefeasible persistency of

---

[20] In "Dual Economy," Johannes Voelz engages in the same comparative reading. My own reading of the ontological efforts present in "The Poet" and "Experience" is clearly inspired by Voelz's Emerson scholarship.

[21] More precisely, I understand "appropriation" in the reception aesthetic connotation of "taking over" (*Aneignung*) of the position of an other, in which reception turns into creative (co-)production.

[22] In the dynamic of appropriation and creation we thus recognize what Julie Ellison calls "detachment and transition" – two terms Emerson uses (rather ambivalently) in "Art" – as the essence of art and the appearance of power. See Ellison, Part 3, Chapter 8.

the individual to be himself," as he notes in "Quotation and Originality" (*LSA* 191) – a persistency which serves, in the logic of my essay, as the communal's ultimate enabler. We have to "disclose our originality" (Kateb 167), and thus need to refrain from ourselves and excel against the backdrop of our communal being. To be *with* someone, for Emerson, means to be *through* someone. It means to be, at the same time, predecessor and successor of another.

In his critique of social reform activism in "New England Reformers," Emerson therefore disdainfully notes that such activism is based on the wrong premise. It puts the cart before the horse, as it tries to change society without changing the self (and its relation to it): "society gains nothing whilst a man, not himself renovated, attempts to renovate things around him" (*EL* 596).[23] "Renovation," in this context, exceeds "reform," for it does not hint at a more or less substantial subversion of social being but at its self-scrutinizing getting-to-the-bottom. It is a power that is, as Emerson notes in "Power," "conservative, as well as creative" (*EL* 974); it restores its authentic being and excels into the new. It is, in the words of Branka Arsić, "the joy of seeing new meaning" (89). Proper quotation thus means to surround and infuse oneself with originality.[24]

V. Poetic Treatment

Emerson knows that self and society coexist, and so he seeks to find a mode of being that is both present in the self and appears in the occurrences the self is in relation with. We have thus come to a point at which we need to understand that Emerson's ontological hermeneutics of communal being depict a particular mode of dealing with the world. Both in his early lecture on "Politics" and an 1839 journal entry, Emerson evokes a curious image. In "Politics," he writes: "every subject of human thought down to most trivial crafts and chores ought to be *located poetically*" (*Early Lectures 3* 239; my emphasis). Quoting his lecture excessively, he notes in his journal: "Every thing should be *treated poetically*" (*Journals* 329; my emphasis). Within the spectrum of his own thinking, Emerson changes the metaphor from poetically "locating" to

---

[23] For a more extensive discussion of Emerson's reform criticism see Levin, esp. Chapter 1.

[24] As social relations, friendships, for Emerson, come closest to this mode of creative appropriation and mutual originality. On Emerson and friendship see Lysaker, *Emerson and Self-Culture*, Chapter 6; Lysaker, ed., *Emerson and Thoreau*.

"treating," thereby not contradicting but expanding the image of what could be subsumed as being-in-the-world poetically. At first glance, Emerson is trying to explore an all-pervasive (and utterly Romantic) change in our relation to the world that lets the utilitarian be absorbed in the playfully "inventive," as he notes in both texts. But one realizes quickly that poetic treatment of the world and, thus, poetic being of the self expand decidedly upon the eccentricity of Romantic being. That being said, what interests me in the context of my essay is the way in which Emerson experiments with the metaphor of poetic treatment, in which he does not wish to overthrow the self's relations to its world but to reconcile authentically and ecstatically (that is, philosophically) the self with its social relations – "conservative, as well as creative."[25]

If for Emerson the self is the essential premise of communality and if being one's self is its mode of self-understanding, communality must be represented in the representation of the self. "Poetic treatment" must thus be deemed the processual (i.e., translatory) representation of the self as creative representation (and affirmation) of its relations. Again, in the mutual working of appropriation and creation, Emerson no longer negates one's necessary involvement in social relations. Yet, he urges his readers to "treat things poetically," which constitutes the most promising (if not existential) mode of action in which self and society, each in its turn, express their most productive mode of interrelatedness. Treating and locating things poetically allows the self to productively distance itself from itself while at the same time drawing society into a sphere of transformative self-explication – where appearance is a community without a place.

In this logic of contextual abandonment, Emerson wants to provide "things" with something more and something different, thereby turning them into ever-new sources of interpretation and, hence, poetic treatment. Only through such treatment, his argument goes, can self and world encounter and explore each other in unexpected appearances, in the equiprimordial abandonment of community without community. To rephrase, what sounds like a call for the self-extension of romantic Genius (as the most anti-conventional force of resistance), turns out to be Emerson's attempt to mark *and* reconcile the essential rift between self and society in an ontological hermeneutics of communal (and, hence,

---

[25] One could further try to assess whether Emerson, whenever the communal breaks into his reflection of self and experience, basically seeks to establish a philosophy of life forms, i.e., whether he looks for, in the words of Günter Figal, "that particular coherence of life in which everything owns the curious familiarity of that which is self-understanding [*das Selbstverständliche*]" ("Übersetzungsverhältnisse" 103; my translation).

creative) being. And in a logic of communal selfhood, to treat a thing poetically must necessarily be more than just emphasizing this thing's aesthetic effect and social appeasement. Rather, it *is* the mutual relatedness of one's being in new relations and, at the same time, producing them. In "Inspiration," Emerson notes: "The man's insight and power are interrupted and occasional; he can see and do this or that cheap task, at will, but it steads him not beyond" (*LSA* 257). But to leap within the "series" of one's inspirational experiences is to *be* "by lyrical facility" (257). Only in poetic treatment is one truly attentive to the "thing" and at the same time enabled to be beyond oneself (i.e., self-abandoned).[26] It is, in other words, an active power that, as John Lysaker puts it, "must bring the sallies of genius into the various activities of life, thereby giving them proper direction, our direction" (57).

For Emerson, such a state of poetic (self-)treatment of abandonment as communal being marks the premise of all philosophical thinking and worldly interaction. And even though both are ultimately incompatible, locating them poetically is one way of relating them. As Ross Posnock notes, Emerson's philosophy is characterized by "a formal resistance that mirrors its refusal to resolve the opposites it poses" (296). In and through aesthetic semblance of thinking and this thinking's formal expression is it that the essence of a greater claim – a "new circle," so to say – appears. Self-understanding is thus not primarily a result of proper public or social conduct, but a mode of communal being. This being said, Emerson perpetually tries to philosophically determine the power of the self's autonomy within the normative (and inextricable) limitations of the social. As it reminds us of his critique of reformist communities, Emerson's thinking – his being-in-a-world-of-thought – cannot possibly accept the romance of concord and harmony, of "concert," as he writes in "New England Reformers" (*EL* 598). His vision of "locating poetically" is radically opposed to all manners of idyllic longing and communal embeddedness. Instead, communal being can only be fully powerful when it is its own refusal to be pinned down, when it is the perpetual abandonment of its own relations. Community, in this sense, can never solely be its "reliance on Association" (597).

---

[26] As Emerson writes in "Poetry and Imagination," to "become[] lyrical" is "the mind allowing itself range" (*LSA* 55), which, ultimately, brings us back to the equiprimordial appearance of presence and distance. As misleadingly Cartesian as Emerson's reference may sound, he is clearly not interested in the relation between mind and world, subject and object, *res cogitans* and *res extensa*. Quite the contrary: As has been shown, Emerson wants to understand the essence of their mutual translatability into each other. He wants to *think* communal being as self and vice versa.

Instead of deeming this a bleak outlook, we may understand it as an invitation for promising future discussions – especially in the field of American studies. In times of excited debates about recognition, identity politics, communal empowerment, cultural resistance, and questions of social participation, Emerson's philosophy of communal being – not least due to its celebration of creative philosophical disengagement and self-distancing – may, on the one hand, help us reassess the role of hermeneutic philosophy for the study of literature, culture, and society. On the other hand, we may make use of the ways in which Emerson addresses the tension between individual self-empowerment and communal interaction as a dilemma that can never be solved but may perhaps be productively dynamized within the force field of its presence. One may, for example, very well argue that the productive nature of this self-produced dilemma features quite prominently within such different power dynamics as that between artistic autonomy and creative collaboration, between individual self-fashioning and pop-cultural group affiliation. Against this backdrop, we may thus want to understand Emerson's ontological hermeneutics of communal being as a recurrent reminder that community is not a more or less stable social entity within which one flourishes as an individual actor, but that community always already is "power over and behind us, and we are the channels of its communications" (*EL* 607). At which point we are essentially determined to ask: Where do we find ourselves?

References

Arsić, Branka. *On Leaving: A Reading in Emerson*. Cambridge and London: Harvard University Press, 2010.

Bercovitch, Sacvan. *The Puritan Origins of the American Self*. New Haven: Yale University Press, 1974.

Breitenwischer, Dustin. *Dazwischen: Über Wesen und Wirken ästhetischer Erfahrung am Beispiel amerikanischer Kunst und Literatur von Hopper bis Hustvedt*. Paderborn: Fink, 2017 [forthcoming].

Buell, Lawrence. *Emerson*. Cambridge and London: The Belknap Press of Harvard University Press, 2003.

Cavell, Stanley. "Thinking of Emerson." *Emerson's Transcendental Etudes*. Ed. David Justin Hodge. Stanford: Stanford University Press, 2003. 10-19.

———. "Emerson, Coleridge, Kant." *Emerson's Transcendental Etudes*. Ed. David Justin Hodge. Stanford: Stanford University Press, 2003. 59-82.

Dewey, John. *Art as Experience*. New York: Penguin, 2005.

Ellison, Julie. *Emerson's Romantic Style*. Princeton: Princeton University Press, 1984.

Emerson, Ralph Waldo. "The Emancipation of the Negroes in the British West Indies." London: John Chapman, 1854.

———. *The Complete Works of Ralph Waldo Emerson. Vol. 8. Letters and Social Aims*. Boston: Houghton Mifflin, 1884.

———. *The Complete Works of Ralph Waldo Emerson. Vol. 7. Society and Solitude*. Boston: Houghton Mifflin, 1904.

———. *The Journals and Miscellaneous Notebooks 1838-1842*. Cambridge: The Belknap Press of Harvard University Press, 1969.

———. *The Early Lectures. Vol. 3, 1838-1842*. Cambridge: The Belknap Press of Harvard University Press, 1972.

———. *Essays and Lectures*. New York: Library of America, 1983.

Figal, Günter. "Übersetzungsverhältnisse." *Der Sinn des Verstehens*. Stuttgart: Reclam, 1996. 102-12.

———. *Martin Heidegger: Phänomenologie der Freiheit*. Tübingen: Mohr Siebeck, 2013.

Friedl, Herwig. "Fate, Power, and History in Emerson and Nietzsche." *ESQ* 43 (1997): 267-93.

Frothingham, Octavius Brooks. *George Ripley*. Boston: Houghton Mifflin, 1883.

Gadamer, Hans-Georg. *Truth and Method*. Trans. Joel Weinsheimer and Donald G. Marshall. New York: Continuum, 2006.

Golomb, Jacob. *In Search of Authenticity: From Kierkegaard to Camus*. London and New York: Routledge, 1995.

Haugeland, John. "Heidegger on Being a Person." *Noûs* 16.1 (1982): 15-26.

Heidegger, Martin. *Nietzsche. Vols. 1 and 2*. Trans. David Ferrell Krell. New York: Harper, 1991.

Holmes, Oliver Wendell. *Ralph Waldo Emerson*. Boston and New York: Houghton Mifflin, 1892.

Kateb, George. *Emerson and Self-Reliance*. Thousand Oaks: Sage, 1995.

Keiling, Tobias. "Zirkel und Kreise des Verstehens: Gadamer, Emerson, Kant." *International Yearbook of Hermeneutics* 14 (2015): 42-79.

Levin, Jonathan. *The Poetics of Transition: Emerson, Pragmatism, and American Literary Modernism*. Durham and London: Duke University Press, 1999.

Luhmann, Niklas. *Art as a Social System*. Trans. Eva M. Knodt. Stanford: Stanford University Press, 2000.

Lysaker, John T. *Emerson and Self-Culture*. Bloomington and Indianapolis: Indiana University Press, 2008.

———, ed. *Emerson and Thoreau: Figures of Friendship*. Bloomington and Indianapolis: Indiana University Press, 2010.

Newfield, Christopher. *The Emerson Effect: Individualism and Submission in America*. Chicago and London: The University of Chicago Press, 1996.

Packer, Barbara. *Emerson's Fall*. New York: Continuum, 1982.

Posnock, Ross. *Renunciation: Acts of Abandonment by Writers, Philosophers, and Artists*. Cambridge and London: Harvard University Press, 2016.

Schirmeister, Pamela. *Less Legible Meanings: Between Poetry and Philosophy in the Work of Emerson*. Stanford: Stanford University Press, 1999.

Voelz, Johannes. *Transcendental Resistance: The New Americanists and Emerson's Challenge*. Hanover: Dartmouth College Press, 2010.

———. "Ralph Waldo Emerson and the Dual Economy of Recognition." *Amerikastudien / American Studies* 57.4 (2012): 553-80.

From Brook Farm to Burning Man: Alternative Communities in the United States

Agnieszka Soltysik Monnet

Since the Puritans founded their original colonies as the first "alternative communities" in the New World, America has continually reinvented itself through an ongoing series of experiments in how to live together as groups united less by ethnic or traditional ties and more by choice, affiliation, common purpose, and political and/or religious values. I am interested in two specific aspects of intentional communities: religion and environmentalism. Taking as a point of departure the observation that the most successful communities have been united by a common faith or sectarian religious practice, I intend to explore the question of whether alternative communities are always necessarily sites of alternative or heightened religious practice. Secondly, I am interested in how these issues of spiritual being in the world have been historically linked on the part of alternative communities to an ecological engagement and concern with the land and living environment. Finally, I will suggest that the recent skepticism about community, well-intended and necessary as it is, threatens to undermine our ability to accurately understand the legacy and lessons of intentional communities, which may yet turn out to be an important resource for the future.

The question of community has been at the heart of how the United States defines itself from the very start. Since the first European settlers arrived, America has continually reinvented itself through an ongoing series of experiments in how to live together as groups united less by ethnic or traditional identity ties and more by choice, affiliation, common purpose, and political and/or religious values. What I propose to do in this essay is present a short history of alternative communities in

American Communities: Between the Popular and the Political. SPELL: Swiss Papers in English Language and Literature 35. Ed. Lukas Etter and Julia Straub. Tübingen: Narr, 2017. 123-44.

the United States up to the present, examining in particular the principal kinds of impulses that have led people to decide to withdraw from conventional society. Given the frequency and enduring success of intentional communities organized around a common religious faith (e.g., the Mormons, the Quakers), one of the questions I intend to explore is whether alternative communities are always necessarily sites of alternative and/or heightened spiritual/religious awareness/practices. A second question concerns the fact that most such communities have also been uniquely concerned with their physical and natural environment, the design of their homes and lands, and developing values we would now call sustainability and stewardship. The final question motivating this inquiry is whether there is any vital connection between the spiritual and the ecological dimensions of alternative intentional communities, and if so – *what is it?*

First of all, what do I mean by alternative community? The current word for this is "intentional community," and there is probably no formula for how to define this except as a community that consists of people that have purposefully joined together to live in a manner they believe is better than the prevailing social structure. So the basic principles are that of *affinity* as opposed to simply accident of birth, and the choice to join with a *group* of like-minded people, as opposed to simply attempting to live your values on your own. In his study of communes of the 1960s, Timothy Miller proposes seven principles: 1. *A sense of common purpose and of separation from the dominant society*, 2. *Some level or form of self-denial, suppression of individual choice in favor of the good of the group*, 3. *Geographic proximity*, 4. *Personal interaction*, 5. *Economic sharing*, 6. *Real existence*, and 7. *Critical mass*, by which he means an intentional community should have at least five individuals (*60s Communes*, xxiii-xxiv). A point that could be added to these principles is that intentional communities or alternative communities have often regarded themselves as potential models for others, showing people that different ways of organizing life are possible. In rejecting "the dominant society," alternative communities tacitly set themselves up as blueprints for a better alternative.

According to Jonathan Dawson, a leading sustainability writer and educator, the first intentional communities could be dated back to either the Bible, to the prophet Amos, who believed strongly in economic justice, or Pythagoras, who founded a community dedicated to asceticism and fairly strict restrictions in relation to diet and behavior. Dawson also cites Celtic Christian monasteries off the Scottish and Irish coasts in the sixth, seventh, and eighth centuries CE (Dawson 15). In an important respect, then, alternative communities have often been linked to religion, and moreover, they have also often sprung from a rejection of materialism and class. One could say that, from a British perspective, the American colonies were founded as an intentional community by the Puritans, who wanted to live according to what they regarded as a more "pure" interpretation of the Bible, going back to the practices of the early Church.[1] They also saw themselves as a model, in John Winthrop's words from 1630, as a "shining city upon a hill." Also like later intentional communities, the Puritans were strongly critical of the poverty generated and tolerated by capitalism, and sought to create a fully egalitarian society with respect to the material standing of each family. A final way in which they anticipated later communitarian projects – many of which experimented with early forms of feminism – is that they advocated literacy for all members including women. In these respects, the Puritans – at least in their intentions – shared with later communards an intense desire for a truly egalitarian community in which every individual feels valued and respected, something that liberal capitalism has never been able to provide.

Just as the Puritans set out to realize their social and spiritual project in the New World, so did many European immigrants in the centuries that followed. No other nation has been home to as many intentional communities as what came to be the United States, since its first settlement. Many came from present-day England, France, Switzerland, Holland, and other countries to create communities that offered an alternative to the injustices and atomism and other shortcomings of life under capitalism. Most of these communities were religious – such as the Quakers, the Shakers, the Mormons, the Mennonites, etc. – and some have been successful and long-lasting. Uniting all of these movements was a strong dissatisfaction with capitalism, class division, excessive individualism, and private property. Here, too, many looked to the teachings of the Early Christian Church and passages in the Book of Acts, which suggest that Christ advocated a system of common property and redistribution of wealth among followers (Jennings 51-52). One of the most interesting and enduring religious communities in the United States have been the Shakers. Founded in America in the 1770s by Ann

---

[1] The Book of Acts (especially 2-5) has been particularly important to activists and Christians as it describes followers of Christ being instructed to share all property in common, and the rich to sell their possessions and give the proceeds to the apostles to redistribute among all equally. Not surprisingly, many contemporary American Christian commentators have sought to interpret these passages as ambiguous, claiming that they only suggest acts of charity from time to time, rather than actually proposing a socialist model of common property as they seem to do.

Lee, a cotton mill worker from Manchester, the Shakers created – in the following decades – twenty-five "well-built and prosperous villages" throughout most of the settled regions of the country (Hayden, *Seven* 65) and served as an inspiration to many communities that followed, offering concrete proof that "successful Communism is subjectively possible," as John Humphrey Noyes, founder of the famous Oneida community in the nineteenth century, put it (quoted in Hayden 65). The fact that Noyes would look to the Shakers, rather than his own communal experiment, as proof of the viability of communitarianism illustrates how influential this group was in the nineteenth century.

The Shakers offer an ideal example of how religious faith and discipline could contribute to a group's cohesion and longevity. A millennial sect, they believed that the millennium – Christ's thousand-year reign on earth – had already begun. Like many early religious communities, the Shakers were fascinated by the earth-heaven dichotomy and sought to bridge the gap between the two spheres in their own lives. In practical terms, the earthly sphere was characterized for the Shakers by a thoughtful but strict regimentation of daily life, including every aspect of personal behavior, dress, and domestic economy. The Shakers became well-known for their carefully made furniture and elegantly functional architecture and designs, concrete manifestations of how they adapted their living environment to their spiritual ideas.

Their name, however, comes from the other aspect of their religious practice, that which attempted to imagine and imitate heaven, and which took the material form of joyous and sometimes abandoned celebrations that included singing, dancing and rolling, or twirling and shaking. The dances, which could be witnessed by outsiders and which were drawn by artists, were heavily rhythmic and could be called trance-inducing. Some of the dances thus emphasized the pleasures of what William H. McNeill has called "keeping together in time," one of the most satisfying physical aspects of ritual (2-5). In preserving the spirit of individual identity and expression, Shakers could also break out into individual forms of ecstatic dance or speak in tongues. They were also encouraged not to harmonize their voices while they sang, but to sing in the key that they personally preferred, according to the principle that God has given each one the gift of voice. In this way, Shakers created a religious practice that strongly emphasized community in its daily performance but still allowed room for intense physical and verbal expression on special occasions.

In offering both strict bodily discipline – including celibacy – and occasions for cathartic sensual release, Shakers attempted to create a spiritual practice that balanced the needs of the body with the need for connection and higher purpose. The community created by Shakers was an egalitarian one, organized into "families" of 30 to 100 people, with members calling each other "Brother" and "Sister." The families were not based on kinship (and the celibacy requirement meant that there were never many children in the movement) but organized according to members' relative advancement on the scale of spiritual "travel." If "family" was one important trope to describe the community, another was that of a "living building," in which each member was both builder and building block. This second trope is particularly interesting because it fuses the community and its physical space ("building") into an image that sees the group and its environment as one and the same. This inaugurates the recurrent concern with physical grounds and design that characterizes the history of intentional communities and foreshadows their currently pioneering role in sustainable farming and living.

In a broad sense, Shakers anticipated recycling and what is now called "permaculture" in their relationship to their land and grounds, which was one of careful stewardship, sustainability, and circularity. Millennial in their religious beliefs, they sought to create a heaven on earth, and one that would endure. One of Ann Lee's most cited quotes is "Do all your work as though you had a thousand years to live, and as you would if you knew you must die tomorrow" (Andrews 24). As a result, they considered carefully what crops to sow on the kind of land they possessed, they practiced crop rotation and contour plowing, they cared for woodland as carefully as their tilled land, they captured rainwater for crops, used human waste for compost, and created a "sacred, closed system" of careful and intense land use that closely resembles what contemporary advocates of permaculture and sustainable farming recommend (Hayden, *Seven* 76).

Although not all intentional communities were as thoughtful and systematic in their use of their natural environment as the Shakers, most intentional communities have had a far more protective and complex relationship to their land than conventional farmers. Because most tacitly opposed American capitalism, especially its competitiveness and social inequality, they have often wanted to be both self-sustaining (not dependent on the dominant capitalist economy) and an alternative model of egalitarianism and cooperation. Since intentional communities often envision or at least hope for long-term futures for themselves, there tends to be an inherent concern with sustainable and regenerative farming. However, many communities have started off with limited funds and were obliged to buy less-than-ideal land. Some were skillful and knowledgeable enough to regenerate their land, while many others faltered because of poor crops, hard winters, or other practical problems. Many nineteenth-century communities explicitly envisaged their project as creating a kind of earthly Eden (as did the Shakers), and grew disappointed with the initially meager results.

In the nineteenth century, new ideas about reform, human perfectibility, socialism, and revolution created a more secular foundation on which people dissatisfied with the dominant order could found alternatives, yet all maintained some religious or spiritual dimension. Henri de Saint-Simon, Étienne Cabet, and Robert Owen all had an impact to varying degrees on the United States, though none of them more so than Charles Fourier. Over thirty Fourierian communities called "phalanxes" were founded in the United States, and although most only lasted a few years, the North American Phalanx operated from 1843 to 1855 (https://www.britannica.com/topic/utopia#ref1041400).

Like most planners of intentional communities, Fourier found conventional nineteenth century society – and especially capitalism – deeply dissatisfying. As a boy, he learned in his father's textile shop that selling was often indistinguishable from lying and swore an "eternal oath" against commerce (Jennings 181). Specifically, he considered capitalist competition as wasteful, incoherent, and unproductive, and subsequently imagined communities organized on industrial and domestic *cooperation* instead. He also felt that conventional society stifled all of human beings' God-given emotional and relational needs, creating mental illness and other pathologies, and imagined a community in which people spent most of their time pursuing their interests and creative expression, as well as cultivating a wide range of rich human relationships and friendships according to the natural laws and principles of what he called "passional attraction" (his theory of the operation of human emotion and desire). In practical terms, Fourier saw people living in a phalanx working only a few hours a day, at tasks attributed according to their natural talents and interests, and the rest of the time devoted to activities that correspond to the five senses, including music, painting, drawing, sculpture, and eating, as well as hunting, fishing, libraries, picnics, mass, etc. Women would have the same scholarly and physical activities as men, as well as complete sexual freedom, one of Fourier's many proto-feminist ideas that were far ahead of his time.

Although there is a strong scientific bent to Fourier's vision, which is extremely systematic and even obsessively numerological, there is nevertheless a religious or spiritual substrate to his philosophy. At the foundation of his theory of human nature is the argument that the existence of God is sufficient proof of the perfectibility of man and the inevitable goodness of his needs and desires. Fourier's philosophy is based on what he calls the three "unities," which consist of the unity of man with himself and his nature, the unity of man with God, who gave man his nature and passions, and the unity of man with the Universe (Poster 8-9). By devoting one's self to cultivating one's "passional" needs and happiness, one is actually acting in highest accordance with what God intended for humans. Fourierism also resonated with the principles of Romanticism and especially Transcendentalism, which saw the divine as present inside every individual. The dichotomy between daily life and communal celebration would diminish, making every action in a typical day an iteration of communal belonging.

Nowhere was this fusion of the practical and the communal more apparent than in the way Fourier imagined the layout and design of the phalanx grounds. Believing that the arrangement of human society was correlated to the "health" of the earth and the cosmos, Fourier regarded the universe as a "coherent mechanism created by a beneficent and omnipotent God" (Jennings 167). Accordingly, Fourier saw the natural and built landscapes as interdependent and inseparable, and specified that the ideal phalanx would be located in a picturesque, varied location, "provided with a fine stream of water, intersected by hills, adapted to varied cultivation, contiguous with a forest" (Hayden, *Seven* 154). What was especially important was spatial distribution of various productive activities to encourage communal and personal contacts. To this end, he proposed a pattern of interlaced cultivation. Work groups would identify the specificities of the soil and microclimate, and then lines and patches of cultivation would extend out from the central area. The point was both to make use of varied terrain and to create opportunities for social interaction, that is, to "bring different groups together on the same grounds" so that workers could meet and interact (154). Fourier's landscape thus imagines the natural and the built features of the land to be arranged to maximize both their agricultural potential (hence the concern with microclimate and soil) and the social and relational potential of people.

The largest, longest-lasting, and most promising of Fourier's living communities was the North American Phalanx in Colt's Neck, New Jersey. Founded by Albert Brisbane in 1837 with the financial backing of non-resident sponsors and sixty resident founders, the community endured for thirteen years before financial problems brought it to a close. Ironically, these problems stemmed less from a failure to prosper than from pressure by the sponsors to build a giant edifice that would supposedly create a sense of community. Residents resisted this impractical plan, resulting in a drastic reduction in the sponsors' financial contribution (Hayden, *Seven* 172). Instead, the residents of the phalanx constructed a pleasant three-story wooden structure built on local models that served as the main building and was still standing a hundred years later. Around this building, they developed their estate according to Fourier's principles, leaving woodland intact, and creating an interlaced area of cultivation that produced fruits and vegetables that sold well across New York (Hayden, *Seven* 161).

Even more famous than the North American Phalanx is the community founded by George Ripley, Brook Farm, which was initially a Transcendentalist community and then adopted Fourierian associationism for the second half of its six-year existence. This community is amongst the most famous nineteenth-century experiments thanks to its connections to American literati, including Nathaniel Hawthorne, who lived there for six months and seems to have especially resented having to perform manual labor. Brook Farm is thus remembered best for its satirical description in Hawthorne's *The Blithedale Romance* (1852) and for its various problems, including poor crops. Apparently the soil was not very good and the system of voluntary work (often by writers and intellectuals with few farming skills) made self-sufficiency more elusive than at the North American Phalanx. Nevertheless, in the course of six years, thanks largely to its prosperous school, it had added four attractive buildings and was solvent. It was only after a fire destroyed a large new but uninsured building that Brook Farm folded. Admittedly, however, Brook Farm is something of an exception to the tendency of nineteenth-century communities to espouse proto-ecological ideas. Perhaps because its goals were more closely tied to social equality, education, and the cultivation of the arts, and its revenue depended largely on its school and manufacturing activities, Brook Farm residents were less explicitly concerned with their natural environment than other communities and Fourierian phalanxes.

Yet, like most intentional communities, Brook Farm attempted to invent a more "whole" and balanced life for residents. According to George Ripley, the stated goals of the community were to reject competition and to attenuate class differences by asking all residents to perform manual labor as well as leaving them time for study and leisure. In a letter to Ralph Waldo Emerson, Ripley explains his wish to combine the "worker" and the "thinker" in one individual (Ripley, "1840 Letter" 23). In another letter, Ripley tells Emerson that he believes in "the divinity of labor," articulating a vital link between the spiritual, practical, and economic dimensions of the project, a link that seems to characterize many American intentional communities (Ripley, "I believe" n. pag.). All were to be paid the same for any kind of work, including women. In addition, residents enjoyed picnics, theatricals, card games, weekly dances, and a variety of artistic activities. Although Brook Farm was not explicitly a religious community, they performed a nightly ritual of holding hands and vowing "truth to the cause of God and Humanity." This was called the "symbol of Universal Unity," a phrase that recalls Fourier's three-fold "unities" and resonates with the frequent expression among founders of intentional communities of a desire for a more whole and connected life, less fragmented and divided by class and social hierarchy.

One of the criticisms of the idea of community that has been made in recent years is that it is a highly romantic notion that often hides a more sinister political agenda. Thus, while celebrating wholeness and natural or spontaneous connectedness, the notion of community in fact implies an exclusion of those who are different and a reification of identity. In a similar vein, Miranda Joseph argues in *The Romance of Community* that "the rhetorical invocation of community and the social relationships that are discursively articulated as community" are actually "imbricated with capitalism," by which she means they are complicit with it even as community is often invoked as a form of resistance to capitalism (viii-ix). While a blind idealization of community is certainly a dangerous thing, and notions of community have often been invoked by American nationalists and nativists who posit America as a "Christian" or a white nation, often also in response to forces of industrialization or now globalization, it seems impractical to scrap all notions of community altogether. If we do so, we will be hard pressed to find a vocabulary to understand the deepest longings and intentions as well as the subjective experiences and objective achievements of communitarian pioneers.[2]

---

[2] As for Joseph's point regarding exclusionary aspects of the notion of community, it must be acknowledged that the members of the intentional communities discussed in this essay were predominantly white, and that some socialist communities in California explicitly refused African American members (e.g., Llano del Rio). Productive counter-examples to this bias are hard to find – the highly mediatized Jonestown cult, for instance, being too bleak to serve as a positive example, and also much too complex to be

While Joseph's articulation of community and capitalism may reflect the complexities of how this term is often deployed ideologically, the history of intentional communities in the United States suggests that capitalism has rarely been so thoroughly repudiated as by the groups discussed above. Almost every intentional community, whether religious or secular, has expressly rejected the principle of individual and class competition, citing the atomism, inefficiency and injustice of the principle of competition itself. All have embraced a deep structural reliance on cooperation and mutual aid, and many used the aforementioned Book of Acts (2-5) as a model for altruism. For example, Mormons initially upheld a principle of shared property stored in communal storehouses administered by bishops, who would distribute according to need. All new members were to deed ("consecrate") their property to the church, which could then bestow lands or farms on members in "stewardship" in order to earn their living but donating all extra proceeds to the church again. These practices were later dropped but the movement had begun with a radical attempt to challenge the inequalities created by capitalism (May 141-51).

The Mormons' Law of Consecration is one of many ways nineteenth-century intentional communities sought to bridge a variety of systemic dichotomies and create a more integrated and "whole" life experience. Intentional communities almost invariably strove to be self-sustaining and therefore required members to be both residents and workers as opposed to having work outside. Many were feminist in the sense that they advocated certain forms of equality between men and women, most strove to find labor-saving or labor-pooling solutions to reduce women's work, and most rejected the nuclear family model or what John Humphrey Noyes called "the little man and wife circle" as too isolating and inefficient (Hayden, *The Grand Domestic Revolution* 37). In some communities, integration of the functional and the aesthetic happened spontaneously, while in others it was to showcase the community for visitors, and in other cases because residents were inspired by the idea of creating an Edenic space on earth, a practical garden where people and nature co-exist symbiotically. A song at the Oneida

---

done justice to here (cf. Chidester) – though the reasons are less hard to find. African Americans historically did not have access to the mainstream capitalist life that white communitarians were fleeing, and often already had a strong sense of community, frequently centered around their church. Since the 1960s, many intentional communities have consciously sought to be racially integrated, and some African American communes existed, but true diversity continues to elude the intentional community movement (Miller, *60s Communes* 171).

community founded by John Humphries Noyes describes a place where work, worship and daily life are fused into a single whole: "We have built us a dome/On our beautiful plantation/And we all have one home/And one family relation" (Holloway 179). With the parallelism of the dome, plantation, and home, the song expresses the desire for fusion among the spheres of religion, work, and domesticity, combining the main aspects of an integrated life into one physical space.

One should recall that the idea of setting "nature" aside as an untouched preserve was not fully articulated yet at the time of the antebellum communes and would come at the end of the century, after the closing of the frontier and the dedication of national parks. Although the conservation movement has done Americans a valuable service in protecting areas of wilderness, the way in which the American landscape is thereby divided into "protected" parks, agricultural land which can be ruthlessly exploited, and urban areas where humans are packed far away from both turned out to be problematic. This fragmentation of the landscape and of life into sharply differentiated categories reflected the compartmentalization of modern life more generally, where spirituality, connection, and play were as carefully cordoned off from daily life as the national parks were far from urban and farming areas. These neatly policed divisions between work, home, and play – which promoted soulless conformity to professional identity and highly conventional social roles – were among the many sources of dissatisfaction for young Americans in the 1960s, when the next great wave of communitarian experiments appeared.

The surge of 1960s "communes," as they were often called, emerged from a thorough and devastating critique of the failures of American capitalism in the wake of WWII. This critique of American technocratic and consumerist society began in the 1950s with the Beats. Allen Ginsberg's "Howl" (1955) depicted America as a concrete prison where poets and other non-conformists went mad. The image he uses of America as "Moloch," the Canaanite god associated with child sacrifice, evokes the structural violence of a society that required everyone to live in a hetero-normative nuclear family and have a corporate job, while regularly sending its young off to die in foreign wars (e.g., Korea in the early 1950s). Similarly, Jack Kerouac's *On the Road* (1957), the more romantic flip side of Ginsberg's "Howl," described a longing to leave mainstream society and its rigid structures and explore the rest of the country and its many less travelled roads.

The Beats' disinterest in a nuclear family and a consumerist work model paved the way for the wholesale disaffection from that lifestyle in the 1960s, a disaffection that took on greater urgency when the war in Vietnam escalated after 1964 and revealed the dark underside to American prosperity. While the military-industrial complex, as Dwight Eisenhower had called it in his 1961 farewell address, drained government coffers to build bombs and toxic chemicals to drop on peasants in Southeast Asia, and as the number of American and Vietnamese deaths climbed daily, the Civil Rights movement at home revealed the emptiness of American claims of national community and coherence, and young people began to abandon conventional American society (Braunstein and Doyle 8-9). The counterculture of San Francisco, the epicenter of the hippie movement, emerged from a rejection of the rigidity, emptiness, and hypocrisy of middle class life and undertook a broad-ranging exploration of group living and alternative values, both in the city and the neighboring countryside. By the late 1960s, many thousands of people were living in intentional communities either as a way of taking political activism to a new level, by living the values they believed in, or as a way of simply withdrawing their energy from what they saw as a murderous, unjust and soul-killing system.

The 1960s commune movement was thus every bit as existential and spiritual as it was political. Some communes were explicitly Christian, devoted to the more progressive teachings of Jesus Christ as counterculture model. Miller writes that in fact the "Jesus communes" may have been "the largest identifiable communal type of the 1960s" (*60s Communes* xxiv). Others looked to Native American or eastern religious traditions to find models for imbuing the everyday with a sense of the sacred (see Krech; Smith). All were appalled by the empty materialism of American life and outraged by the hypocrisy and violence behind the white suburban family model for American national community while African Americans, Native Americans, and others were being exploited and excluded (Miller, *The Hippies* 8).

The intentional communities that resulted differed from the nineteenth-century experiments in several important respects. First of all, 1960s communards were not interested in the model of an earthly Eden or garden of paradise, as many of the antebellum experimenters had been. Founders of the 1960s communes embraced a philosophy of "back to the land" instead, which looked to historical and not Biblical roots. Most of all, they looked to Native Americans for practical knowledge in sustainable and self-sufficient farming skills as well as a model on how to live in a more spiritually balanced way. While many hippies and communards romanticized Native American life, to be sure, they generally did so out of a respect for a cultural heritage that had been mostly erased up until that time, and out of an awareness of the ongoing struggle of Native Americans to reclaim their land sovereignty and civil rights (the American Indian Movement was founded in 1968). Many other communes hoped to invent a more sustainable, satisfying, and equitable life on their own, solving problems as they came up with new ideas and design structures (such as the geodesic domes that characterized Drop City in southern Colorado).

According to Timothy Miller, foremost historian of the hippie movement and counterculture, there were several thousand communes during the 1960s era, with incredibly diverse goals, structures, compositions, and achievements (*The Hippies* 88). Nevertheless, one generalization that can be made is that, like their predecessors, 1960s communes grew out of a strong conviction that American capitalism was a failure as a social system. Competition and consumerism had fragmented people's lives into empty routines of work, leisure, and consumption, wholly devoid of real meaning, real playfulness, and real connection to other people, while producing foreign wars and domestic exploitation. Like the founders of intentional communities of the nineteenth century, the hippies and commune creators of the 1960s sought to create communities that offered true equality to all members, often offering membership to anyone who wanted it, redefining the meaning of "family," and attempting to invent a more whole and integrated way of life (*The Hippies* 93).

They were also interested in creating a relationship with the land that was respectful, healthy, and sustainable. Rachel Carson had published her terrifying study of pesticides used in industrial farming, *Silent Spring*, in 1962, and had created an awareness of the urgent need to rethink farming and its dependence of toxic chemicals. At the same time, the capitalist model of land as private property for extraction of resources and industrial farming was openly questioned for the first time. One response that exemplified the spirit of the times was Lou Gottlieb's. A musician and scholar, Gottlieb founded in 1966 Morning Star Ranch, a free-wheeling commune outside of San Francisco, and in 1969 deeded the land to God. Although a local judge objected that God was "not a person, natural or artificial, in existence at time of conveyance and capable of taking title," the concept of open land (related in spirit to the so-called crash-pad in urban areas) was popular among the 1960s generation, who questioned the logic and legitimacy of private property in general (Miller, *60s Communes* 51). Another response was the bioregionalism movement, which looked back to Native American culture and sought to redefine community in terms of naturally coherent biomes and regions (see Arnsperger in this volume).

Although most communes lasted no more than a few years, some have endured and thrived up to the present. The Farm was conceived in Haight-Ashbury and finally established in Tennessee, and has existed since 1971. According to Timothy Miller, it epitomizes "most perfectly . . . the spirit of the communal 1960s era" (*60s Communes* 118). Founded by Stephen Gaskin, a university instructor and spiritual leader, the Farm was rooted in "prototypical hippie spirituality and religiosity, espousing a unique faith that drew from the deepest insights of all the world's major religious traditions" (118). Members took vows of poverty and dedicated themselves to helping the poor in the third world, and the commune has had an international program in place since 1974. Environmentalists from the start, they sought self-sufficiency in food and practiced veganism, avoiding all animal products including leather and honey. They also established a public-interest law firm which filed lawsuits on behalf of victims of exposure to nuclear radiation, fought the Army Corps of Engineers plans to control wild rivers, and published climate change research.

The Farm still exists today and its mission statement of core beliefs still heavily emphasizes spirituality as well as an expanded vision of community. The first value listed is:

> We believe that there are non-material planes of being or levels of consciousness that everyone can experience, the highest of these being the spiritual plane . . . We believe that we are all one, that the material and spiritual are one, and the spirit is identical and one in all of creation" (http://www.thefarm.org/about-our-community/basic-beliefs-agreements/).

If The Farm represents the prototypical 1960s commune, then this statement conveys several exemplary aspects of hippie spiritual belief and practice. First of all, it rejects secular materialism and affirms the existence of a spiritual dimension or "plane." It claims that "everyone can experience" this plane, alluding to the notion of personal subjective experience of a "higher level of consciousness," situating the spiritual in "states of consciousness" which can be accessed (through meditation, mind-altering drugs, or other consciousness-altering techniques). The claim that "everyone" can experience these planes emphasizes the democratic and participatory aspect of 1960s religiosity, located in each individual and not in an institution or spiritual leader.

Nevertheless, not to overstate the correlation between intentional community and religion, there have been many communities that are fully secular and not concerned with spirituality in any overt form. One of these is the Los Angeles Eco-Village (LAEV), founded in 1993 in Los Angeles just west of downtown. The community is comprised of around 40 people who live on the premises in two apartment buildings that Eco-Village owns as a cooperative. Members are assigned an apartment according to their needs, which may evolve as their family grows or changes. Since 1993, the LAEV has been "eco-fitting" the buildings for sustainability, encouraging residents to bike instead of drive, make soil through composting, and reaching out to the neighborhood in a variety of ways. The Eco-Village has several on-site workshops and crafts spaces, including for soldering and sowing. It uses solar cookers and captures rainwater. The courtyard garden features a variety of local or edible plants and serves as the main gathering place for outdoor events. The LAEV is also heavily invested in teaching, offering weekly tours and frequent conferences on topics related to sustainability. The main focus of the LAEV is reducing residents' carbon footprints and developing the processes of community-building and development.

Like other intentional communities which have sought to create more integrated or "whole" life experiences, the LAEV explicitly uses a method called "Whole Systems Approach," which it defines on its webpage as a "whole-systems or permaculture approach to community development, integrating the social, economic and ecological or physical aspects of neighborhood life with the goal of raising the quality of life while radically reducing environmental impacts" (http://laecovillage.org/crsp/). The emphasis here is on integrating social and environmental concerns, which has always been a key feature of intentional communities, as we have seen, only here the environment is urban rather than rural.

Although the LAEV is ostensibly secular, I would argue that there is nevertheless a tacitly spiritual dimension to their project, articulated most clearly in the first of their seven core values (first formulated in 2011 and regularly revisited). These values include "Learn from nature and live ecologically" and "Create balanced opportunities for individual participation & collective stewardship," but the one that speaks in a quasi-religious register is "celebrate and include joy in all our endeavors" (http://laecovillage.org/home/about-2/).[3] This value resonates with

---

[3] The complete list of values: "1. Celebrate & include joy in all our endeavors / 2. Take responsibility for each other & the planet through local environmental & social action /

spiritual import. The word "joy" is not a term that evokes mainly an ethical or political stance, but emanates from a register that is affective and potentially religious. The word "celebrate" makes the tone and lexicon of the phrase even more explicitly linked to worship. I would argue that even in this most pragmatic and secular of intentional communities, values that cannot be called anything except spiritual nevertheless lie at the heart of their project and communal spirit.

A final contemporary example of an intentional community is the annual festival at Black Rock Desert, Nevada, called Burning Man. Initiated in 1986 as a small party on a beach near San Francisco, Burning Man is now an event that attracts over 60,000 people annually. This is not an intentional community in the same sense as the others, since it exists geographically for only one week a year, but it arguably springs from similar impulses and addresses similar yearnings (see Junger). A subtitle of Burning Man sometimes is "a festival of radical self-expression," which points to the fact that the creation of temporary artwork and performance has been at the core of how Burning Man has developed. The festival takes its name from the wooden sculpture in the form of a giant man that is built every year and ceremoniously burned on the last day, in an event that recalls fire-based pagan seasonal events. Although the festival now commissions certain artists to come and create their art-pieces before the five-day official event begins, all participants are encouraged to bring things they have made or to express themselves creatively. There is no money at the festival (except to buy ice and coffee in the central tent) and everyone is invited to volunteer for one of the many tasks that contribute to the functioning of the event, including greeting people, providing information, running the lost and found service, working at the central café, and providing security. The festival organizers do not pitch the festival like a concert (though there is a lot of music) or an art show (though there is also a lot of art), but as a temporary city that is meant to serve both as foil to contemporary society and as a model for a responsible alternative community.

The festival lists 10 core values, namely, radical inclusion, gifting, de-commodification, radical self-reliance, radical self-expression, communal effort, civic responsibility, leaving no trace, participation, immediacy. Like most other intentional communities, Burning Man springs from a

---

3. Learn from nature and live ecologically / 4. Build a dynamic community through diversity & cooperation, giving & forgiving / 5. Inspire compassionate, nurturing, & respectful relationships / 6. Create balanced opportunities for individual participation & collective stewardship / 7. Engage our neighbors and broader community in mutual dialog to learn, act and teach" (source: http://laecovillage.org/home/about-2/).

conscious rejection of capitalism and the kind of culture and subjectivity that develops around it.[4] The values of "gifting" and "decommodification" refer to the prohibition on money transactions, the encouragement of barter, and an attempt to temporarily suspend the economic logic that structures much of our lives. Recalling the Diggers' experiments with free medical services and free goods in the donation-based "Free Store" in San Francisco, Burning Man encourages participants to interact with each other on a basis other than consumerism and exchange. "Radical self-reliance" and "leaving no trace" both allude to the protective relationship with nature that participants are required to have: everyone must bring everything they need to survive a week in the desert, and they are asked to take everything with them when they leave. The goal of the festival is to "leave no trace" on the desert after the festival in order to preserve the local eco-system and natural environment.

If "no trace" is to be left on the desert after the departure of tens of thousands of "burners," as festival participants are referred to, the community that they build there is meant to endure throughout the rest of the year in a different form. Participants can stay in touch with each other, meet locally and even create local versions of the festival called "burns." The values that are promoted during the one colorful and joyous week of celebration in the desert are intended to be cultivated throughout the year in one's daily life. The yearly event is imagined like a coming together of the tribes, recalling the Human Be-in of 1967 in San Francisco, except that the somewhat nostalgic notion of a "tribe" – enthusiastically embraced by the hippies in honor of earlier Native American cultures – does not resonate with the Burning Man ethos as well as does the image of a temporary city, as can be seen in the value of "civic responsibility."

However, there is one important element of tribalism at the festival: the ritual of burning the wooden effigy on the last night, a pyromaniac's dream of a pagan ceremony, with fire-breathers and fire-dancers and fire cannons and the bonfire of the giant wooden man. This brings me to the question of religion and spirituality. To be sure, Burning Man is not a religious event, nor even explicitly spiritual in the manner of The Farm. Nevertheless, there is an element of the religious in the quest for collective celebration through art and ritual, the desire to alter one's

---

[4] There is of course a certain irony that the main participants are well-educated and fairly well-off. According to the Burning Man census figures, most participants have at least a B.A. degree and 31 percent of 2016 participants have a graduate degree. Most also earn between 50,000 and 100,000 dollars per year (source: https://drivegoogle.com/file/d/0BxJfvV_7__jqRTlpVHRWbGZIMkE/view, 16-18).

consciousness through art, dance, meditation, drugs (including alcohol), or other means, and a general interest in participating in a heightened experience of shared community. Durkheim in his *Elementary Forms of Religious Life* saw one of the first forms of religion and culture emanating from group life as the division of time into the profane and sacred, with the former consisting of daily life and the latter organized into periodic moments of coming together for ritual and group worship, arousing in participants a heightened emotional state that Durkheim called "effervescence" (Durkheim 427-28).

Burning Man is nothing if not a weeklong condition of effervescence and heightened emotional, sensory, and social experience. The core value listed as "immediacy" alludes to the importance of mindfulness, being in the present, being "awake" (a key principle of Buddhism, which comes from "bodhi" or "to wake up" in Sanskrit), or simply being attentive and fully engaged with one's immediate environment as opposed to being submerged in the automated and routinized experience of everyday working life. Burning Man's particular form of spirituality, like that of the Shakers and many other communards, is based on the belief (and putting into practice) that every individual has a unique voice (as the Shakers put it) and gifts; is simply unique; and should share this uniqueness and these gifts with the world, which will receive and somehow answer. This is the foundation of the value of "radical self-expression," as Larry Harvey describes it in a 2014 interview (https://www.you-tube.com/watch?v=x54s_G0NYG8).

Making the connection to religious experience nearly explicit, Harvey argues that the "ultimate experience" that draws people to Burning Man is for "transcendence, being connected to something much larger than you are." He explains that many people come for the artwork or for the prospect of a weeklong desert rave but they end up staying "for the community." The set of values espoused by the Burning Man festival, according to Harvey, adds up to "a whole life and an ethos," an "authentic life," and that "people come from all over the globe to see what that feels like." Asked if Burning Man has ever changed anyone's life, he replies: "Incessantly . . . it's like a conversion experience," evoking the way that intense experiences of community seem to generate religious rhetoric and affect (https://www.youtube.com/watch?v=x54s_G0NYG8).

Although Burning Man is not a community where people live physically all year long, it offers participants a temporary experience of intentional community of sorts and the possibility to remain in contact throughout the year with people who have shared that experience. It is possible to argue that the yearning for more meaningful encounters with like-minded friends and strangers and for an alternative to the deadening mechanisms of work and consumption-driven capitalism is the same for Burning Man participants as for people who actually move into a "real" collective living experiment.

Although there is a strong ethos of leaving "no trace" on the playa, the use of heavy generators for lights and sound systems, trucks spewing water for people to revel in, and the gratuitous destruction of the Burning Man effigy itself, reveal that other impulses besides environmentalism are driving the event. These include, I would argue, a yearning for ritual, for creativity, playfulness, connection, and for the sacred. The fact that many participants come to Burning Man to celebrate their weddings (including numerous group weddings for the San Francisco crowd) suggests that the festival has succeeded in creating an occasion that functions as a meaningful ritual, a true "holiday" and moment of collective effervescence. With their whimsical costumes and mutant vehicles, Burning Man participants may seem on the surface as different from the Shakers as anyone could be, yet in the underlying impulse to create a community of radical horizontal participation and a space for "radical self-expression," burners are acting out of a similar need as the Shakers when they whirled and danced and spoke in tongues.

In describing the intentions and longings of American communitarians, and paying less attention to the problems and dissatisfactions they encountered, I do not mean to imply that alternative communities were always or even often successful. Most struggled with economic problems and internal conflicts, experiments with egalitarian labor distribution often fell short of true gender equality, and efforts to replace monogamous marriage arrangements with "free love" were often mixed at best. Nevertheless, to dismiss intentional communities as founded by naïve or manipulative eccentrics, as Hawthorne's *The Blithedale Romance* left generations of American readers feeling about Brook Farm, is to do a profound disservice to American history and to future generations which may need to look to these communities for ideas on how to live less destructively than we currently do. Recent critiques of community have attempted to complicate a concept that is indeed often invoked rather uncritically. Miranda Joseph points out that it is almost inconceivable to use the term "community" in any but a romanticized and positive sense despite the fact that it often carries a strongly exclusionary dimension. Joseph argues that in fact modern invocations of community are strongly implicated with capitalism (viii-ix), and Roberto Esposito makes a similar case when he proposes that community and its connotations of *belonging* are strongly linked to property and *proprium* (2-3).

Despite these legitimate concerns and critiques, American intentional communities deserve to be taken seriously. In repudiating the competitive and exploitative relationships created necessarily and by definition under capitalism as it developed in Europe and North America, intentional communities have attempted to realize social life without private property, class inequality, or sexual hierarchy. Though not always successful, their example offers valuable lessons. Many adopted an attitude of careful and sustainable cultivation of their land as a mirror to the attitude of care and protectiveness of their individual members as well as the group as a whole. In doing so, many also found a sense of higher purpose, human connection and sacredness that sociologists and other observers have reported as largely lacking in modernity (Taylor 367-68). The recent surge in intentional communities suggests that these lacks have only grown more intolerable as people realize that our current forms of inhabiting the planet are not only unsatisfying but destructive and, worse for us, suicidal. This is why throwing the community baby out with the romanticized-community bathwater does us no service in terms of looking for the solutions we need now to regenerate a sense of connection to each other and the planet we share as a species before it's too late.

References

Andrews, Edward D. *The People Called Shakers: A Search for the Perfect Society*. New York: Dover, 1953.

Braunstein, Peter and Michael William Doyle. "Historicizing the American Counterculture of the 1960s and '70s." *Imagine Nation: The American Counterculture of the 1960s and 70s*. Ed. Peter Braunstein and Michael William Doyle. New York: Routledge, 2002.

Chidester, David. *Salvation and Suicide: Jim Jones, the Peoples Temple, and Jonestown*. Revised edition. Bloomington: Indiana University Press, 2003.

Dawson, Jonathan. *Ecovillages: New Frontiers for Sustainability*. Devon: Green Books, 2006.

Durkheim, Emile. *The Elementary Forms of the Religious Life*. Trans. Joseph Ward Swain. New York: Free Books, [1915] 1965.

Esposito, Roberto. *Communitas: The Origin and Destiny of Community*. Stanford: Stanford University Press, 2010.

Hayden, Dolores. *Seven American Utopias: The Architecture of Communitarian Socialism, 1790-1975*. Cambridge: MIT Press, 1976.

———. *The Grand Domestic Revolution: A History of Feminist Designs for American Homes, Neighborhoods and Cities*. Cambridge: MIT Press, 1981.

Holloway, Mark. *Heavens on Earth: Utopian Communities in America 1680-1880*. New York: Dover, 1966.

Jennings, Chris. *Paradise Now: The Story of American Utopianism*. New York: Random House, 2016.

Joseph, Miranda. *Against the Romance of Community*. Minneapolis: University of Minnesota Press, 2002.

Junger, Sebastian. *Tribe: On Homecoming and Belonging*. New York: Twelve, 2016.

Krech, Shepard. *The Ecological Indian: Myth and History*. New York: Norton, 1999.

May, Dean L. "Communal Life Values Among the Mormons." *America's Communal Utopias*. Ed. Donald E. Pitzer. Chapel Hill: University of North Carolina Press, 1997.

McNeill, William H. *Keeping Together in Time: Dance and Drill in Human History*. Cambridge: Harvard University Press, 1995.

Miller, Timothy. *The Hippies and American Values*. Second edition. Knoxville: University of Tennessee Press, 2011.

———. *The 60s Communes: Hippies and Beyond*. Syracuse: Syracuse University Press, 1999.

Poster, Mark, ed. *Harmonian Man: The Selected Writings of Charles Fourier*. New York: Doubleday, 1971.

Ripley, George. "1840 Letter to Ralph Waldo Emerson." *Sharing the Earth: An International Environmental Justice Reader*. Ed. Elizabeth Ammons and Modhumita Roy. Athens and London: University of Georgia Press, 2015. 23-26.

———. "I believe in the divinity of labor." Letter to Ralph Waldo Emerson (1840). http://historymatters.gmu.edu/d/6592/ Accessed on 13 February 2017.

Smith, Sherry. *Hippies, Indians, and the Fight for Red Power*. New York: Oxford University Press, 2012.

Taylor, Charles. *A Secular Age*. Cambridge: Harvard University Press, 2007.

Communities of Reinhabitation: Bioregionalism, Biogeography, and the Contemporary North American Reflection on Sustainability

Christian Arnsperger*

The 1960s and 1970s saw the birth, in the United States and in particular in California, of a movement called bioregionalism. It was rooted in a both backward- and forward-looking ethic of "reinhabitation," linked to the rediscovery of Native American perspectives on living within landscapes seen as coherent biomes – as opposed to the administrative borders inherited from Anglo-European colonization and land grabbing. Bioregionalism emerged in the wake of the countercultural contestation already begun by the hippie movement. It offered the possibility to rethink North America as a potentially more sustainable civilization venture anchored in what key authors in the movement called "applying for membership in a biotic community." Community in America should have a cultural as well as a natural core, so the idea goes; humans should live in harmony with each other and with nonhuman species, in ecologically and biogeographically delineated areas experienced as "native life places." This essay draws on the thoughts of key thinkers of the movement and uses California as a critical example, in order to argue that bioregionalism constitutes one of North America's most in-depth theoretical and practical contributions to creating new foundations for a notion of community that is informed by the contemporary necessities of sustainability.

---

* The author is grateful to the editors of this volume, Julia Straub and Lukas Etter, as well as to an anonymous referee for being of invaluable assistance in improving both the form and the argument of this article.

American Communities: Between the Popular and the Political. SPELL: Swiss Papers in English Language and Literature 35. Ed. Lukas Etter and Julia Straub. Tübingen: Narr, 2017. 145-64.

*

Bioregionalism emerged in the United States in the 1960s as a worldview and movement rooted in a both backward- and forward-looking ecological ethic of "reinhabitation." As this essay argues, comprehending bioregionalism is essential in order to understand how a notion of community based on ecological and biogeographical elements can make sense in modern North America. It serves as one crucial element forming the backdrop for many initiatives that have sprung up since the 1960s, such as alternative intentional communities (see e.g., Bernard and Young; Boal, Stone, Watts and Winslow; Campbell) or movements towards economic re-localization (see e.g., Shuman; Estill; Wicks). These initiatives will not, in themselves, be the object of this essay; rather, a general framework is offered here that will be useful in understanding how "biotic community-making" rooted in ancient remnants of a native "sense of place" has served, and continues to serve, as an important building block of many of these *community-based sustainability practices* in postwar North America.

1. Addressing North America's "Un-sustainability"

At a time when both the civil rights movement and the Vietnam war were in full swing, generating levels of division and uncertainty unheard of in the postwar United States, a small collective of Californian countercultural activists – some of whom, like Peter Berg, had been key actors in the Summer of Love and the Diggers movement while others, like Gary Snyder, would go on to become highly influential poets – sought to explicitly connect community with local geography as well as biodiversity. It was an attempt at wresting the notion of community from the political conservatives as well as the religious communitarians by looking to land and landscape, as well as fauna, flora, and ancestral culture as the defining domains of American communities.

Appearing to take their cue from, among others, the *Port Huron Statement* published in 1962 by Students for a Democratic Society (SDS) (see Hayden), the collective I am speaking of espoused a radical critique of American imperialism, militarism, and capitalism, along with their combined catastrophic social, political, as well as environmental impacts. They used this critique to argue that US society needed to reinvent itself deeply through a rediscovery of its citizens' lost connection to the soil and to the ecological web of life. Neither place nor landscape nor nonhuman species were to be viewed as mere supports and "resources" for instrumentalization and objectification. Rather, reaching back to a partly historically accurate and partly mythologized Native American perspective on human settlement and ecology, this small countercultural group sought a concrete, workable, and spiritually attractive alternative to what they identified, already back then, as the key drivers of America's lack of sustainability: the massive overextension of the US's globe-spanning military and economic domination enterprise, the gigantism of many of its core institutions and of many of its major cities, and the resulting ecological destruction and tenacious blindness to social inequality and – to borrow the title of Rob Nixon's recent book – to the "slow violence" being inflicted both on humans and on nonhuman species (see Nixon).

These countercultural thinkers and activists ultimately argued that the pathologies in question were rooted in a process of deep existential loss – namely, the loss of a *sense of inhabitation*. In the name of progress, growth, and the "American dream" of limitless material prosperity, the United States had gradually destroyed what had ensured the sustainability and endurance of most indigenous cultures on the American continent before the several waves of Spanish and Anglo invasion and occupation. The nation-state had fast become an entity of both internal and external predation. Just like older states such as France or Spain, the United States had attempted to homogenize local domestic cultures in the name of "nationhood." Seeming to merely emulate older colonialist models such as Spain's or England's, the United States had also attempted to colonize and dominate foreign cultures in the name of "internationalization."[1] Borders, so the argument went on, were political and, even more so, economic in nature. They were generated by the increasing abstraction brought about by the requirements of both internal and external extraction and production.

The task of critiquing capitalist abstraction was made somewhat more complex in the context of the 1960s civil rights movements. The Reconstruction and its reverberations all the way into the Jim Crow laws and the persistent racial segregation in US society had demonstrated the ability of American capitalism to integrate and metabolize the structural injustice bequeathed by conflicts of the antebellum period. Roughly a century after the end of the Civil War, the US was facing the fallout from never truly having dealt with the "original sins" of how its economy, its political system, and its cultural values emerged out of a racist

---

[1] On these aspects of "nationhood" and "internationalization," see e.g., Lopez.

and militaristic sacralization of materialism and imperialism (see Baptist; Beckert and Rockman).

The hippie movement, for all its multiple facets, fundamentally saw itself as the polar opposite of such a retrograde worldview, and promoted an ethic that sought to overturn and transcend it (see Miller). Therefore, merely reaching back to inherited historical and political post-1865 categories in order to promote "localism" and "rootedness" would have been unthinkable for those who sought to combine civil rights, anti-capitalism, the liberation of sexuality and the broadening of consciousness with a critique of what American culture had become. The racist and colonial "good old times" needed to be overturned and transcended – and in this case this meant looking back, in a creative and forward-looking way, to *even older "times"* when it had been neither racist segregation nor extractive greed that would drive the American people's community-building. Part of this was rethinking who the "American people" were in the first place.

2. The "Old Ways": Seeking Timeless Wisdom

Much has been said and written about how influential the partial blurring of boundaries between white Anglos and African Americans was in giving birth to the counterculture of the 1960s. Less has been said and written until now about how the allure of what Gary Snyder called "the Old Ways" of the original Native American settlers impacted the whole back-to-the-land movement, the communes movement of the 1960s, and especially the rediscovery of landscapes, biotopes, basins, and watersheds as relevant entities of a form of "natural," and therefore simple and peaceful, existence within self-contained, non-imperialistic, regional entities.

In a striking book entitled *Tribe*, the contemporary cultural and political critic Sebastian Junger has documented how, at the very heart of the brutal destruction of Native American nations and tribes in the mid-nineteenth century, there lay a paradoxical denial of the sheer fascination that tribal belonging and the "Indians [who] lived communally in mobile or semi-permanent encampments that were more or less run by consensus and broadly egalitarian" (1-2) exercised on Anglo "settlers." What surprised and infuriated early anti-Indian propagandists was that quite a number of new settlers chose to join Native American tribes and live with them permanently (and were mostly welcome to do so) whereas not a single native willingly espoused the "modern" way of life imported from Britain and continental Europe. Early on in the colonization process, quite a few new "settlers," so Junger argues, developed a deep attraction of Native American community-building and the associated ways of inhabiting the land.

A century later, quite a number of hippies sided with the Native Americans both existentially and politically – a fraternization which was treated with scorn by those who coined the derogative term "red hippie." One case in point was Jake and Susanne Page's detailed account, published in the early 1980s, of how they were invited by the Hopi Indians in the mid-1970s and sought, as journalists and photographers but also as "children" of the 1960s, to understand and document in a meticulous but fundamentally positive light the Hopi way of living and seeing the world (see Page and Page). A certain naïve idealization of Native American ways of life by ecologically-minded Americans has occasionally been pointed out and criticized (see e.g., Krech). With or without idealization, it is clear that what was perceived as Native American gentleness, nobility, frugality, and cosmocentrism played a central role in shaping the rules of certain hippie communes, their views of the world, and even their habitats (see e.g., Bosk). The Indians were admired and also envied by the average white bourgeois kid of the mid-1960s – much like the enthusiastic cultural appropriation of African American culture in 1960s white-dominated popular culture. And much like what occurred in the case of African Americans, the cause of Native Americans was espoused by a large number of young people (both white and black) who rightly pointed to the oppression of the Native American nations alongside that of slaves from the African continent. Even before the full extent of the actual "parallel" enslavement of the Indians was rigorously documented (see e.g., Reséndez), the "Red Power" movement had gained adherents in many strata of American progressivism (see Smith).

There was clearly a political dimension to all this, but just as clearly a cultural and ecological one. In fact, the two were not completely distinct even though emphases differed. The countercultural activists I mentioned at the beginning were convinced that overturning and transcending America's contemporary violence and gigantism, which was in large part rooted in its dark past of colonialist slavery, required returning to pre-colonial ways of settling, using, and inhabiting the land. This "return," however, was never viewed as a form of backtracking. Rather, it was seen as a way of criticizing the prevailing, naïve notion of progress and linear growth and the American cult of "prosperity" – by showing that progress and prosperity had better be approached through a striving for knowledge and spiritual resources that were "outside of history," as argued by Gary Snyder with the now classic phrase in August of 1976:

> Mankind has a rendezvous with destiny in outer space, some have predicted. Well: we are already traveling in space – this is the galaxy, right here. The wisdom and skills of those who studied the universe firsthand, by direct knowledge and experience, for millennia, both inside and outside themselves, are what we might call the Old Ways. Those who envision a possible future planet on which we continue that study, and where we live by the green and the sun, have no choice but to bring whatever science, imagination, strength, and political finesse they have to the support of the inhabitory people – natives and peasants of the world. In making common cause with them, we become "reinhabitory." And we begin to learn a little of the Old Ways, which are outside of history, and forever new. ("Reinhabitation" 28)

This notion of timelessness was central in the group's critique of American progress. Around the same time (the mid-1970s), the architect Christopher Alexander was working – also in California, which is probably not coincidental, as I will argue further down – on what he called a "timeless way of building," rejecting modernist notions of progress and claiming to have uncovered a "pattern language" whose elements get repeated and recomposed in any *genuinely livable and enlivening* community – building, neighborhood, or city (see Alexander, *A Pattern Language*, and Alexander et al., *The Timeless Way of Building*).

Both the countercultural hippies and the anti-modernist architects have, at various times, been labeled as primitivists. Their naïve glorification of timeless patterns – whether it be patterns of settlement or patterns of construction – is predicated, so the standard critique goes, on a regressive and "artificial" existential stance because it is rooted in nostalgia for what can never return, and was not even so wonderful to begin with. Critics routinely point to the brutality of certain Indian tribes and to their ecological ineptitude, only concealed by the low technical means they possessed for doing any extensive harm to their environment, just as they point to the oppressiveness of the traditional village square and to the squalor and non-functionality of Renaissance Venice or pre-Haussmannian Paris. On another note, one of the eminent thinkers of Anglo-American neoliberalism, Friedrich August von Hayek, presented "tribalism" as the core flaw of all anti-liberal societies, in which the free flow of goods and humans across regional and national borders is hampered by tradition and parochialism, and in which free thought – seen mainly as the financially and economically competitive exercise of instrumental rationality – is stopped in its open tracks by sentiments of belonging and community (see Hayek).

Here is not the place to delve at length and with any degree of nuance into the pros and cons of Hayek's and the anti-tribalists' positioning. No analysis of pre-modern groupings and traditional values should be borrowed without the crucial and critical question whether it contains glorifications and the pitfalls of the "noble savage" discourse, to be sure. But neither can a blanket defense of (neo)liberal subjectivity and anti-communalism be valid in the face of what the countercultural activists I am speaking of here were witnessing: the piecemeal "destruction," as they called it, of their landscapes and communities by ruthless urban growth, commercialism, and war. Americans had become destructive, they claimed, because they had lost their native ancestors' sense of how to live within the broader community of mineral, vegetable, animal, and human species, supported in myriad ways by the entire biosphere.

3. Reinhabitation: Toward a Notion of Biotic Community

Crucial to Snyder's point about the timeless ethic of the Old Ways are the concepts of "inhabitation" and "reinhabitation." It is around these concepts that the so-called "bioregional" movement was born by the middle of the 1970s.[2]

With regard to its roots within the 1960s counterculture, bioregionalism was never a homogeneous or centrally governed movement. Nevertheless, it relied on a relatively unified field of physical and metaphysical orientations concerning the deeper qualities of human settlements – with reference to the figure of the *peasant*, whose etymological roots refer to the land (*pays, paese*) and to the landscape (*paysage, paesaggio*): the peasant is he or she who knows how to dwell in the land, how to *genuinely be a part of the land as part of a broad and deep biotic community*. This includes Native American tribes who were nomad or semi-nomad hunter-gatherers and, therefore, not agricultural agents in modern terms – but who were, in a very deep sense, "native to their places" and, therefore, peasants. This capacity for place-based, multispecies community – this cultural trait gradually lost in modern Americans' relation to their lands – is what "inhabitation" mainly refers to, as two of bioregionalism's main thinkers wrote around 1978:

---

[2] For relatively recent, detailed as well as critical articles on bioregionalism, see Aberley, "Interpreting Bioregionalism" as well as Parsons.

> Reinhabitation involves developing a bioregional identity, something most North Americans have lost, or have never possessed. [. . .] The term refers both to geographical terrain and a terrain of consciousness – to a place and the ideas that have developed about how to live in that place. Within a bioregion the conditions that influence life are similar and these in turn have influenced human occupancy. A bioregion can be determined initially by use of climatology, physiography, animal and plant geography, natural history and other descriptive natural sciences. The final boundaries of a bioregion are best described by the people who have lived within it, through human cognition of the realities of living-in-place. [. . .] [T]here is a distinct resonance among living things and factors which influence them that occurs specifically within each separate place on the planet. Discovering and describing that resonance is a way to describe a bioregion. (Berg and Dasmann 82)

One of the authors of this passage was Peter Berg, a New York native who grew up in Florida and in 1964 hitchhiked to San Francisco, where he later became very active during the Summer of Love and was a prominent member of the Diggers, even making an extended appearance as an arrogant and much maligned young hippie agitator in Joan Didion's abrasive 1967 essay about the Summer of Love, "Slouching Towards Bethlehem." Berg became one of the main – and most vocal – thinking heads behind the bioregionalist Planet Drum Foundation, which emerged in San Francisco in 1973 and exists to this day.

The other author of the above passage was Raymond Dasmann, a professional conservationist and, at the time, chief ecologist at the International Union for the Conservation of Nature (IUCN), then based in Morges, a few miles from Lausanne in Switzerland. Dasmann, who was born in San Francisco, had previously authored numerous articles and books about the unraveling of wildlife in his native California and had, in 1965, published a landmark book entitled *The Destruction of California*, in which he observed and predicted the trends of sprawling urbanization, resource deterritorialization, and massive ecological overshoot that are nowadays a hallmark of Los Angeles in particular, and of much of the rest of California as well, especially in its southern part.

The essay co-authored by Berg and Dasmann was, in fact, entitled "Reinhabiting California." It breaks with the growth obsession that, as they argue, has been driving California's development since the incorporation of Los Angeles as a US city in 1850, and offers a radically *regenerative perspective* on being an inhabitant of the California landscape:

[R]egardless of the "endless frontier" delusion and invader mentality that came to dominate in North America, removing one species or native people after another to make-a-living for the invaders, we now know that human life depends ultimately on the continuation of other life. Living-in-place provides for such continuation. [...] Once California was inhabited by people who used the land lightly and seldom did lasting harm to its life-sustaining capacity. Most of them have gone. But if the life-destructive path of technological society is to be diverted into life-sustaining directions, the land must be reinhabited. *Reinhabitation* means learning to live-in-place in an area that has been disrupted and injured through past exploitation. It involves becoming native to a place through becoming aware of the particular ecological relationships that operate within and around it. It means undertaking activities and evolving social behavior that will enrich the life of that place, restore its life-supporting systems, and establish an ecologically and socially sustainable pattern of existence within it. Simply stated it involves becoming fully alive in and with a place. It involves applying for membership in a biotic community and ceasing to be its exploiter. (81-82)

Direct aim is taken, here, at the myth of the United States as a community with a "manifest" destiny rooted in a shared drive by rugged individualists to push back the Frontier and possess as well as exploit ever-expanding tracts of land for agriculture and industry. What supposedly makes America a mythic capitalist, market-driven community of anonymous participants in the greatest wealth accumulation project in history was portrayed by the bioregionalists as the very thing that destroys genuine biotic community: the sharing of space, resources, and time with many human generations and many nonhuman species. What hard-nosed scientific ecologists such as Dasmann brought to the table is the incontrovertible fact of ecological interdependence, showing that any "manifest destiny" can only make sense if the humans who pursue it protect and regenerate, or even venerate, the life-support systems that make any community possible.

The connection between such hard-nosed ecological science and the Native American ethic of reinhabitation, the "Old Ways," was explicitly made by Gary Snyder in a talk given in 1993 at the University of California at Davis. In this talk, entitled "The Rediscovery of Turtle Island," Snyder begins by reaching for the insights of ecology:

We human beings of the developed societies have once more been expelled from a garden – the formal garden of Euro-American humanism and its assumptions of human superiority, priority, uniqueness, and dominance. We have been thrown back into that other garden with all the other animals and fungi and insects, where we can no longer be sure we are so privileged. [...]

> Ecological science investigates the interconnection of organisms and their constant transactions with energy and matter. Human societies come into being along with the rest of nature. There is no name yet for a humanistic scholarship that embraces the nonhuman. I suggest (in a spirit of pagan play) we call it "panhumanism." (236-37)

Thomas Berry, in his essay "Bioregionalism: The Context for Reinhabiting the Earth," similarly embraces ecology as a framework for creating regenerative communities in which nonhuman beings are viewed as full members:

> A bioregion is an identifiable geographical area of interacting life systems that is relatively self-sustaining in the ever-renewing processes of nature. The full diversity of life functions is carried out, not as individuals or as species, or even as organic beings, but as a community that includes the physical as well as the organic components of the region. Such a bioregion is a self-propagating, self-educating, self-governing, self-healing, and self-fulfilling community. Each of the component life systems must integrate its own functioning within this community to survive in any effective manner. (166)

The panhumanistic foundations of a new sense of American community are to be found, Snyder argued later, in the Native American view of the renewal of North America – a view both forward-looking and rooted in a past when the continent was called "Turtle Island." Recalling a conversation in 1969 with a representative of the Navajo nation, Snyder ties directly into the connection between bioregional reinhabitation and the regeneration of community:

> It was instantly illuminating to hear this continent renamed "Turtle Island". [. . .] I was reminded that the indigenous people have a long history of subtle and effective ways of working with their home grounds. [. . .] The landscape was intimately known, and the very idea of community and kinship embraced and included the huge population of wild beings. Much of the truth of Native American history and culture has been obscured by the self-serving histories that were written on behalf of the conquerors, the present dominant society. (242)

As we will see in the next section, it is precisely because the intention of bioregionalists was to root community within the limits and synergies of nature that their approach was organically opposed to territorial expansionism and economic growth.

4. Questioning Borders, Re-mapping the Life-world, Limiting Expansion and Growth

The cultural/ecological critique of America's empty and aggressive "national community" rhetoric was accompanied by a radical questioning of political borders. In two papers published with IUCN in 1972 and 1973, Dasmann "discussed the need for a combined ecological and biogeographical approach to the classification of natural regions of the world" and suggested a "scheme based on the concept of biotic provinces" ("Defining and Classifying" 1). This meant essentially discarding political and administrative borders when it came to conserving species integral to biotic communities that spread across these borders. Considering it was the middle of the Cold War, Dasmann was undoubtedly provocative from a political viewpoint when he asserted, on biogeographical grounds, that "[b]oth North America and Eurasia share the same biomes" and that "[t]he similarities between northern North America and northern Eurasia have long been noted by biogeographers" ("Defining and Classifying" 2).

A few years later, in 1975, still at IUCN – and in not less of a politically provocative, ecologically grounded gesture – Miklos Udvardy published a now classical memorandum in which he redrew the map of the Earth according to what, drawing on Dasmann, he called "biogeographical provinces of the world" (Udvardy). Twenty-six years later, a team of conservation scientists and ecologists published an updated version of Udvardy's and Dasmann's initial effort at reconfiguring the planet's borders through ecological and biogeographical, rather than historical or political, criteria: "Ecoregions [. . .] are classified within a system familiar to all biologists – biogeographical realms and biomes. Ecoregions, representing distinct biotas (Dasmann, 1973; Dasmann, 1974; Udvardy, 1975), are nested within the biomes and realms and, together, these provide a framework for comparisons among units and the identification of representative habitats and species assemblages" (Olson et al. 933). It is these assemblages of habitats and species which, ultimately, function as *effective community generators* – as the biotic communities to which we humans need to apply for membership. Reinhabitation, so Dasmann and his successors argue, is to be defined on the basis of knowledge about "biogeographical realms and biomes" (Olson et al. 933). When it comes to the biogeographical bases of American communities, bioregionalism views geographers and biologists as the contemporary purveyors of an actualized version of the Native American's "Old Ways."

So bioregional thought was, from the onset, a politically and culturally as well as ecologically critical endeavor. David Simpson wrote as much in 2015 in his recollections of Berg, entitled "The Mechanics of Reinhabitation: Remembering Peter Berg along the Bioregional Trail":

> Behind us [environmentalists in the late 1960s], casting a long shadow, sat a history and a dominant frame of reference haunted by the archaic politically drawn boundaries upon which nation-states have been founded. There as a strong need for this established geographical and psychological perspective to give way so that the underlying shapes of the biosphere and the realities of the natural world might be felt. This task was almost feverishly political. We sought a perspective that transcended anything resembling the artificial geopolitical boundaries within which we had grown up. We saw ourselves working in the service of an emerging consciousness based in planetary reality and the terrain of our own psyches. This budding perspective pointed at how humans might reclaim an appropriate place in the natural world, something other than that of [an] industrial leech sucking on the tender flesh of the mother planet or brute creatures that, left unregulated, could not help but desecrate the last remnants of the "wilderness" heritage – while all the time reproducing without measure. (231)

This ecological, or biospheric, cosmopolitanism coexisted in bioregionalism with an acutely localist orientation. In keeping with Simpson's idea of "reclaim[ing] an appropriate place in the natural world," Doug Aberley has called bioregional mapping an act of "mapping for local empowerment," creating what he calls the "boundaries of home" (see Aberley, *Boundaries of Home*). As contemporary scholars like Mitchell Thomashow and Christopher Uhl have shown, global ecological consciousness remains largely abstract without a local anchoring in a landscape one can explore, know intimately, and become "native" to – which is precisely what bioregionalism aims for (see Thomashow; Uhl).

In his well-known book *Becoming Native to This Place*, the agricultural and localist philosopher Wes Jackson argues against the abstractions of cultural erudition and in favor of making our cultural references and our educational institutions much more inhabitation- and thus community-centered. In line with Jackson's warning, it has been of paramount importance to the bioregionalists from the very beginning to root human community neither in an abstract collective project of economic growth and prosperity, nor in an equally abstract collective project of ecological cosmopolitanism, but in a concrete collective project of regional reinhabitation. This is a politics of place that emphasizes ways in which the proverbial American tendency to esteem only the individual and the national but nothing in between can be healed, so to speak, by reintroducing two facts which that tendency has led modern Americans to ignore: the fact of a biotic community between humans and non-human species and the fact that many Native American traditions honor this biotic community deeply. In this way, bioregionalists argued, the collective can re-enter the American culture in a manner akin to the ethos suggested by the hippies (see Miller) and radically different from forms of Marxist collectivism or communism.

Bioregionalism never presented itself as economic regionalism, in the sense of a project for localities and regions to center themselves on their own growth and development at the expense of the regional biosphere and the majority of the regional human population. In other words, bioregionalism never colluded with the ideas – now becoming popular in certain circles of economists and territorial planners – of regional development through economic growth. In fact, from a bioregional viewpoint, *economic* growth is incompatible with *biological* growth and with the basic finiteness of the biosphere. Globalization is a contest between nation-states – and, within them, between regions – to attract capital from other parts of the globe and to buy and sell products in other (and potentially *most* other) parts of the globe. Put together, all these competing national and regional attempts to participate in globalization add up to more material flows than what the Earth is able to supply and metabolize, and this generates a pressure on the global biosphere as well as, disproportionately, on certain regional biospheres.

Because the sum-total of material flows is increasing over time, that pressure on the biosphere bears the name "economic growth." By design, bioregions are envisioned as relatively self-sustaining entities that seek self-nourishment and homeostasis – and therefore function, as all ecosystems do, through cycling, recycling, and regeneration – rather than expansion. Biological growth exists in ecosystems, but it is limited in time and space. According to Thomas Berry, the bioregional function of self-nourishment

> . . . requires that the members of the community sustain one another in the established patterns of the natural world for the well-being of the entire community and each of its members. Within this pattern the expansion of each species is limited by opposed lifeforms or conditions so that no lifeform or group of lifeforms should overwhelm the others. (166-67)

"Reinhabitation" essentially means recognizing these very basic insights coming from biotic homeostasis and considering the model of "Old Ways" to be re-integrated into principles of social organization. They need to be recognized – according to the bioregionalists – at a depth where they will actually re-shape political communities and their fundamental aims. And this, Berry argues, flies in the face of modernist views of nation-building in terms of competitive expansion and growth:

> The massive bureaucratic nations of the world have lost their inner vitality because they can no longer respond to the particular functioning of the various bioregions within their borders. A second difficulty within these large nations is the exploitation of some bioregions for the advantage of others. A third difficulty is the threatened devastation of the entire planet by the conflict between bureaucratic nations, with their weaponry capable of continental, and even planetary, devastation. To break these nations down into their appropriate bioregional communities could be a possible way to peace. (169)

When applied to the United States, Berry's discussion implies a bioregionalist critique of (a) the US's internal expansionism during its whole colonial past; (b) its external colonialism and imperialism, including its attempts to turn Europe and Asia into its markets, and the Middle East into its source of fossil fuels so as to remain growing economically; and (c) the overall globalized growth model the US has been promoting through international institutions and treaties. The angle of critique here is that, were the United States to recover and actualize its bioregional heritage, its citizens would discover an alternative way of community-building no longer centrally based on the problematic couple of individual and nation.

The bioregionalists of the 1960s and 1970s realized that this alternative to expansion and growth was part and parcel of American culture but had long been hidden from sight by the manner in which, for at least a century and a half, the US had built on the myth of a conquering, expansionist Frontier people.

5. California and its Bioregional Inhabitation

California was clearly a hotbed of bioregionalist sensibilities. Northern California – notably San Francisco, the whole Bay Area, as well as Santa Cruz – evidenced intense intellectual and political activity around issues of environmental conservation and countercultural critiques of capitalism. To a significant extent, the image of a resource- and wealth-guzzling Los Angeles metropolis in Southern California echoed the deeper pathologies of the Frontier – it became the epitome of destructiveness towards nature and native peoples, of shallow materialism, and of a growth-obsessed gigantism, a gigantism rooted in the myth of "perpetual growth in the land of abundance" (Mackin 19). Northern Californians sought to set themselves apart from the culture that prevailed in LA – as many still do today – by offering a seemingly mellower, more organic, and more spiritual perspective on inhabitation. Ecological as well as cultural specificities, it can be argued, made California the container of two separate regions: the North and the South. Symptomatically, a now famous collective volume from the Planet Drum Foundation, in which Berg's and Dasmann's "Reinhabiting California" essay was republished in 1978, was entitled *Reinhabiting a Separate Country: A Bioregional Anthology of Northern California*. Edited by Berg, it sported on its cover a color drawing of Northern Californian wildlife but also of the physical region as delimited by the state's main mountain ranges, making Northern California appear like a watershed-defined biotic community in its own right. This self-fashioning is brought to the fore in the volume's introduction:

> There are countries that can't be found in a World Atlas although they can be seen at a glance out the window, countries whose soft borders remain invisible to governments even though travelers easily sense crossing them. They are the natural countries founded on specific soils and land forms, exposed to a particular climate and weather, and populated by native plants and animals which have endured since the last Ice Age. Each is a separate living part of the unified planetary biosphere; tissues and organs in the current manifestation of Earth's anatomy. They exist as a live geography more distinct than the nations and states whose borders shift to arbitrarily include or divide them. One separate natural country is at the western edge of North America bounded by the Pacific Ocean, Tehachapi Mountains, Sierra Nevada, and Klamath-Siskiyou Mountains to the Chetco River. It lies almost wholly within California reaching into Oregon only as far as the Chetco. [. . .] Whether it's called "Northern California" by everyone living here isn't important (and another name isn't the most critical issue), but recognizing its wholeness as a living entity is imperative. Only a bare survivor of the place before statehood remains now, a sketchy outline of the rich portrayal given in early accounts, and it can no longer withstand the extractive demands put on its life in the past. The country needs people who share its life to begin acting in its behalf; their behalf. The heaviest demands are likely to come from outside, and people need a form of agreement or culture-of-place to withstand them. ("Introduction" i)

The North-South division, which makes for two rather large separate "communities" in the form of separate "countries," can be and has been refined in many ways. Gary Snyder addressed the California Studies

Center at Sacramento State College in 1992 in a talk entitled "Coming into the Watershed" where he offers a striking description of the ambiguities of administrative borders that override bioregional ones. From a bioregional standpoint, Snyder argued, California should not be viewed as one or two, but rather six different regions:

> I am not arguing that we should instantly redraw the boundaries of the social construction called California, although that could happen some far day. But we are becoming aware of certain long-range realities, and this thinking leads towards the next step in the evolution of human citizenship on the North American continent. [. . .] With the exception of most Native Americans and a few non-natives who have given their hearts to the place, the land we all live on is simply taken for granted – and proper relation to it is not considered a part of "citizenship." But after two centuries of national history, people are beginning to wake up and notice that the United States is located on a landscape with a severe, spectacular, spacy, wildly demanding, and ecstatic narrative to be learned. Its natural communities are each unique, and each of us, whether we like it or not – in the city or countryside – lives in one of them. (222-24)

This fascinating collision of citizenship and the natural community is, in Snyder's case, more than merely ideological. It bases itself, as we saw earlier, on a penetrating recognition and cultivation of ecological consciousness – making American bioregionalism and its idea of the human membership in a biotic community an eminently important stream of thought and practice[3] through which to (re)connect community with ecological impact and biogeographical cohesiveness.

6. Redefining Community on the Basis of a One-planet Ecological Footprint

Bioregionalism is not eco-fascism, although some critics have suggested as much in the wake of Ernest Callenbach's controversial 1975 novel, *Ecotopia*. This novel portrays the Pacific Northwest – of which the region that Berg calls "Northern California" is a part – seceding from the United States and establishing an ecologically radical republic strongly suggestive of a network of regenerative ecovillages. The novel suggests

---

[3] This essay has, admittedly, not been focused on practices. The cited survey articles by Parsons and by Aberley, as well as Kirkpatrick Sale's *Dwellers in the Land* and Robert Thayer's *LifePlace*, can provide the reader with ample information about groups that practice bioregionalism and campaign for it at the everyday, political level.

that bioregionalism is fundamentally reconstructive, and more resolutely utopian – or, rather, *eutopian* (in search of "good places") – than dystopian. It uses biogeographical awareness and cartographical representation in order to *provide an imaginary map of the life-world humans share with other species and the elements:* "imaginary" in the strong sense of a territory based on images and desires that generate a creative impulse. Bioregionalism, in this sense, is an exercise in the reimagination of community on the basis of territory. It is territorial community-making. It gives territory and its reinhabitation a central place in re-mapping boundaries of belonging. Thus it is *an imaginary re-writing of territory as a performative gesture of ecologically informed identity renewal.*

Bioregions do not exist officially or administratively, they do not confer legal rights or duties, but they might elicit deep loyalty and an "underground" attachment that through its imaginative potency surpasses the force of legal and administrative bonds. The prefix *bio-* in bioregionalism refers to the biotic coherence of a region – to a region delineated by the invisible boundaries born of what systems theorists call its "operational closure": the myriad ways in which ecosystems bond to generate a perpetual, permanent, and specific flow of life-support. Bioregionalism is part of an existential biogeography. The bioregion is therefore a "domain of rule" (*regio* stemming from Latin *regere*, to rule) where the "rules of the domain" – the etymological roots of the word *economy* – are dictated by the "*bios.*" As such, bioregionalism may well be North America's most significant contribution to a movement of thought and practice that seeks to redefine community on the basis of a one-planet ecological footprint. This refers to the idea that any collective needs to organize according to the following criterion (cf. Merkel; Thorpe): If everyone else lived in the same fashion, the overall ecological footprint of humanity would be one single planet. In a sense, this notion of "one-planet living" connects bioregional practices with a concern for the whole planet, hence with the fate of humanity as a whole. But it does so through a hypothetical, not a categorical, imperative: Each biotic community – and, within it, each household and possibly each individual – needs to find ways to adopt a *universalizable* way of life, that is to say, a way of life which, if universally adopted, would lead to a one-planet footprint.

References

Aberley, Doug. *Boundaries of Home: Mapping for Local Empowerment*. San Francisco: New Catalyst, 1998.

———. "Reinterpreting Bioregionalism: A Story from Many Voices." *Bioregionalism*. Ed. Michael Vincent McGinnis. New York: Routledge, 1999. 13-42.

Alexander, Christopher. *A Pattern Language: Towns, Buildings, Construction*. New York: Oxford University Press, 1977.

———, Sarah Ishikawa, and Murray Silverstein. *The Timeless Way of Building*. New York: Oxford University Press, 1979.

Baptist, Edward E. *The Half Has Never Been Told: Slavery and the Making of American Capitalism*. New York: Basic Books, 2016.

Beckert, Sven and Seth Rockman, eds. *Slavery's Capitalism: A New History of American Economic Development*. Philadelphia: University of Pennsylvania Press, 2016.

Berg, Peter. "Introduction." *Reinhabiting a Separate Country: A Bioregional Anthology of Northern California*. Ed. Peter Berg. San Francisco: Planet Drum Foundation, 1978. i.

——— and Raymond Dasmann. [1977]. "Reinhabiting California." *Envisioning Sustainability*. Ed. Peter Berg. San Francisco: Subculture Books, 2009. 81-88.

Bernard, Ted and Jora Young. "What We Have in Common is the Salmon: The Mattotle Watershed, California." *The Ecology of Hope: Communities Collaborate for Sustainability*. Ed. Ted Bernard and Jora Young. Gabriola Island: New Society Publishers, 1997. 128-47.

Berry, Thomas. "Bioregionalism: The Context for Reinhabiting the Earth." In Thomas Berry, *The Dream of the Earth*. San Francisco: Sierra Club Books, 1998. 163-70.

Boal, Iain, Janferie Stone, Michael Watts and Cal Winslow, eds. *West of Eden: Communes and Utopia in Northern California*. Oakland: PM Press, 2012.

Bosk, Beth. *New Settler Interviews: Vol. 1 – Boogie at the Brink*. White River Junction: Chelsea Green, 2000.

Callenbach, Ernest. *Ecotopia: The Notebooks and Reports of William Weston*. Berkeley: Banyan Tree Books, 1975.

Campbell, Brian. "Growing an Oak: An Ethnography of Ozark Bioregionalism." *Environmental Anthropology Engaging Ecotopia: Bioregionalism, Permaculture, and Ecovillages*. Ed. Joshua Lockyer and James Veteto. New York: Berghahn, 2013. 58-75.

Dasmann, Raymond. *The Destruction of California*. New York: Macmillan, 1965.

———. "A System for Defining and Classifying Natural Regions for Purposes of Conservation." *Morges: IUCN Occasional Paper* 7 (1973).

———. "Biotic Provinces of the World: Further Development of a System for Defining and Classifying Natural Regions for Purposes of Conservation." *Morges: IUCN Occasional Paper* 9 (1974).

Didion, Joan. [1967]. "Slouching Towards Bethlehem." In Joan Didion, *Slouching Towards Bethlehem: Essays*. New York: Farrar, Straus and Giroux, 1968. 84-128.

Estill, Lyle. *Small Is Possible: Life in a Local Economy*. Gabriola Island: New Society Publishers, 2008.

Hayden, Tom. *The Port Huron Statement: The Visionary Call of the 1960s Revolution*. New York: PublicAffairs, 2005.

Hayek, Friedrich August von. *Law, Legislation and Liberty*. 3 volumes. Chicago: Chicago University Press, 1973-1979.

Jackson, Wes. *Becoming Native to This Place*. Lexington: University of Kentucky Press, 1994.

Junger, Sebastian. *Tribe: On Homecoming and Belonging*. New York: Twelve, 2016.

Krech, Shepard. *The Ecological Indian: Myth and History*. New York: Norton, 1999.

Lopez, Barry. *The Rediscovery of North America*. Lexington: University of Kentucky Press, 1990.

Mackin, Anne. *Americans and Their Land: The House Built on Abundance*. Ann Arbor: University of Michigan Press, 2016.

Merkel, Jim. *Radical Simplicity: Small Footprints on a Finite Earth*. Gabriola Island: New Society Publishers, 2003.

Miller, Timothy. *The Hippies and American Values*. Second ed. Knoxville: University of Tennessee Press, 2011.

Nixon, Rob. *Slow Violence and the Environmentalism of the Poor*. Cambridge: Harvard University Press, 2013.

Olson, David, Eric Dinerstein, Eric Wikramanayake, Neil Burgess, George Powell, Emma Underwood, Jennifer D'amico, Illanga Itoua, Holly Strand, John Morrison, Colby Loucks, Thomas Allnutt, Taylor Ricketts, Yumiko Kura, John Lamoreux, Wesley Wettengel, Prashant Hedao, and Kenneth Kassem. "Terrestrial Ecoregions of the World: A New Map of Life on Earth." *BioScience*. Vol. 51 (2001): 933-38.

Page, Jake and Susanne Page. *Hopi*. New York: Abrams, 1982.

Parsons, James. "On 'Bioregionalism' and 'Watershed Consciousness'." *The Professional Geographer* 37 (1985): 1-6.

Reséndez, Andrés. *The Other Slavery: The Uncovered Story of Indian Enslavement in America*. New York: Houghton Mifflin, 2016.

Sale, Kirkpatrick. *Dwellers in the Land: The Bioregional Vision*. Second ed. Athens: University of Georgia Press, 2000.

Shuman, Michael. *Going Local: Creating Self-Reliant Communities in a Global Age*. New York: Routledge, 1998.

Simpson, David. "The Mechanics of Reinhabitation: Remembering Peter Berg along the Bioregional Trail." *The Biosphere and the Bioregion: Essential Writings of Peter Berg*. Ed. Cheryll Glotfelty and Eve Quesnel. New York: Routledge, 2015. 228-47.

Smith, Sherry. *Hippies, Indians, and the Fight for Red Power*. New York: Oxford University Press, 2012.

Snyder, Gary. [1976]. "Reinhabitation." *Earth First!*, 23 September 1987. 28.

———. "The Rediscovery of Turtle Island." In Gary Snyder, *A Place in Space: Ethics, Aesthetics, and Watersheds*. New York: Counterpoint, 1995. 236-51.

———. *The Old Ways*. San Francisco: City Lights Publishers, 1977.

———. "Coming into the Watershed." *A Place in Space: Ethics, Aesthetics, and Watersheds*. Ed. Gary Snyder. Berkeley: Counterpoint Press, 1996. 219-35.

Thayer, Robert. *LifePlace: Bioregional Thought and Practice*. Berkeley: University of California Press, 2003.

Thomashow, Mitchell. *Bringing the Biosphere Home: Learning to Perceive Global Environmental Change*. Cambridge: The MIT Press, 2003.

Thorpe, David. *The "One Planet" Life: A Blueprint for Low-Impact Development*. New York: Routledge, 2015.

Udvardy, Miklos. "A Classification of the Biogeographical Provinces of the World". *Morges: IUCN Occasional Paper* 18 (1975).

Uhl, Christopher. *Developing Ecological Consciousness: The End of Separation*. Second ed. Lanham: Rowman and Littlefield, 2013.

Wicks, Judy. *Good Morning, Beautiful Business: The Unexpected Journey of an Activist Entrepreneur and Local Economy Pioneer*. White River Junction: Chelsea Green, 2013.

The Common Community Made Uncommon in Brian Sousa's *Almost Gone*

Roxane Hughes

This essay complicates the notion of commonality on which definitions of community are based, and focuses on the dissonant, disparate, and discontinuous elements at the heart of communities in settings of migration. Taking as a starting point the definition of *uncommon community* given by the American Portuguese Studies Association in the context of its 2016 conference, this essay explores the literary representation of the disconnected Portuguese American community as exemplified in Brian Sousa's *Almost Gone* (2013). This novel-in-stories approaches Portuguese migration from the multiple and conflicting viewpoints of three generations of Portuguese American immigrants. Through the narration of fragmented yet intertwined stories, Sousa portrays the personal and familial struggles faced by Portuguese immigrants in their search of self, and comments more generally on the complexity of the immigrant experience as the protagonists' individual and collective sense of alienation paradoxically separates and unites them across generations. By depicting a conflicted community in perpetual transit between time and place, as well as submerged in literal and metaphorical waters, Sousa subverts notions of unified, exclusionary, and common grounds that permeate definitions of communities and instead proposes a more nuanced representation of what makes a community in the context of migration.

A community is generally defined by its commonality, be it a shared place, language, ethnicity, religion, set of values or experience (*Merriam-Webster*). Little attention has, however, been granted to the internal space of the disparate and uncommon in theoretical approaches to communities. By reflecting on the notion of *uncommon community* for its biennial conference (October 2016, Stanford University), the American Portuguese Studies Association (APSA) emphasized the necessity to discuss "the increasing emergence of communities based on intense differences" in "settings of multilingualism, immigration and transnationalism" (n. pag.). The Association urges us to consider "the disparate elements within a common collective," and focus on "the dissonance in consonance" (n. pag.). APSA thus revises notions of unified, exclusionary, and fixed grounds and looks instead at the fragmentation, heterogeneity, multiplicity, and fluidity of communal places and identities to offer "alternative forms of togetherness" across differences and ruptures (Liska 8).

How is the uncommon community, as defined by APSA,[1] constructed and represented in literary terms? What are the techniques used by writers to revise definitions of communities based on commonalities and address contemporary problems of being together across differences? I propose to discuss this theoretical concept through the example of Brian Sousa's "novel-in-stories" *Almost Gone*.[2] The genre of novel-in-stories mirrors the uncommon community it depicts as the fragmented whole simultaneously sets apart and unites the independent stories told, while amplifying the *uncommon* grounds, temporality, and viewpoints that divide *and* join protagonists. Indeed, *Almost Gone* presents the Portuguese diasporic community of Narragansett, Rhode Island, from the multifarious viewpoints of protagonists whose relation varies in time and space but connects Portugal and the American continent, then and now. Sousa complicates commonality as he focuses on this diasporic community's inherent oppositions, continuous relocation, and fragmentation. The temporal, spatial, and generational shift from one story to the next accentuates the theme of migration that permeates the novel-in-stories, as the protagonists individually relocate – or wish to relocate

---

[1] This essay does not refer to the religious connotation of the term "uncommon community" that has been used more extensively in Christian studies to represent the diversity of the Christian community united across differences. Joey Letourneau, for instance in *The Power of Uncommon Unity*, draws attention to the uncommon community of apostles discussed in the Bible (Acts 4) that "came together in an uncommon unity that Jesus Himself had prayed for, and that the Spirit was willing to lead them and empower them from. They *came together diversely, but with one voice*. They were shaken from their old ways, and supernaturally bound together within something – or someone – new" (13-14; my emphasis). In the context of this essay, I complicate the notions of unity and oneness to draw attention instead to the plurality of dissonant voices at the heart of uncommon communities.

[2] Many thanks to Brian Sousa who commented on an early version of this paper and gave me invaluable insight into his work.

– to new grounds to escape the loss of loved ones and/or their irredeemable past errors (infidelity, forbidden love, murder). Yet relocation, or self-exile, does not bring them relief but rather magnifies their traumatic memories. These multifarious shifts thus capture the protagonists' conflicting positions within the community: While their inability to escape their haunting past isolates them from one another, it is their experience of individual alienation that paradoxically unites them across differences. Indeed, what binds them together throughout *Almost Gone* is not their cultural identification as Portuguese in a diasporic context, but their shared relocation and sense of fragmented identity, estrangement, and un-belonging.

The uncommon community of Sousa's *Almost Gone* is further embodied by the water imagery that dominates the novel and complements the discontinuous temporality and geography in subverting notions of fixed and unified grounds. Bodies of water in diasporic contexts are ambivalent spaces that refuse fixity and categorization and thus aptly portray the fluidity of the diasporic subject, caught between movement – physical and imagined – and a contrasting sense of paralysis. Literally and metaphorically set in the middle of the ocean, Sousa's Portuguese American protagonists, submerged – if not drowned – by countercurrents, *meander* between here and there, now and then, in their perpetual endeavors to reconstruct their self-identity and come to terms with their old secrets and lies. The multifaceted ocean thus epitomizes the variegated mental states and inner conflicts of the characters grappling with their sense of guilt and contrasting longing for redemption and relief. By using water images to complement the temporal and geographical conflicts permeating *Almost Gone*, Sousa thus offers a nuanced depiction of what makes a community in the context of migration, as he paints an image of a drifting community whose disconnection and dissonance better illustrate the lasting effect of trauma on the forging of individual and collective identities across borders.

Sousa's genre of novel-in-stories is akin to what Forrest L. Ingram called the "short story cycle" in the 1970s. This genre presents the collection of independent and interconnected stories that combine the brevity, intensity, lyricism, and fragmentation of the short story, with the narrative wholeness, continuity, and unity of the novel (Patea 9-10). In other words, it is a hybrid and "disruptive" genre (Lundén 20) that refuses fixity, as the debate regarding its definition and precise denomination, started fifty years ago, attests.³ Its destabilizing nature lies in its juxtaposition of "variety and unity, separateness and interconnectedness, fragmentation and continuity, openness and closure," and in the tension such juxtapositions create, as Rolf Lundén explains (12). Oppositions between singularity and plurality, as well as individuality and collectivity, can also be noted through the genre's "double tendency of asserting the individuality of its components on the one hand, and of highlighting, on the other, the bonds of unity which make the many into a single whole," as Ingram observes (19). This genre is therefore particularly suited to explore the relationship of the individual to the community, as its interconnected yet independent stories situate the individual within and against the community to which s/he belongs (Davis 8). Its hybridity and multiplicity of forms, as well as its destabilizing nature, thus offer myriads of possibilities for Sousa to explore the private and collective conflicts and tensions at the heart of the Portuguese diasporic community depicted in *Almost Gone*.

Almost Gone is divided into fifteen stories that can be read independently but remain connected when read together; a separation and connection that highlights, on the one hand, the protagonists' attempt at self-assertion, and, on the other, the ineluctable presence of the community. When read individually, the short story depicts an intense and dramatic fragment, or a "slice or snapshot of reality," in Viorica Patea's words (11), that becomes representative of the protagonist's larger world (Pasco 420). The fragmented and elliptical nature, as well as the intensity and dramatic potential of the short story, are emphasized in *Almost Gone*, as a majority of stories are internally fragmented (11 out of 15), with the storyline often interrupted by flashbacks and/or juxtapositions of episodes. Offering a collage of fragmented and discontinuous narratives, the stories of *Almost Gone* refuse linear progression, and epitomize the internal fragmentation and conflicts of the protagonists, whose self-fulfillment is often thwarted by their inescapable trauma and resulting sense of estrangement from and un-belonging to the community.

The fragmentation of *Almost Gone* into independent stories is contrasted with the simultaneous interconnectedness and inseparability of the stories that mirror the protagonists' connection across differences.

---

[3] This genre has been renamed over the years as "short story sequence" by Robert Luscher in 1989, "composite novel" by Maggie Dunn and Ann R. Morris in 1995, and as "short story composite" by Rolf Lundén in 1999, just to mention a few. It is now more neutrally called "linked stories." For a detailed analysis of the debate surrounding this terminology, see Lundén 12-19.

The novel-in-stories follows a Portuguese American family spanning over four generations: Nuno and Helena, a married couple who left Portugal in 1941; their American-born son Paulo and his wife Claire; their grandson, Scott and his wife Hailey, and Emily, their deceased great-granddaughter. The stories of this extended Portuguese American family are complemented by the stories of Catarina, a thirty-year-old first-generation Portuguese immigrant; and Mateo, Helena's haunting lover who suffered a tragic death in Portugal at Nuno's hands before their migration to the United States. Catarina's and Nuno's stories give sense to the transnational struggles of the community, as they link Portugal and the United States, past and present. Moreover, as the eight protagonists' lives are interconnected, so are the stories they tell. Similar anecdotes and memories are told in a "kaleidoscope collage of different perspectives," as Sousa declares (qtd. in Ledoux n. pag.), the kaleidoscope figuratively epitomizing the variegated and constantly changing narrative standpoints juxtaposed in the novel-in-stories. By telling the same stories from a variety of perspectives, Sousa amplifies the Portuguese diasporic community's internal divergence and isolation, while simultaneously emphasizing the protagonists' inevitable interconnection with the rest of the community.

The tension between individuality and community, commonality and difference enacted by Sousa's novel-in-stories is furthered by the juxtaposition of first-person and third-person narrations, as well as external and internal points of view. Ten out of fifteen stories are told from an omniscient third-person narrative voice, which approaches the individual stories of the first and second generations of Portuguese immigrants represented in *Almost Gone*. This omniscient narrator resonates, so to speak, with the communal voice of the community, which, from an external position, looks into the individual lives of its members. Yet, this external point of view is also confused. These third-person narratives are dominated by internal monologues presented in free indirect discourse that destabilize the binaries of objective and subjective, external and internal, past and present. Indeed, although the ten stories are told in the past tense, the internal monologues give a sense of present-ness to these past stories, magnifying the older generations' nostalgia, as well as their continuing – if not timeless – feelings of alienation and entrapment. This tension between past and present dominating *Almost Gone* reveals how first and second generations are haunted by memories of a past long gone that affects them individually and collectively in the present.

The third-person narratives are accompanied by five stories told by a first-person narrative voice: Scott's introductory, internal, and concluding stories, Hailey's email, and Mateo's brief story written in letter form. While Hailey's and Mateo's first-person narratives are related to the epistolary genre in which the stories are written, Scott's first-person voice frames and dominates the novel-in-stories. His stories – along with Hailey's email – are the most recent, as they stretch from 2009 to 2010.[4] Juxtaposed to his forbearers' third-person narratives, Scott's first-person voice dramatizes his conflicting journey to self-assertion, and more generally, the third generation of Portuguese immigrants' search for self-definition and fulfillment outside of the community's collectivity.

With its structural juxtaposition of different narrative forms and perspectives, Sousa's novel-in-stories is particularly befitted to represent issues related to migration, notably the alienating effect of displacement on the formation of individual and communal identities across borders and generations (Nagel 225).[5] Its subversive and destabilizing form, which isolates and unites, dramatizes the individual fight against a common collective. Seen in this light, the tensions at the core of this genre can also represent, when left unresolved, the collection's possible "failure to form and define a community," in Rocío Davis's words (9), and to bring together the "things pulling apart" (9). This failure of unification is at the core of Sousa's *Almost Gone* as the independent, yet interconnected, stories and viewpoints magnify protagonists' individual trauma, often to the detriment of the communal whole.

However, despite the generational gap inferred by the contrasting first and third person narratives, as well as past and present narrations, the stories remain focused on the characters' individual grief, as they are all haunted by a darker past that impinges on their self-development in the present. In this respect, the juxtaposition of these narrative techniques has a double and more ambivalent function. While it widens the

---

[4] Conversely, Mateo's letter written in 1941 is set in the furthest past, which stresses its lasting effect in the present of the characters involved (Helena and Nuno).

[5] As Nagel highlights, the short story cycle attracted migrant writers throughout the twentieth century to explore issues related to "immigration, acculturation, language acquisition, assimilation, identity formation, and the complexities of formulating a sense of self that incorporates the old world and the new, the central traditions of the country of origin integrated into, or in conflict with, the values of the country of choice" (15). Dealing with immigration, displacement, alienation, and identity conflicts, *Almost Gone* finds space in a larger field of diasporic writings in the United States, which expands the notion of uncommon community beyond the Portuguese American community on which this novel-in-stories is centered.

discrepancy between the individual and the community, it also breaches the intergenerational gap separating the protagonists, thus drawing attention to the formation of an uncommon community whose members are united by their communal sense of individual trauma and longing for the past.

It is precisely in this feeling of longing and grief, or in other words, in this shared sense of *saudade*, that the diasporic community's Portuguese identity is the strongest. *Saudade* – a Portuguese term that refuses translation – can be described as a mixed feeling of "longing, grief, sadness, pain and enduring love," an "aching absence" inherent to the "Portuguese soul," as Robert Henry Moser and Antonio Luciano de Andrade Tosta state (4-5). This mixture of sorrow and nostalgic longing permeates Portuguese American literature dealing with the immigrant experience as it captures the difficult condition of the immigrant deeply affected by lasting feelings of love for the people, culture, and land left behind. The haunting, yet absent, presence of the loved ones in *Almost Gone*, while contributing to building a Portuguese cultural identity across borders, equally holds the protagonists back or in a state akin to paralysis as they seem unable to let go of the past and move forward. This ineluctable traumatic past gives a darker twist to the notion of *saudade*: Longing dissipates under grief, anguish, and heartache for all protagonists alike as they are unable to redeem themselves from their past actions.

The protagonists' separation and connection across generations, as well as their mutual entrapment in a distressing past, are equally emphasized by the uncommon temporality governing *Almost Gone*. The stories move back and forth between 1941 and 2010. While the first six stories take place in the 2000s (1: 2010; 2: 2008; 3: 2000; 4: 2000; 5: 2000 and 6: 2010), the following nine stories alternate between 2010 and a variety of dates between 1941 and 1976 (7: 1945; 8: 2008; 9: 1965; 10: 2010; 11: 1976; 12: 1941, 13: 2000; 14: 1941 and 15: 2009). Although *Almost Gone* does not offer a decreasing chronology, it nevertheless moves further back in time in its second half, as it explores more deeply each character's dark secrets and past experience at the roots of their individual alienation.

The novel-in-stories' discontinuous temporality is complicated by the reverse chronology governing each character's storyline. While Scott's story starts on the beach of Fortaleza in 2010, his last story concludes with his daughter's death that occurred in Rhode Island in 2009. A similar chronological decrease takes place in Catarina's narratives. While her first two stories are set in 2008 – the first story taking place a few months after the second one – her last story goes back to 2000 when she migrated to the United States. More time elapses in the case of Paulo's storyline that moves from 2000 to 1976 and retrospectively explores traumatic moments of his childhood. This return to the past culminates with Nuno's stories that move from 2000 to 1975 to 1941, the year he killed Mateo and migrated to the United States, which forges the temporal gap separating him from the younger generations. Similarly, the reverse chronology overseeing each character's storyline locates the various protagonists' lives in different and distant temporalities. However, while this reverse chronology sets them apart, it also highlights their shared sense of alienation across difference and rupture. Indeed, the future seems "perpetually unreachable" for all protagonists alike, as Ethel Rohan states (n. pag.).

The *uncommon grounds* that protagonists inhabit between Portugal and the United States echo the discontinuous temporalities of their lives. The characters' reverse chronology that fixes them in the past – however fluctuating it may be – is contrasted with their continuous physical and mental relocation between geographies linking the United States (Narragansett, Rhode Island), Brazil (Fortaleza), Portugal (Lagos, and Sintra) and Spain (Granada). In so doing, *Almost Gone* draws attention to the Portuguese diasporic community's transnational bonds and inability to settle in one unique place, thus destabilizing the notions of common land or territory that often dominate definitions of community. Moreover, although resonating strongly with the theme of migration permeating the novel-in-stories, the protagonists' constant movement also points to their pervading sense of un-belonging that spurs them to move physically and imaginatively in time and space in the hope of finding a better – yet ultimately unreachable – future outside of communal bonds. The concentricity of the stories, however, brings the characters back to Narragansett where they live or once lived, and to Portugal through numerous flashbacks – two sites of longing and trauma for the respective generations. The protagonists' physical relocation is thus opposed by their reverse migration – not physical but imagined – that continuously brings them back to their point of departure or origins.

For first-generation immigrants, Portugal is associated with traumatic memories of loss and death that appear enmeshed with other cherished recollections of a past long gone. This intertwining of haunting trauma and *saudade* prevents them from moving forward with their lives. References to Portugal are mostly made through Nuno's and Helena's previous lives in Lagos, a maritime city carefully selected by Sousa. Located in the region of Algarve and facing the Atlantic Ocean, Lagos considerably developed during the fifteenth century with Portuguese maritime discoveries and conquests. Because of its strategic location, Lagos became an important harbor and trading post in this era of maritime expansion and developing trade routes (see Coutingo). The protagonists' migration to the United States – although taking place between the mid-twentieth and early twenty-first centuries – is subtly inserted in this larger legacy of maritime discovery. Yet, Sousa gives a negative twist to this heroic history of Portuguese migration. The protagonists' dream of *terra prometida* – here associated with the United States – is demystified. Haunted by their past and discovering an often-disabling America, Portuguese immigrants are unable to find self-realization in the United States, thus deconstructing the American Dream of the first generation. Helena's love affair with Mateo in Lagos, whom Nuno involuntarily killed, haunts Nuno beyond Helena's death. Helena's memories of Mateo similarly hold her back and negatively impact her relationship with her husband. Her attempt to assimilate into American culture and prove worthy of Nuno's attention – as narrated in her story "The Dog" – is juxtaposed to her memories of Lagos, interwoven with her reminiscence of the pleasure found in Mateo's arms – a sexual *jouissance* contrasted to her sexual paralysis with Nuno.

Catarina also returns to the traumatic time of migration and relocation that permeates her stories, from her mother's sudden migration to the United States when she was a child, to her own immigration to Rhode Island upon her father's death, as well as to her escape from the United States in search of an *elsewhere*. Her desired elsewhere resembles a middle ground between Portugal and the United States: "There was nothing in Portugal for her anymore, and now, nothing left in the United States. But inbetween? Inbetween perhaps there was everything" ("Teach Me" 21).[6] The juxtaposition of nothing and everything depicts this inbetweenness as a place of possibility and self-fulfillment. Her search for an elsewhere throughout the novel-in-stories, exemplified by her constant movement, in body and thoughts, dramatizes her sense of un-belonging now and then, here and there. Yet, in contrast to Nuno and Helena who clearly never made it back home, Catarina *almost* returns – yet not quite – as she considers settling in Portugal's nearest neighbor, Spain. By presenting Portugal as a site of nostalgia, but especially as a place of trauma and suffering that the first generation seeks to

---

[6] For the sake of specificity and clarity, the parenthetical citations list the titles of Sousa's individual stories throughout this essay. In contrast, the bibliography does not provide an individual entry for each story, but only refers to the whole novel-in-stories.

escape, Sousa once again deploys *and* complicates the Portuguese notion of *saudade* and sheds light on immigrants' difficulty to forget and move forward.

As the first generation of immigrants escaped Portugal in the hope of finding a better future in the United States, American-born Portuguese immigrants turn to Brazil to escape the pressures of the family and community. Brazil interestingly emerges as an alternative to the United States and Portugal – a middle ground in second-generation Paulo's story "Almost Gone": "Brazil had been his favorite; he found it easy to get around, meet interesting people, sleep with women. He'd never made it to Portugal, he wanted to go, and he got the sense that his father had wished he had" (59). Paulo describes Brazil as a place where he could taste a little bit of Portuguese culture and language without returning to his ancestors' land. Read in this context, it is not arbitrary that Scott, Paulo's son, also chooses to flee to Brazil upon his daughter's death. His father's photograph of Brazil, which he finds when going through his daughter's belongings, depicts it as a promised land with "green water, thatched roofs on the beach, stretches of golden sand dotted with brown bodies" ("Jerusalem" 123). The ocean he imagines in Brazil *a priori* contrasts with the submerging and engulfing water that took his daughter's life – and his with hers, at least metaphorically so.

Yet, as with his elders, Scott's relocation fails to relieve his trauma. Scott's framing stories, told in the present, are juxtaposed to detailed accounts of fragments of his life in Brazil to dramatic flashbacks of his daughter's death that he relives in his dreams, and his alcohol-induced loss of consciousness that relentlessly carry him back to Rhode Island. Moreover, Scott's attempt to escape his community ironically brings him closer to his family as he confronts a similar alienating experience of relocation. *Almost Gone* opens with Scott's emphatic sense of physical, cultural, and linguistic alienation in Brazil. Read in contrast to Helena's discomfort with the English language that Nuno forces her to speak to *fit in*, Scott's discomfort with Portuguese underlines the pressures of assimilation on the Portuguese community in diaspora and the loss of ancestral language and culture across generations. Scott's whiteness and blond hair also demarcate him from the Brazilian population and grants him the title of "gringo" (1). To this interpellation is added the chaotic Rio de Janeiro, which he feels "assault[s]" him with its "maniac honking and squealing tires" (2) that make him "jumpy" and "skittish" (2). Scott finds refuge in the Northeastern city of Fortaleza – a symbolic fortress or stronghold, which, far from providing him with comfort, figuratively connotes his entrapment. Scott's life thus mirrors the lives of his forbearers, whose haunting past erases any sense of future healing. Scott ultimately and ironically connects with his ancestors through his shared sense of alienation from the community.

The ocean that permeates *Almost Gone* also complicates the notion of firm or fixed ground at the heart of definitions of community and identity, and contributes to depicting the Portuguese American community of Narragansett as being adrift between different temporalities and geographies. The Atlantic Ocean that geographically links *and* separates Portugal and Rhode Island acts as a symbolic frame to the stories told. The novel-in-stories is paratextually enclosed by water: The same black-and-white photograph of water introduces and concludes the novel-in-stories (internal title page and last page of the book).

Literally set in the middle of the ocean, the stories are not only contextualized within a larger maritime history of migration, but also engulfed, if not submerged, in this body of water. Oceans are sites of multiple contradictions and tensions formed by tumultuous crosscurrents (Fajardo 39). They are spaces of migratory flows and diaspora connecting here and there, now and then. Indeed, oceans refuse temporal fixity. They are sites of history, and memory;[7] sites where identities *meander* between conflicting spaces and temporalities (Baucom 17). The fluidity of the ocean seems to appeal to Sousa as it not only simultaneously divides and joins the various grounds occupied by the Portuguese diaspora, but also contributes to the blurring of past and present temporalities that keep the protagonists caught in a state of trauma. Indeed, by literally setting the stories in the middle of the ocean, Sousa questions a notion of firm place or ground for the Portuguese community that does not seem to be at home in any of the locations they come to inhabit. He thus points to the *meandering* of the protagonists' identities, which fluctuate between past and present, individuality and collectivity, as well as between various localities.

The drowning stories that open and conclude *Almost Gone* complement the paratextual submersion enacted by the oceanic photographs framing the novel-in-stories by subverting notions of fixed grounds, and by locating the Portuguese diasporic community in the middle of the ocean. This also accentuates the fragmentation of the protagonists, who appear to metaphorically drown in their traumatic past. The opening story "Fortaleza" juxtaposes Scott's memory of his daughter's drowning

---

[7] See, for instance, Paul Gilroy's, Gabeba Baderoon's and Omise'eke Natasha Tinsley's writings on the Middle Passage; as well as James Clifford's, Kale Bantigue Fajardo's and Clare Anderson's works on colonialism, imperialism and transit.

– which he reconstructs episodically in his three stories "Fortaleza," "Jerusalem" and "Where to?" – to his own drowning experience in Brazilian waters. While Scott felt a "strange dizziness" and was "breathing harder than usual" when he started swimming, his heart now "pound[s]," his skin "itches and crawls," his "head spins" ("Fortaleza" 5), as he grapples with the rough and strong undercurrent encountered – an undercurrent that metaphorically symbolizes his sinking under the weight of memory. Indeed, it is the thought of his deceased daughter Emily and his family left behind that accentuates his palpitations and prevents him from swimming. His feeling of dizziness is accelerated when a little boy, whose young age reminds him of Emily and makes her absence even more difficult to bear, swims next to him:

> But *my legs* scramble, and *my feet* flail and touch nothing but emptiness. *My hands* open and close, *my arms* spin frantic circles, and suddenly I feel cool water rushing into *my lungs* as I choke and cough, slapping *my hands* against the water as the boy did. I can't breathe this air, but for some reason pulling *my head* up is too difficult. I want to press it further and further down into the cold, to sink down and rest. ("Fortaleza" 6; my emphasis)

The fragmentation of Scott's body renders the drowning scene more vivid as it draws attention to the slow decline of his fighting spirit. His battle is replaced with a desire to "sink down and rest" at the bottom of the ocean, to metaphorically end both the trauma caused by the loss of his daughter, and his own sense of guilt for her death.

Scott's drowning continues as the scene proceeds, when Emily appears as a literal and metaphorical weight on his shoulders pushing him down:

> I close my eyes and choke and see you, Emily, climbing onto my shoulders so I can run around the house with you again and again. Hailey's laughing from the kitchen, yelling "Be careful, be careful!" I feel my heart chugging slowly, but Emily, your feet are pressing me down and I'm sinking into the blackness again – should I let myself go? ("Fortaleza" 7)

His previous assertive desire "to sink down and rest" (6) is replaced by an apostrophe to his daughter – "should I let myself go?" (7) – putting his fate in his daughter's hands as he is neither able to absolve himself from the guilt of her death, nor to move on. His daughter thus becomes the cause of his drowning, as she metaphorically pulls him toward her.

Unable to distinguish the boy from his imagined daughter, Scott mistakes the boy's struggle to drag him back to shore with his daughter's pushing. Scott's state of internal bewilderment is mirrored at the narrative level as reality and illusion blur, leading to a confused description of his fight for air:

> My eyes sting in the salt and the sun, I feel his hands pressing down – but why down? Why pressing down? – on my chest *and* then my shoulders, *and* my eyes flash open as I flail my arms *and* kick, *and* with my last bit of strength I grip his skull as I go under, gasping, choking, and then pull him under me, my fingers clutching at his open mouth, Emily's hand pushing too, her face flashing above me, my knees digging into his back, one of his arms pressing my throat, then air filling my lungs. ("Fortaleza" 7; my emphasis)

The repetition of the conjunction "and" at the beginning of this long sentence not only re-connects his body (chest, shoulder, eyes, arms) to make it whole again, but also emphasizes his regaining control over the action as he makes himself the subject: *He* feels, flails, kicks, grips, and goes under. The repetition of this conjunction is, however, replaced half way through this long sentence by an asyndeton that juxtaposes gerund clauses separated *and* linked together by commas. The asyndeton, in addition to representing his gasping for air, emphasizes the confusion of the scene, as Scott fights against the boy and his imagined daughter, who are conflated in their pushing. The narrator, the boy and Emily are reduced to fragmented body parts, as their limbs intermingle, pushing up and down, thus contrasting with the narrator's temporary feeling of wholeness expressed at the beginning of the sentence. This juxtaposition of wholeness and fragmentation echoes Scott's conflicting state as he grapples with his daughter's death and his own sense of guilt. The chiasmic structure of the juxtaposition of Scott's fighting and Emily's appearance – "*my fingers* clutching at his open mouth, *Emily's hand* pushing too, *her face* flashing above me, *my knees* digging into his back" (my emphasis) – interweaves father and daughter, while accentuating Emily's immateriality, as she is represented as framed, if not contained, by her father. In contrast, the boy, whose presence concludes this chiasmic fragment, appears as disentangling from father and daughter, ultimately saving Scott from drowning and figuratively sinking into madness. This opening drowning scene gives a dark and sad tone to the novel-in-stories and comes to epitomize figuratively the struggle of protagonists internally fragmented between the here and there, the now and then.

Scott's literal drowning in "Fortaleza" is followed by his symbolic drowning in alcohol in his hope of evading reality and forgetting Emily – a metaphorical drowning experienced by many characters throughout the novel-in-stories.[8] Yet, Scott's endeavor to forget her is futile; alcohol gives Emily flesh. Whereas the first drink makes her "whole" (9), the second helps Scott relax and distance himself from his own life and self as he contemplates the "Before and After" of his life (9) – an after that, interestingly, starts when Emily is diagnosed with leukemia. The third drink, although giving him a fleeting sense of relief from his family's judgment, accentuates his confusion, blurring his vision of the past, and mixing "Portuguese and English" voices in his head (9) – voices that metonymically represent his family fading into the background. The fourth drink plunges him deeper into daydreams as he hopes to rewind his life to the moment preceding Emily's death. This rewinding is actually a new beginning – a beginning without Hailey, his parents, and grandparents; a beginning for him and his daughter exclusively (10). Far from evading Scott's mind, Emily reappears with more strength and passion, eluding the soothing escape Scott sought in alcohol.

The literal and figurative drowning of Scott narrated in "Fortaleza" is contrasted with Scott's lighter description of his daughter's drowning at Jerusalem beach reported in the last story "Where to?". In this brief story, Scott recounts how he took his daughter out of the hospital, at her request, and brought her to her favorite beach. Despite the sadness of the episode narrated, the story concludes on a happier note, as Scott remembers Emily feeling better, entering into the water and happily dancing one last time (177). The ocean is not depicted as menacing or engulfing in Scott's recollection; the tide is low and the waves "whispering" (177). Scott's fear of seeing his daughter disappear in the water is counterpoised with her "slipping under the waves with ease" (178) before being taken away by another "curling sheet of water" (178). The light, although literally "dying," continues to "shimmer" (178) at the surface, as the waves lastingly carry Emily's voice in an echo.

The story – and the entire novel-in-stories – concludes on an open note, as the narration takes a new direction and moves to a more recent

---

[8] Hailey talks about her drinking problem in her story "Smile": "I know I started drinking more. (OK, I know it became a problem and I'm saying right now, I'M SORRY, but Dr. Rich says that it's a drinking mechanism [sic] that a lot of people use. I don't drink like that anymore [. . .].)" (76). Nuno also heavily drinks throughout his stories – using alcohol to forget his wife's affair with Mateo and his involuntary killing of the latter, as well as to cope with his own affair in Narragansett with one of his friends' wives. See "Just One Night" (89).

time between 2009 and 2010, a time of departure, hope, and new beginning for Scott, as he leaves for Brazil, taking his daughter with him: "When I decided to leave, I knew that you'd come with me, Emily. Tonight, I can feel you in the empty seat next to me as the plane trembles and then takes off against the cold winter wind" ("Where to?" 178). Emily – gone, but not quite – continues to live in Scott's mind and memory as she travels with him to distant shores. Together, they head toward an elsewhere where their bonds and complicity can survive unaltered. This elsewhere is equated with the ocean that "surges and beckons" them (179), when Scott remembers merrily spinning around with Emily on his shoulders. Called by the ocean, Scott ultimately and symbolically comes to inhabit this fluid oceanic space of memory that subverts fixed geographies and temporalities.

The open-endedness of the story, echoing the question formulated in its title "Where to?" while also hinting at the possibility of a new beginning for Scott and his daughter, brings the reader back to the beginning of the novel-in-stories, where similar images are deployed in the opening story "Fortaleza": "You never leave my mind, Emily. I can hear you exhale with every step I take. You're always up on my shoulders, where you loved to sit, your hands buried in my hair, your swinging weight pressing down on me" (2). The circularity of the novel-in-stories – if we consider the decreasing chronology of each protagonist's story – dramatizes the stasis of the characters as time worsens their condition and entraps them in their illusions. Scott does not appear pressed down by his daughter's weight in the last story, but inspired by his daughter's ghostly presence, as he chooses dreams over reality, escape over responsibility. Conversely, a year later in Fortaleza his daughter's ghostly presence has not receded but increased, and is slowly pushing him down. Moreover, the elsewhere he was hoping to find in Brazil remains illusory, as his trauma evades time and relocation, but appears magnified "in light of a new land" in Sousa's words.[9] Likewise, by concluding with a drowning scene, the last story literally engulfs the novel-in-stories, thus precluding any sense of escape or figurative re-surfacing. The stories once again plunge the protagonists into the middle of the ocean – in this dark and profound fluctuating space between – a place of history and memory that ultimately refuses fixity. Yet the happier imagery and tone concluding the last story gives a sense of relief, even if temporary, from the traumatic repetitions of the cycle, thus ending the novel-in-stories on a lighter note and leaving the reader with a sense of hope.

---

[9] Personal conversation dating to 4 January 2017.

This drowning frame finds resonance throughout *Almost Gone* in the figurative representations of the protagonists' trauma. Hailey and Scott's attempts to cope with their daughter's death in "Jerusalem" are punctuated by threatening water images, as they return together to the beach where their daughter drowned – in a symbolic, if not spiritual, journey toward acceptance and forgiveness. "Well, Dr. Rich *did* say that this trip might inspire some deep thought," Hailey says in the opening of the story (123). However, "Jerusalem" does not portray Scott's and Hailey's *deep thinking* but their individual retreats into the past, despite their common endeavor to cope with their daughter's death. Drowning images that isolate and join them in their experience of alienation depict their metaphorical sinking into trauma. Hailey seems engulfed, in Scott's eyes, by the waves surrounding the jetty on which she is walking: "the further she goes, the deeper the water is, the bigger the waves are that crash on either side," observes Scott (128). Her slow movement is soon counterpoised with her paralysis as she stops: "Hailey is on one knee, paralyzed. [. . .] The waves pound at the rocks all around her. If she stumbles and hits her head, slides into the water that's brown and heavy with seaweed and yellow foam, she could drown. She could drown" (129). Scott's distance from Hailey amplifies the threatening aspect of the ocean that seems to be waiting to take her away. The lingering thought of her drowning – like their daughter – scares him and spurs him to react, to "sprint" and "move quickly" (129) toward her to save her. This constitutes a first step toward resolution. Yet, his running *toward* her is followed by his running *away* from her as she violently accuses him of having killed their daughter: "You took her away, Scott! *My daughter!*" (130). Blind to their daughter's sickness and to her daughter's last wish that Scott fulfilled by bringing her to her favorite beach, Hailey does not find peace in the physical and spiritual journey she imposes on Scott, but enlarges the gap that separates them. Scott's resulting desire for escape culminates at the end of the story as he leaves Hailey on the jetty. The juxtaposition of his running toward and away from her speaks of the limbo he inhabits, caught between his traumatic past and hope for a better future.

The story concludes with yet another drowning simile infused with a touch of hope, however, as Hailey proceeds toward Scott: "Hailey begins to *try* to run toward me, *digging in* and *fighting* the currents of wind, but she barely moves. It is as if she is drowning. Or *learning* to swim" (130; my emphasis). Her previous paralysis is opposed to her movement and physical fight against the wind that figuratively symbolize her attempt to bridge the gap between them. Her movements are barely visible – the drowning imagery still dominating and hindering her metaphorical progress toward him. However, her drowning is counterpoised by her learning to swim, which brings hope of a new beginning. The fragment "or learning to swim," which is grammatically isolated from the drowning statement, while offering a touch of hope, also stresses its incompleteness. The juxtaposition of the contrasting "drowning" and "swimming" – with their gerund form expressing an action in progress – ultimately reinforces the liminal position that both Scott and Hailey occupy, stuck between the traumatic memory of a past "gone wrong," to use Rohan's terms (n. pag.) and their desire – although *almost* impossible – to move on. This last juxtaposition also echoes Scott's paradoxical running toward and away discussed above. Their symbolic return to Jerusalem, a place rife with symbolic and religious connotation in the context of diaspora studies, thus fails to give them a sense of wholeness. It ironically contributes to their *dispersion* and separation as any return to a life in unison is impeded by their personal guilt and inability to communicate. The ocean once again underlines their movement *and* paralysis, as well as connection *and* separation. Their inevitable separation is accentuated as the story unfolds, as they literally sink under the weight of their individual yet mutual trauma. Caught in this fluid space between, they are left to drift alone between their inescapable past and an unreachable future together.

The ocean similarly submerges Nuno in "Just One Night" as he grapples with the haunting memory of his wife's affair with Mateo, and his equally traumatic desire – yet inability – to tell Helena he knew about her love for Mateo. Nuno's memories of Lagos – awakened by "the salt in the air" he inhales (83) – culminates as he joins his wife in bed and feels submerged by a choking feeling: "Nuno wanted, suddenly, to hold onto her [Helena] as tightly as he could to stop the feeling that was washing over him, as if he was adrift in those waves again, being tossed by the current" (84). The oceanic simile concluding the sentence complements the water lexicon preceding it ("washing away") to emphasize Nuno's inability to forget the traumatic episode that submerges him time and again. Panic takes possession of his body – "his heart [is] drumm[ing] under the covers" (84), spurring him to pull the covers down, in an effort to resurface from the metaphorical water that surrounds him. The passage concludes with Nuno rolling onto his back, as Helena wakes up, and with a description of his upper lip that is said to be "wet" (84). In addition to nodding to the water imagery used to describe his panic attack, the focus on his wet upper lip also foregrounds his trauma, as this unidentified moisture calls attention to his strong bodily response; his sweat, tears, or excess of saliva.[10]

For Helena, the smell of the ocean in Narragansett reminds her of home, thus bringing her temporary comfort from her alienating experience of displacement and forced assimilation in the United States. In her mad confrontation with the dog, which she desperately wants to capture to save Nuno's garden, Helena quiets down as she hears "the rise and fall of the ocean and the faint scream of the gulls outside" ("The Dog" 111); a familiar sound that temporarily transports her home. Yet despite the temporary escape and sense of home it might provide, the ocean looks once again menacing, as its breeze takes "somewhere else" the smell of the food she has smeared all over the garden to attract the dog, thus threatening to ruin her master plans that would bring her closer to Nuno (117). Magnifying her trauma, the ocean figuratively accompanies her sinking into madness and links her to the other characters, whose lasting memory of a traumatic past engulfs them time and again and leaves them adrift between different grounds and temporalities.

Accordingly, *Almost Gone* presents a divergent, heterogeneous, fragmented, geographically disconnected, and drifting community. Through the narration of fragmented yet intertwined stories that refuse common grounds, Sousa portrays the personal and familial struggles faced by Portuguese immigrants and their descendants in their search of self. Sousa approaches the conflicting present of a community that appears in endless diaspora – as a sense of home and self-fulfillment continues to evade them. The discontinuous temporality of the stories that often carries us backward instead of forward, as well as the circularity of the whole novel-in-stories, dramatizes the characters' continuing relocation, or self-exile, in search of an elsewhere and a better future. Yet, the characters' movement in time and space intensifies their stasis and inertia, as they are unable to come to terms with their old secrets and the loss of loved ones. It is this shared sense of un-belonging and estrangement, as well as their movement and paralysis – amplified and embodied by wa-

---

[10] In contrast to his father, Paulo finds a sense of comfort in the ocean. Paulo associates the ocean with a temporary fantasy in "Almost Gone" that provides him with relief from the constraints of his marriage. At a moment when his wife tries to arouse him, Paulo's body shuts down, and his mind wanders to other shores as he fantasizes about his father's neighbor Catarina: "Paulo slowed his breathing and stayed perfectly still, waiting for her to stop, and on the beach next to him lay Catarina, her black skin glistening with saltwater" (59). The beach he imagines figures as a temporary elsewhere or refuge that also recalls the Brazil that Paulo once saw, with its green water, long beaches, and brown bodies lying in the sun immortalized in the photograph that Scott is to find years later ("Jerusalem" 123).

ter imagery – that connects them across difference. The notion of uncommon community, therefore, offers a better look at the conflicting and polyvalent relations of the individual to the community and revises the concepts of unity, common grounds, and fixed cultural identities that continue to permeate definitions of communities, while providing a more complex perspective on migration.

References

Anderson, Clare. "Subaltern Lives: History, Identity and Memory in the Indian Ocean World." *History Compass* 11.7 (2013): 503-7.

Baderoon, Gabeba. "The African Oceans – Tracing the Sea as Memory of Slavery in South African Literature and Culture." *Research in African Literatures* 40.4 (2009): 89-107.

Baucom, Ian. "Charting the 'Black Atlantic'." *Postmodern Culture* 8.1 (1997): n. pag.

Clifford, James. *Routes: Travel and Translation in the Late Twentieth Century*. Cambridge: Harvard University Press, 1997.

"Community." *Merriam-Webster*, 2017. www.merriam-webster.com/dictionary/community. Accessed 18 April 2017.

Coutingo, Valdemar. *Lagos e o Mar Através dos Tempos*. Lagos: Câmara Municipal de Lagos, 2008.

Davis, Rocío. "Identity in Community in Ethnic Short Story Cycles: Amy Tan's *The Joy Luck Club*, Louise Erdrich's *Love Medicine*, Gloria Naylor's *The Women of Brewster Place*." *Ethnicity and the American Short Story*. Ed. Julie Brown. New York: Garland, 1997. 3-24.

Dunn, Maggie and Ann R. Morris. *The Composite Novel: The Short Story Cycle in Transition*. New York: Twayne Publishers, 1995.

Fajardo, Kale Bantigue. *Filipino Cross Currents: Oceanographies of Seafaring and Masculinities in the Global Economy*. Minneapolis: University of Minnesota Press, 2011.

Gilroy, Paul. *The Black Atlantic: Modernity and Double Consciousness*. Cambridge: Harvard University Press, 1993.

Ingram, Forrest L. *Representative Short Story Cycles of the Twentieth Century*. The Hague: Mouton, 1971.

Ledoux, Abigail. "Portuguese-American Culture Examined in Book." *Emerson College Today*. 29 January 2013. www.emerson.edu/news-events/emerson-college-today/portuguese-american-culture-examined-book#.WL_fDRRqlhM. Accessed 16 December 2016.

Letourneau, Joey. *The Power of Uncommon Unity: Becoming the Answer to Jesus' Prayer*. Shippensburg: Destiny Image, 2013.

Liska, Vivian. *When Kafka Says We: Uncommon Communities in German-Jewish Literature*. Bloomington: Indiana University Press, 2009.

Lundén, Rolf. *The United Stories of America: Studies in the Short Story Composite*. Amsterdam and Atlanta: Rodopi, 1999.

Luscher, Robert. "The Short Story Sequence: An Open Book." *Short Story Theory at a Crossroads*. Ed. Susan Lohafer and Jo Ellyn Clarey. Baton Rouge: Louisiana State University Press, 1989. 148-67.

Moser, Robert Henry and Antonio Luciano de Andrade Tosta, eds. *Luso-American Literature: Writings by Portuguese-Speaking Authors in North America*. New Brunswick: Rutgers University Press, 2011.

Nagel, James. *The Contemporary American Short-Story Cycle: The Ethnic Resonance of Genre*. Baton Rouge: Louisiana State University Press, 2001.

Pasco, Allan H. "On Defining Short Stories." *New Literary History* 22.2 (1991): 407-22.

Patea, Viorica. "The Short Story: An Overview of the History and Evolution of the Genre." *The Short Story Theories: A Twenty-First Century Perspective*. Ed. Viorica Patea. Amsterdam and New York: Rodopi, 2012.

Rohan, Ethel. "Book Reviews: *Almost Gone*." *Necessary Fiction*. 15 April 2013. necessaryfiction.com/reviews/AlmostGonebyBrianSousa. Accessed 12 December 2016.

Sousa, Brian. *Almost Gone*. Dartmouth: Tagus Press, 2013.

Tinsley, Omise'eke Natasha. "Black Atlantic, Queer Atlantic: Queer Imaginings of the Middle Passage." *GLQ* 14.2-3 (2008): 191-215.

"Uncommon Communities." *The American Portuguese Studies Association (APSA)*, 2016. apsa.us/uncommon-communities. Accessed 12 December 2016.

Contemporary Anglo-American Drama of Exile[1]

Philipp Reisner

The motif of exile as a symbol for the human condition in contemporary Anglo-American literature has taken on special significance in recent American plays. Playwrights use dialogue to emphasize folly rather than the absurd, by showcasing the characters' failure to be at home in their communities. Intense parallel conversations and the polyphony of voices in rapid succession reveal the general condition of exile to be an exile from language: Following the theater of the absurd, playwrights have now returned to the deep psychology of language exchanges. With verbal misunderstandings and misconceptions, they show characters having lost their home in language and their communities. The characters' desire for community and communion and their sense of being lost in the world become tangible in their interaction on stage. This suggests that drama, too, reflects the sacralization characteristic of contemporary Anglo-American literature. This trend is evident especially in the increasing, but subtle presence of religious symbolism, often misconstrued as the "postsecular." Exile in drama refers to the first exile from the Garden of Eden. Investigating how a new sense of home emerges from these interactions can contribute to our understanding of contemporary definitions of community.

Recent scholarship on contemporary Anglo-American drama has examined the concepts of sexuality, violence, dialogue, audience participation,

---

[1] This essay is based on a lecture given at the University of Bern, 5 November 2016. The author would like to thank the organizers and the Swiss Association for North American Studies for the invitation to the conference and the opportunity to publish this article. He would also like to thank Ebtehal Elrashidy and Aaron Shoichet for their valuable comments on the first draft.

American Communities: Between the Popular and the Political. SPELL: Swiss Papers in English Language and Literature 35. Ed. Lukas Etter and Julia Straub. Tübingen: Narr, 2017. 187-203.

ethnicity, character and subjectivity, media culture, the role of animals, and metatheater (cf. Malkin; Klaver; Delgado-García). It has been suggested that "postmodern synthetic realism" (Sauer 1) is an apt description of dramatic realizations of the polystylistic (or "synthetic") drive of contemporary art more generally. However, these general rubrics rarely capture what unifies contemporary plays and gives them structure, aside from pointing to their experimental and innovative textual strategies. If we are justified in grouping these plays together in one category, then it is necessary to identify a more fundamental unifying theme. I believe it can be shown that the motif of exile may constitute just such a unifying theme. Anglo-American plays of the past decade from a variety of backgrounds deal with the question of human existence as exile from diverse perspectives.

While the relation between contemporary drama and exile has not gone unnoticed (cf. Meerzon), the complex theological implications of exile in contemporary Anglo-American drama have still not been examined in great detail. Exile is central to the plays by David Adjmi, Marcus Gardley, and Young Jean Lee that were published together in an anthology documenting "a variety of cultural perspectives on America" in contemporary drama of the early twenty-first century (Benson vii). While dealing with the theme of historical exiles on the surface, these authors probe on a deeper level especially the theological implications of exile. These plays may be seen as instances of performative theology, which come to replace, subvert, and question simpler understandings in drama of the experimental, political, or absurd. At the same time, their works engage with the Bible on several levels, revealing the influence of sacralization on contemporary dramatic writing. This suggests that current accounts of sacralization in twentieth-century (Zalambani 251) and contemporary culture (Ostwalt, Jr.) will have to be refined and corrected. Conrad Ostwalt Jr. in particular has depicted sacralization as a kind of late modern counter-movement to the anti-church tendencies of the Enlightenment (24-29). Yet we are compelled to ask whether the impetus of sacralization is more profoundly related to originating impulses of the Enlightenment itself and to be grasped in its institutional and not merely economic context, as both Zalambani and Leypoldt have pointed out (cf. Leypoldt; Holifield; Stievermann, Goff, and Junker). This would entail calling into question claims of the post-secular that frame the current discourse on contemporary drama (Megson). The three playwrights chosen for the present analysis – Adjmi, Gardley, and Lee – demonstrate that theology and mythology, more so than hyphenated or hybrid cultural identities, are the defining factors of contemporary Anglo-American dramatic writing. It is thus important to go beyond the theorizing impulse motivating questions of identity, which are often understood in ethnic, generational, and particularizing terms. By contrast, a theological perspective reveals that religious allegiances and motifs are more fundamental than narrow conceptions of identity politics and aesthetics, and that they lead to a substratum of contemporary art in which these very different dramatic approaches share a concern and interest in communities of religious, particularly biblical, engagement. These three examples show that the political relevance of theater is connected to questions concerning the convergence of historical and theological exile that transcend the genre. A similar concern with biblical text, of the Old Testament in particular, can be observed in much of contemporary Anglo-American literature, especially in short prose and poetry. The dramatists whose work is examined here share an interest in basic questions on the theological underpinnings of contemporary society. Seen in this light, contemporary drama demands much more than particular interpretations of identity – it requires that we explore the phenomenon of exile across genres in its diverse literary and historical contexts. Such an undertaking will aim to uncover the unifying strand of contemporary artistic interpretations of the communal. The present analysis may serve merely as a beginning of a broader critical engagement with the tendency in drama criticism and research, especially prevalent since the 1980s, of interpreting the communal in ethnic rather than religious terms (cf. Bruck). Peter Bruck has exemplarily shown in reference to the work of African American playwright Ed Bullins how contemporary drama persistently avoids and pits itself against the idea of community theater. Engaging with exile from a "universal" perspective – if there is such a thing – will allow us to reevaluate the function of religious motifs in contemporary drama. Research must raise these questions, for these motifs serve not merely as rhetorical embellishment, but instead quite possibly lead to the central ideas of these plays.

Theologizing Contemporary Drama of Exile

In this context, and in light of the plays in the focus of the present analysis, the relation between community and exile needs to be considered theologically: In Genesis, the first steps towards community raise the question of the first occurrence of plurality. In Genesis 1:1, God or the divine, potentially plural itself because of "Elohim" (Hebrew), is juxtaposed with the plurality of "the Heavens" and the singularity of the

Earth: "In the beginning God [Elohim] created the heavens and the earth."[2] This frequently mistranslated passage, for which the singular "heaven" is given in the King James Version and some recent Bible translations, may be read to show a "divine surplus," namely the plurality of the heavens, as created in the first creative act in Genesis by a Godhead that is potentially plural within itself. It does not create a binary opposition, but instead "heavens" and a singular "earth," as a primary plurality upon which all other creation as well as the Trinity is based. In the following verses, man is created in a plural world with a plurality of heavens, waters (Genesis 1:2), days, nights (the fourth day, Genesis 1:16), plants (the third day, Genesis 1:11), and animals (the fifth day, Genesis 1:20). From the perspective of Genesis as the origin of theological thought on exile, the question of plurality and divine simplicity may be seen as the most complex task for Trinitarian theology, which establishes the spiritual relationality of man and which serves as the basis for the creation of a plurality of men and women, and hence of community, in the subsequent biblical narrative (Genesis 1:27 and 2:18). The Fall as the first exile (Postell 120) is necessary because of the original plurality of men and women in both creation stories in Genesis; the woman is the cause of the Fall and also opposes the serpent after the expulsion from Eden: "And I will put enmity between you and the woman, and between your seed and her seed; it shall bruise your head, and you shall bruise his heel" (Genesis 3:15). This double dialectic can be seen as the gendering of exile explored in the plays by Adjmi, Gardley, and Lee. The confusion of tongues (Genesis 11) creates the loss of language that the characters must come to terms with, whereas the Babylonian exile depicted in the Books of Isaiah, Jeremiah, and Daniel takes up questions of community and belonging by adding an eschatological dimension. While acknowledging the relation between community and Trinitarian theology and especially placing its eschatological aspects in the foreground, contemporary (Lutheran) dogmatics, too, neglects the dimension of exile (cf. Hinlicky). Like other genres of contemporary Anglo-American literature, drama enters into dialogue with theology, drawing attention to theology's weakness in recognizing societal conflicts. Theological motifs are relevant not merely from the point of view of Liberation Theology. Tracing their role in contemporary literature and especially drama may deepen our understanding of diverse

---

[2] This passage is from *The Holy Bible* (2014; 29). Aside from this passage, *The Holy Bible* (1978) will be used throughout.

communities currently in exile, including North American cultures in their founding context (cf. Nanko-Fernández 41).

These contemporary Anglo-American plays engage the religious dimensions of the term "community." From a Christian perspective, which is foundational for many of the theological aspects of these plays, community is the place where individual exile is overcome. It is to be understood eschatologically as defined in Hebrews 10:24-25, a letter which relates to the topic of exile: "And let us consider one another to provoke unto love and to good works: Not forsaking the assembling of ourselves together, as the manner of some is; but exhorting one another: and so much the more, as you see the day approaching" (cf. Barker, Lane, and Michaels 312). This passage reveals the eschatological bent of contemporary Trinitarianism and contemporary drama, and may be seen as a template against which David Adjmi explores the concept of "sin" in his play *Stunning*.

Probing the Depths of Sin: David Adjmi's *Stunning* (2008)

David Adjmis's play *Stunning* is set in the Syrian-Jewish neighborhood of Midwood, Brooklyn, and written in a deeply satirical tone that is critical of both personal and societal attitudes and deficiencies. It opens with three girls sitting at a card table discussing the life of their absent friend, the fourth girl whom they had expected to join them:

Shelly	She's / finished
Claudine	She committed / suicide
Lily	(Oolie!)[3] /
Claudine	RUINED!
[STOP]	
(*Crunching a carrot stick.*) I like the dip What's in this /	
Lily	Chives.
Claudine (*bright*)	Heeee: I *like* chives. /
Lily	Should we / play?
Claudine (*quick*)	(Did you see Debbie's haih? She cut / it).
(Benson 10)[4]	

---

[3] According to the "Glossary of Syrian-American Terms," the term "oolie" is an "exclamation of shock, worry, horror, discovery – spoken with correlative intonations (reverential worry: 'ooooolllllliiieeeee?,' 'OO!LIE!,' '*OOLIE!*' etc.)" (Adjmi, "Glossary" 8).

[4] Because of minor changes, the play is quoted from the later version in Benson 1-132 throughout the present essay; like the other quoted passages, this one appears with typographical changes in Adjmi, *Stunning* 15-16.

This passage showcases the sarcasm with which Adjmi caricatures the community of exiled Syrian Sephardic Jews to which he belongs. It is evident early on that the general condition of exile refers to an exile from language, reinforced by the parallel conversations and rapid exchanges of numerous voices. Through a series of verbal misunderstandings and misconceptions, the play depicts how characters lose their home in language and their communities. The exaggerated tempo of the everyday language in the dialogues does not forego violent expressiveness. In their interaction on stage, the characters' desire for community and communion and their sense of being lost in the world are made tangible.

This suggests that drama, too, is part of the trend towards sacralization that characterizes contemporary Anglo-American literature. Exile in drama refers to the exile of Adam and Eve from the Garden of Eden. This occurs in the context of a turn towards Old Testament texts, with special emphasis on the Book of Genesis and the Book of Psalms. Discreet references link the plays' renewed emphasis on Old Testament material to New Testament texts, especially the First Letter to the Corinthians. Investigating how a new sense of home emerges from these interactions, which at the same time is constantly in danger of disintegrating, can contribute to our understanding of contemporary redefinitions of community.

In *Stunning*, Adjmi refers to the story of Lot's wife to discuss accusations of alleged sexual "insecurity" or "instability". The protagonist Lily, a sixteen-year-old Syrian Jewish wife of an older man, employs an African American woman as her maid, ironically named Blanche and seemingly over-qualified, who is gay:

Lily (*blunt textbook sanctimony*)	LESBIANS IS WRONG /
Blanche	(And they taught you grammar / too Nice)
Lily	And I know about Sodom and Gomorrah!
Blanche	What do you know?
Lily	They were *Sodomites*!
Blanche	And:
Lily	And they had *sodomy ca-an*?[5] And God said to Lot's wife not to look back and she looked back.

---

[5] According to the "Glossary of Syrian-American Terms," the word "ca-an" is spoken "when challenging the veracity of something. Has a vaguely sarcastic connotation, as in, 'Yeah, right!' Sometimes serves as phatic punctuation" (Adjmi "Glossary" 8). Adjmi's meticulous attention to language inflects theatrical naturalism, adding to the polystylistic texture of the play.

Beat.		
Blanche	Would you look back?	
Lily	God said no.	
Pause.		
Blanche (*internal; faraway*)		I would. (Benson 53-54)

Exile here becomes the attempted exile of homophobic exclusion. It has been claimed that in many ways Lot's wife remains the quintessential representation of the dangers of nostalgia in exile (Hartman 30). Between the female protagonist and the antagonist, a drama of exile unfolds that leads ultimately to Blanche committing suicide out of despair at the prospect of being sent away from her new job with Lily into yet another exile. This new exile is in part a consequence of her criminal history as an attempted murderer, of her potentially abusive father, which is unveiled as the play unfolds (Benson 76, 118).

Acutely and in personified fashion, Adjmi raises the question whether and to what extent exile, as a characterization of the human condition, is ultimately bearable. He carefully links this issue to contemporary society by satirizing a New York Syrian-Jewish community and engaging the Israeli-Palestinian conflict (Benson 31). While his treatment of these topics emphasizes the universality of his dramatic scenes, he goes beyond the societal to raise the deeper question concerning the concept of exile as a characterization of human existence in general. His play is a satirical tragedy that embraces the complexity of contemporary existence from multiple points of view, subtly engaging questions of race, gender, and politics. These different strands are theologically united, leading to a sobering diagnosis of the modern human condition: That people lack charity, they perpetually expulse and exclude themselves and each other.

This becomes even more apparent in Adjmi's play *The Evildoers* (2008), in which he deals explicitly with what he calls Christian fundamentalism (Adjmi, *Stunning* 147). Two Jewish-American couples discover in conversation their personal insecurity and the instability of their relationships. Carol Thernstrom, a wedding counselor, is so cynical and destructive in her claims about marriage, relationships, and human existence in general, that the play's climax is the revenge of Martin Goldstrom, the husband of the other couple: He cuts out Thernstrom's tongue. This punishment is a reference to Psalm 12:3 and Proverbs 10:31 and intricately linked to Babylonian exile expressed in Psalm

137:5.6.[6] The right hand is the one on which Carol presumably wears her ring, which becomes a symbol of her cynical attitude that Martin finds so objectionable. This extreme punishment for verbal "sin" is linked to the origin of the Babylonian confusion of tongues: People no longer understand each other and are exiled in a language of constant misunderstanding. Adjmi's plays realize a theology of exile that transcends satire and tragedy and that thereby eludes Larry D. Bouchard's critical assessment of contemporary theater studies, namely, that the relationship between tragedy and "sin" has been neglected. Adjmi re-establishes the original unity of the tragic and the satirical (Bouchard 10-11) and takes up the complicated relationship between "sin" and exile, which was present in the Jewish tradition (Karlip 256). Of the three playwrights analyzed in this paper, Adjmi's works have received the least academic and, ironically, greatest public attention. This suggests that the public perception of contemporary theater may be useful to theater research by revealing common thematic strands like the topic of exile.

Mythopoetic Syncretisms: Marcus Gardley's *The Road Weeps, the Well Runs Dry* (2013)

Marcus Gardley's play *The Road Weeps, the Well Runs Dry* deals at first sight with the topic of exodus rather than exile from the perspective of the African American tradition. It deals with the migration of the Seminoles, that is, black and Native American people, from Florida to Oklahoma in the mid-nineteenth century, where they established the first all-black town in Wewoka. The epic struggle between the full-blood and half-black Seminoles recalls Old Testament tribal struggles and questions of tribal adherence and belonging. Exile, when seen as the central myth in contemporary drama, highlights the importance of the Bible for contemporary playwrights and opposes the unjustified, but still pervasive, bias of American literary history towards exodus as an explanatory model for early New English settlement. Gardley's mythodrama intervenes in this misperception by engaging questions of identity in a complexity similar to Adjmi's. Like Adjmi from a Jewish perspective, Gardley makes reference to the Old Testament, for example, in the prologue

---

[6] Psalm 12:3: "The Lord shall cut off all flattering lips, and the tongue that speaketh proud things"; Proverbs 10:21: "The mouth of the just bringeth forth wisdom: but the froward tongue shall be cut out"; Psalm 137:5.6: "If I forget thee, O Jerusalem, let my right hand forget her cunning. If I do not remember thee, let my tongue cleave to the roof of my mouth; if I prefer not Jerusalem above my chief joy."

with "Number Two," the black god, wrestling his angel, "OR BLACK BEAR EMBRACES RED COYOTE" (Benson 137). Following an American tradition, he creates a syncretism between mid-nineteenth-century American history and Old Testament mythology, attributing universal and theological significance to minorities and successfully cutting across ethnic particularism. The frequent flashbacks and shifts in time between 1850 and 1866, besides illustrating a historic consciousness in line with nineteenth-century historicism, also mimic the complex temporal structure of the Bible. They emphasize the significance of history for relationships between generations especially in the context of (family) migration. However, the titles of the two acts and their two prologues, "THE OLD TESTAMENT OR WHY THE WELL RAN DRY" (Act One) and "THE NEW TESTAMENT OR WHY THE ROAD WEEPS" (Act Two), preceded by "NUMBER TWO WRESTLES HIS ANGEL OR BLACK BEAR EMBRACES RED COYOTE" (Prologue to Act One) and "THE GOSPEL OF FATE ACCORDING TO RED COYOTE, OR THE SILENT YEARS" (Prelude to Act Two) establish a typological balance and reference to biblical Christianity that runs throughout the play, reinvigorated by a new approach to Old Testament theology (Benson 143, 183, 137, 180). Similar to Adjmi, Gardley pays close attention to language: He expresses the human condition of exile in language by juxtaposing an African American vernacular with King James Version English. By taking up the nineteenth-century fashion of speaking in King James Version English, Gardley mythologizes the mundane and adds to the multilayered complexity also present in Adjmi's plays, while exploring it from a historical and mythological perspective. Unlike Adjmi, Gardley places more emphasis on the notion of community and brings it to a clearer resolve; the characters come to understand their follies and prejudices, and the spectators witness the characters' state of alienation and exile dissolve by the end of the play. But on their way there, they have had to go through "sin," suffering, and self-reflection.

As his other plays testify, including the recent *I Am a Man* (2012), a short one-man play available in a film version online, Gardley, while rediscovering monologue – albeit in a very different way from his contemporary Young Jean Lee – intends to recover spirituality from the shocks of the mundane. Similar to *The Road Weeps, the Well Runs Dry*, in which Gardley examines human relationships over several generations, in *I Am a Man* one male actor plays vignettes of three different males and their roles in society. In both plays, Gardley reveals the cyclical dimension of individual conditions of exile, and points to the spiritual macrostructure that penetrates the microstructure of individual human experience. The topic of exile, which can be found throughout his oeuvre, may offer a much stronger heuristic perspective on his work than rather vague classification such as "post-black plays" (Elam and Jones xxx).

Exile and Community as Experiment: Young Jean Lee's *Pullman, WA* (2005)

In her play *Pullman, WA*, experimental playwright Young Jean Lee takes her hometown as the title for an exploration that combines self-help culture, escapism, religion, and insults directed towards the audience. She thus creates a transtemporal field of tension in which she explores the current manifestations of the "fallen state" of "exilic humanity". Lee stresses the immediacy of her dramatic investigation by stipulating that the characters be named after the actor or actress who is playing them, by employing long monologues that address the audience and reflect the theatrical situation and character experiences, and by making heavy use of anaphoric structure, altered with quick and snappy verbal exchanges. The play opens with Pete, named after the actor of the first performance in its original production:

> Pete   *enters.*
> Pete   I see you out there.
> I see you out there and I can see that you are all different kinds of people.
> You are all going through different kinds of things.
> Some of you may be happy. Others of you may be in hell. I don't know.
> But what I do know is that I know how to live. (Benson 223)

Having established, albeit in a conversational language, a biblical dimension at the very beginning by alluding to hell and the basic ethical question which "Pete" claims to have solved for himself, the play later develops a more decidedly biblical tone by (implicitly) addressing the passage on the shepherds and the sheep in Luke 2:8: "And there were in the same country shepherds abiding in the field, keeping watch over their flock by night." Tom declares:

> There were two shepherds, and the Lord asked them to protect and watch over his lambs in the field.
> The shepherds said, "Yes, Lord, I will obey," and tended the lambs with gentleness and care.

> But soon the shepherds grew weary of their task and began to beat and flay the lambs with their staffs. (Benson 233)

Lee's play thus sets up a counterfactual scenario of religion in exile on Earth in an age that threatens the continuity of the original faith of the shepherds in Luke. As the actors fall in and out of their intermittent religious roles, the spectators are shown how unstable and dangerous faith can be, revealed through the characters' superficial religious language. Confronted with the juxtaposition between passages in biblical language and others written in everyday language, the spectators are forced to reflect on the experimental dimension of existence and the hidden omnipresence of religious motifs in contemporary society. Lee combines these theological references by engaging dramatic monologue. Her reinvention of monologue, which serves as a main device throughout her play, illustrates the importance of redefining characters on the contemporary stage (cf. Delgado-García 48) for which monologue is instrumental, and not merely in underpinning the isolation of the individual. As Deborah R. Geis has pointed out, character development through monologue recedes, and the monologues instead jolt the audience by altering, suspending, or rupturing the narrative "progress" of a play (cf. Geis). In addition, this brief analysis suggests that monologues engage biblical forms of speech, transcending the sermon-like moment by introducing the multi-generic mode of biblical text onto the contemporary stage. Exile then becomes palpable also as an exile from genre into the terrain of the experimental; conventions are permanently put in question, and biblical precepts are subverted in contorted allusions. Exile here becomes a communal theatrical experience in which actors and audience alike are exposed to an inscrutable force-field of estranged biblical texts. They explore and experience the sublime presence of the biblical text in contemporary culture, and at the same time allude to the loss of its presence as a more profoundly and consciously shared knowledge. One might even venture to suggest that Lee's dramatic text raises, in a provocative manner, the subliminal presence and significance of biblical text to the level of consciousness.

A little later, in a passage directed to the audience, Pete and Tom *"get into 'Jesus/God' positions"* while *"Pete is Jesus and Tom is God"* (Benson 242). The unusual use of names, the reference to the second commandment and mystery plays, and allusions to Genesis, 1 Samuel and the book of Psalms form a biblical backdrop that also challenges the audience: This backdrop compels the spectators to think about the depth of their own biblical knowledge and to reflect on where and in which contexts these passages are found in the Bible and why they have been reinterpreted in this way:

Pete	Fear not, for I will walk upon the land.
Tom	I will walk upon the land, in the hills and the valley below.
Pete	I will walk upon the land and shout my name.
Tom	I will shout my name in the desert.
Pete	Over the plains and in the valley, you will hear my name echoing.
Tom	You will hear my name echoing into the hills.
Pete	You will hear my name echoing and fall down.
Tom	You will fall down groveling in the earth.
Pete	You will weep and curse my name.
Tom	You will curse my name and I will smite you down.

(Benson 242)

The anaphoric repetition of the future aspect ("will," which continues beyond this passage) testifies to the eschatological dimension of contemporary dramas of exile. In this way, Lee invites and stimulates reflection on the omnipresence and simultaneous repression of biblical texts in the contemporary consciousness, trenchantly criticizing the superficial and mundane aspects of existence in a way reminiscent of the plays by Adjmi and Gardley. Her experimental approach to writing, which transcends community by exploring the limitations of theatrical community, takes up the experimental style of plays from the latter half of the twentieth century. Yet Lee deals with the exile of contemporary communities of faith from the biblical text itself, which has become submerged by the sacralization of the everyday and the mundane. In this sense, given the profound engagement of contemporary Anglo-American literature with the Romantic era at large, her writing may – despite its experimental surface – revert to motives of Naturalism as a response to individualism and to the theological landscape of Romanticism (cf. Ybarra 513-14). Besides this subversion of theatrical realism and naturalism, with regard to Naturalism and Romanticism as epochs of literary and artistic expression, her work is representative of the turn away from the Old Testament bias of Romanticism and towards the New Testament bias of Naturalism and early Modernism. Not withstanding the somewhat courageous anachronism, this would constitute an explanatory and interpretive framework beyond the descriptive vagueness of "postmodern synthetic realism" (Sauer 1) and may account for the tangible societal concern that is clearly present in these contemporary plays, which on the surface appear very different.

Conclusion

All three playwrights testify in their works to the structural, and not merely thematic, presence of the biblical text. With the use of poetic language, they lend support to Lorca's contention that "a play is a poem standing up" (Collins and Wishna 101). The cyclical element of biblical narrative and song thus translates into contemporary theater, poetry, and narrative, so long as the form itself is cyclical – for example, in the form of short-story and poetry collections or in innovative new plays like the three discussed here. Contemporary Anglo-American drama of exile is a genre-specific expression of the movement of sacralization that defines contemporary literature and culture as a whole, namely, the ever more subtle and subdued, yet nonetheless ubiquitous presence of Scripture in daily life. The plays, like other forms of contemporary literature, shed light on the state of contemporary society, unsettling its certainties by emphatically conveying the theology of exile as a biblical core myth. They creatively bridge the gap between the popular and the political in a quest for spiritual veracity that is driven by a deep but faithful dissatisfaction with status quo beliefs.

While the theological focus on exile can also be observed in biblically informed contemporary Anglo-American literature of other genres such as poetry and short stories, its development in drama – as can be seen from these examples – evolves within the particular rules of the genre. Contemporary Anglo-American drama of exile deals with the biographical experiences of its authors by staging and developing conflicts arising from the human existential condition of exile. The historical settings of the three plays are also remarkable in pointing to eras of particular interest for contemporary society, thus mirroring core literary and historiographical concerns: Adjmi's play is set in the "early 2000s" (Benson 5), possibly pointing to a still inextricably close era of far-reaching societal change, in which new conditions of exile and migratory movements come to the fore; Gardley's play is set in Romanticism and Naturalism, which still have such a powerful hold on contemporary art with its existential questions of belonging and loss; and Lee situates her play in a transtemporal atmosphere of an unspecified present, calling into question the historical contexts of the other plays along with their particular understandings of exile and communities. By taking up contemporary conversational atmospheres (Lee; Adjmi, *Stunning*) and stimulating overlapping mythological imaginaries (Gardley), these playwrights succeed in innovating the stage of contemporary drama by re-casting the relation between the human existential condition and present society. By developing new forms like satirical tragedy (Adjmi, *Stunning*) and a new genre of historical play adding a mythological dimension (Gardley in *The Road Weeps, the Well Runs Dry*) or satirically, experimentally, and allegorically rewriting historical plays (Lee in *LEAR*), these playwrights succeed in speaking not only to their audiences, but also to current societal concerns. Coming from very different backgrounds, they manage to recover both political impetus and author-actor collaborations for a renewed Anglo-American theater that will declare the individual and collective dimensions of the human condition of exile as the focal point for a stage that is both artistically and socially relevant.

References

Adjmi, David. *Stunning and Other Plays*. New York: Theatre Communications Group, 2011.

———. "Glossary of Syrian-American Terms." *Stunning and Other Plays*. New York: Theatre Communications Group, 2011. 8-9.

Barker, Glenn W., William L. Lane and J. Ramsey Michaels. *The New Testament Speaks*. New York: Harper and Row, 1969.

Benson, Sarah, ed. *The Methuen Drama Book of New American Plays*. Methuen Drama Play Anthologies. London: Methuen Drama, 2013.

Bouchard, Larry D. *Tragic Method and Tragic Theology: Evil in Contemporary Drama and Religious Thought*. Philadelphia: Pennsylvania State University Press, 2010.

Bruck, Peter. "Ed Bullins: The Quest and Failure of an Ethnic Community Theatre." *Essays on Contemporary American Drama*. Ed. Hedwig Bock and Albert Wertheim. Munich: Hueber, 1981. 123-40.

Collins, Ken and Victor Wishna. *In Their Company: Portraits of American Playwrights*. Photographs by Ken Collins. Interviews by Victor Wishna. New York: Umbrage, 2006.

Delgado-García, Cristina. *Rethinking Character in Contemporary British Theatre: Aesthetics, Politics, Subjectivity*. Berlin: De Gruyter, 2015.

Elam, Jr., Harry J. and Douglas A. Jones, Jr., eds. *The Methuen Drama Book of Post-Black Plays*. London: Bloomsbury Publishing, 2013.

Gardley, Marcus. *I Am a Man: Performed by Marc Damon Johnson*. Director Hal Hartley, editor Kyle Gilman. 9.11.2012. <https://www.youtube.com/watch?v=hB1mlwr_JD0>. Accessed 28 December 2016.

Geis, Deborah R. *Postmodern Theatric(k)s: Monologue in Contemporary American Drama*. Theatre – theory/text/performance. Ann Arbor: University of Michigan Press, 1993.

Hartman, Stacy. "'A Romance with One's Own Fantasy': The Nostalgia of Exile in Anna Seghers's Mexico." *Edinburgh German Yearbook 3. Contested Legacies: Constructions of Cultural Heritage in the GDR*. Woodbridge: Boydell and Brewer, 2009. 30-46.

Hinlicky, Paul R. *Divine Simplicity: Christ the Crisis of Metaphysics*. Grand Rapids: Baker Academic, 2016.

Holifield, Evander B. "Why Are Americans So Religious? The Limitations of Market Explanations." *Religion and the Marketplace in the United States*. Ed. Jan Stievermann, Philip Goff, and Detlef Junker. Oxford: Oxford University Press, 2015. 33-60.

The Holy Bible: English Standard Version Student Study Bible. Wheaton: Crossway Books, 2014.

The Holy Bible: Containing the Old and New Testaments, Translated out of the Original Tongues and with the Former Translations diligently compared and revised; Commonly known as the Authorized (King James) Version. Philadelphia: National Pub., 1978.

Karlip, Joshua M. *The Tragedy of a Generation: The Rise and Fall of Jewish Nationalism in Eastern Europe*. Cambridge: Harvard University Press, 2013.

Klaver, Elizabeth. *Performing Television: Contemporary Drama and the Media Culture*. Bowling Green: Bowling Green State University Popular Press, 2000.

Lee, Young Jean. *The Shipment and LEAR*. New York: Theatre Communications Group, 2011.

Leypoldt, Günter. "Literature and the Economy of the Sacred." *Religion and the Marketplace in the United States*. Ed. Jan Stievermann, Philip Goff, and Detlef Junker. Oxford: Oxford University Press, 2015. 145-64.

Malkin, Jeanette R. *Verbal Violence in Contemporary Drama: From Handke to Shepard*. Cambridge: Cambridge University Press, 1992.

Meerzon, Yana. *Performing Exile, Performing Self: Drama, Theatre, Film*. Studies in International Performance. Houndmills: Palgrave Macmillan, 2012.

Megson, Christopher. "Is British theatre postsecular?" *Research, 2013*. <https://pure.royalholloway.ac.uk/portal/en/activities/is-british-theatre-postsecular(989a627b-aee1-4560-98a6-3556e3746101).html>. Accessed 2 January 2017.

———. "'Thisworldly wonderment': Contemporary British Theatre and Postsecularism." *Performing the Secular: Representation, Religion and the Public Sphere*. Ed. Milija Gluhovic and Jisha Menon. First edition. London: Palgrave Macmillan, 2017.

Nanko-Fernández, Carmen M. "Alternately Documented Theologies: Mapping Border, Exile and Diaspora." *Religion, Representation, and Politics*. Contemporary Performance InterActions. Ed. Sarah Azaransky. Lanham: Lexington Books, 2013. 33-56.

Ostwalt, Jr., Conrad. *Secular Steeples: Popular Culture and the Religious Imagination*. Second edition. London: Bloomsbury Academic, 2012.

Postell, Seth D. *Adam as Israel: Genesis 1-3 as the Introduction to the Torah and Tanakh*. Cambridge: James Clarke and Company, 2012.

Sauer, David K. *American Drama and the Postmodern: Fracturing the Realistic Stage*. Amherst: Cambria Press, 2000.

Stievermann, Jan, Philip Goff, and Detlef Junker, eds. *Religion and the Marketplace in the United States*. Oxford: Oxford University Press, 2015.

Ybarra, Patricia. "Young Jean Lee's Cruel Dramaturgy." *Modern Drama* 57.4 (2014): 513-33.

Zalambani, Maria. "Literary Policies and Institutions." *The Cambridge Companion to Twentieth-Century Russian Literature*. Ed. Evgeny Dobrenko and Marina Balina. Cambridge: Cambridge University Press, 2011. 251-68.

Timothy Findley's Community of Responsible Readers in *Headhunter*

Sabin Jeanmaire

In his dystopian novel *Headhunter* (1993), the Canadian writer Timothy Findley creates a complex network of intertextual relations between his characters, other literary texts, and real-life events from Canadian history. In doing so, he foregrounds the knowledge that is necessary to recognize the respective connections, and thereby delineates the inclusions and exclusions of the community of those who can be called responsible readers. In part a rewriting of Joseph Conrad's *Heart of Darkness* (1899), *Headhunter* explores topics of responsibility and power, as well as different types of darkness within a psychiatric institution. The implicit community of readers consists of those characters who successfully navigate through the near-apocalyptic version of Toronto the novel presents. Making Kurtz the head psychiatrist of a clinic, Findley raises the question of who or what is considered sane or mentally ill; and he offers a view on how storytelling and access to narrative information are vital in negotiations of power.

A story set in Toronto, a plot revolving around characters who are either doctors or patients at a psychiatric institution, and a subsequent focus on topics of mental illness and power abuse – dark, yes, but not unrealistic so far. However, Timothy Findley's novel *Headhunter*, first published in 1993, presents a dystopian future version of the Canadian metropolis in which many things appear sinister. In addition to its clearly dystopian characteristics, the world of Findley's characters expands beyond Toronto through a myriad of intertextual links to both other literary works and historical events relevant to Canadian culture. At the same time a gripping text about the human psyche, about the ethics and morals involved in psychiatric treatment, and about establishing a series of riddles for people familiar with some of the best-known English-language novels, *Headhunter* offers two quite different types of communities. One is based on spatial proximity and professional necessity: namely, the community of all the characters in this particular psychiatric institution. With the setting in and around this institution, topics of mental illness, but also of power struggles within this clearly hierarchical structure, are foregrounded. It is in this space that the fictional doctors and patients meet for therapeutic sessions, that doctors negotiate their procedures and methods, and that secrets are traded and stories told. This aspect of storytelling, however, is also the basis for the second community, which I will focus on mainly in the present essay. This is a community of reader figures within the novel, established through a shared interest in reading and literature; a community whose inclusions and exclusions are also delineated by their knowledge of literary works, and hence by their ability to trace intertextual connections. My main claim is that in the dystopian world presented by Findley, both this knowledge of cultural history and the ability to become a responsible reader[1] are necessary for survival; conversely, it is precisely the threats to this community of readers and to successful acts of storytelling that make this such a dystopian world. As will be shown, storytelling is threatened by irresponsible readers/listeners, and especially through situations in which those who have a story to tell are denied a voice – a crucial consideration when it comes to witness testimonies.

A successful community is generally one in which communication works, i.e., where people understand each other and are able to respond to what they are told. In the spatial community of the clinic in *Headhunter*, this is not guaranteed, and thus the bond among the members of the community of reader figures is actually much stronger, albeit far more abstract. The novel is set precisely where the two communities overlap and where the private and the public intersect: The interaction between doctors and patients is based on an exchange of stories, in the form of what the patients tell the doctors about themselves. Revealing very personal information and talking about memories of traumatic

---

[1] I suggest that a coupling of empathy and understanding is called for in this particular novel. As Suzanne Keen argues, "conscious cultivation of narrative empathy by teachers and discussion leaders could at least point toward the potential for novel reading to help citizens respond to real others with greater openness and consciousness of their shared humanity" (147). The response as re-action, thus, is one step further than a mere empathetic response on an emotional level, and requires training as a reader.

events create a fragile state that transfers a lot of responsibility onto the character that serves as receiver of the story, namely, the psychiatrist on duty. As for Findley's novel though, it is tempting to expand this toward the real-life reader.

Such an expansion would be as courageous (not to say dangerous) as it would be grounded in the text. It is courageous from a methodological point of view, as it implies bringing into dangerously close connection two levels crucially kept apart in classical narrative theory. I follow this tradition in that I distinguish between "readers" on three levels: the real-life biographical reader, the "implied reader," and characters who are readers on the level of the plot. The role of the responsible reader as it is discussed here applies mainly to characters that are presented as reader figures in the novel, but also points roughly to what is sometimes described as the "ideal" (cf. Culler 51) or "implied" reader (cf. Iser 34) of the novel. What is striking about this particular novel, however, and Findley's moral/ethical imperative as I understand it, is that he seems to be calling upon real-life readers to step into the shoes of the ideal responsible reader his novel constructs. Thus, these two levels cannot always be kept apart neatly. In repeated metafictional gestures and acts of metaleptic interpellation, the novel stages the act of reading on the plot level that mirrors the ideal response requested of the reader of the novel.

The expansion is, at the same time, grounded in the text. As we pick up the novel, we accept the role of readers, and are asked to become members of this community of responsible readers. The opening scene of the novel, our first contact with the book, already presents a meta-reflection on the connections between the different levels of readers:

> On a winter's day, while a blizzard raged through the streets of Toronto, Lilah Kemp inadvertently set Kurtz free from page 92 of *Heart of Darkness*. Horror-stricken, she tried to force him back between the covers. The escape took place at the Metropolitan Toronto Reference Library, where Lilah Kemp sat reading beside the rock pool. She had not even said *come forth*, but there Kurtz stood before her. (3)

What frames the novel as a whole is thus a scene of reading, and this act of intense engagement with a literary text functions as a doubling of our own act of reading, and, as such, as a metaleptic interpellation – from the very start, we are encouraged to compare our reading to Lilah's.

After Lilah, a former librarian and diagnosed schizophrenic, accidentally conjures up Kurtz from the pages of a copy of Joseph Conrad's *Heart of Darkness*, the latter escapes into the streets of Lilah's hometown,

Toronto, and becomes the head psychiatrist at the fictional Parkin Institute, where most of the plot unfolds. This character's literary origin is given in great detail, including the page number from which he escapes, in order to ensure that everyone recognizes the intertext of *Heart of Darkness* from the start – thus making it the most prominent (though by far not the only) intertextual link in *Headhunter*. Kurtz's job at the clinic is a position of power comparable to the one in Conrad's novella, and there is a Marlow to interfere with Kurtz's abuse of power in Findley's text, too. By choosing Conrad's novella as a key intertext Findley evidently also raises questions of responsibility, power hierarchies, and different kinds of darknesses:

> *Headhunter* suggests that each new generation in each invented community must reenter its own particular heart of darkness in search of its own Kurtz – its own shortcomings, its own weaknesses. Books, and by extension art, are the best guides on that journey. (Brydon 61)

For the purpose of the present argument, it might be appropriate to add that books are among the best guides for the journey *through and possibly out of* whichever heart of darkness one has penetrated into – whereas the absence of literary understanding can mean condemning a character to remain trapped in that place of darkness.

In connection to Conrad's key intertext, it is vital to look at the title of the novel, *Headhunter*. We know the word from a professional context, where it refers to a person whose aim it is to find the best people for a given job (cf. OED "headhunting, *n.*, 2"), which in turn is connected to Findley's Kurtz and his position at the clinic, where he is looking for the best people to fit into the roles of doctors, patients and investors. But we might also remember the image in Conrad's novella of the heads impaled on wooden posts that Kurtz collects (164), which links to the first and far more literal definition of "headhunter" the OED provides, namely, "a person who decapitates an enemy and preserves the head as a trophy" ("headhunter, *n*, 1").[2] The word also goes back to the idea of bounty hunters or, to borrow from the OED again, to "a person who pursues wanted criminals, etc., for the sake of rewards offered" ("bounty-hunter, *n.*"). In the first chapter of Findley's novel, the title is echoed literally when we find a description of his Kurtz character with

---

[2] Indeed, as an example sentence for "headhunting, n., 2" from 1961 shows, "headhunter" was formerly used as one of several derogatory terms to denote recruiting firms – others being "body snatchers," "flesh peddlers," and "pirates" – but seems to have passed into value-neutral business vocabulary since.

the following attributes: "Kurtz, the harbinger of darkness. Kurtz, the horror-meister. Kurtz, the *headhunter*" (6; my emphasis). In the context of psychiatry, of course, the idea of hunting for people's heads has the additional layer of meaning that it is all about tracking down people's secrets, capturing them, making them one's own – and, in this modern Kurtz's case, orchestrating them to his own benefit.[3] This Kurtz's trophy collection hence is far more abstract than physical, but no less threatening: It consists of the ideas from inside those heads rather than the actual heads on poles.

The formal structure of *Headhunter*, too, reminds us of the plurality of thoughts expressed during psychotherapeutic sessions. The novel is divided into ten books, each including sub-chapters in which the many plot strands are developed. One easily loses track of the connections between the various characters, but the point where they all cross paths is at the Parkin Institute, and, more precisely, in their interactions with Dr. Kurtz. Given the setting and the episodic structure of the novel, what the real-life reader of the novel is offered is a series of brief stories which allow glimpses into the lives of all those characters. In simple terms, Findley coerces his implied reader to assume a position similar to a prototype therapist's, who also meets his or her patients one by one for relatively short meetings and learns more about them each time, before they disappear again for quite a while. The structural analogy between the positions of the implied reader and that of the prototype therapist invites the former to respond to the patients' stories just as the latter does, namely, by taking them seriously and trying to see overall coherence in their accounts. If we allow this – again, admittedly courageous – transfer a right to exist, it works the other way around, too: The therapist is also shown as a reader figure, who is confronted with texts in the form of his or her patients' testimonies and needs to have the

---

[3] For a discussion of how the patient might question the power hierarchy in doctor-patient relationships, see Lupton (114-20). May further uses Foucault's idea of the clinical gaze to distinguish between the visible (and thus more easily categorizable) physical symptoms of the illness (591) and the personal information about the self which the patient can withhold: "Unlike the 'truth' of the disordered body, visible through examination or biochemistry, the truth of the subject cannot be exposed without the explicit permission of the subject concerned. It cannot be exposed or fixed without positive action on the part of the patient, who may lie or remain silent in the face of such enquiry. The question 'do you want to talk' offers the possibility of answering 'no'" (600). In the psychiatric context in particular, the accessibility and reliability of information can be severely affected by the mental health of the patient or be manipulated more subtly by those in power.

necessary readerly competence to recognize links to other texts, and patterns within the same.

To fully concentrate on the intradiegetic communicative levels again: The moment all characters set foot in the clinic, they enter a shared space and thus become members of the spatial community of the Parkin Institute. It is made up of a sub-community of mental patients on the one hand, and of doctors responsible for them on the other. Parkin is an institution in which hierarchies are to be strictly obeyed, and in which power is linked to authority. Authority can also be read as author-ity, i.e., as a response to the question of who has a voice, who is allowed to tell and own a story, and who is not, which in turn leads to the question of what kind of power is conferred upon the listeners. This power in any case comes with response-ibility[4] – the ability to respond to what one is being told in a way that shows understanding and an appropriate reaction. In Findley's novels, the psychiatrists do not behave the way they should in terms of medical code. As outlined by Judith Herman in her classic *Trauma and Recovery*, therapists ought to

> use the power that has been conferred upon [them] only to foster the recovery of the patient, resisting all temptations to abuse. This promise, which is central to the integrity of any therapeutic relationship, is of special importance to patients who are already suffering as the result of another's arbitrary and exploitative exercise of power. (134-35)

Herman thus highlights the importance of integrity and the responsibility that comes with the position of power that the psychiatrist has. By being the recipients of so many stories, so much personal knowledge, the sub-community of doctors has a type of power that can easily be abused. It is thus in the moment of storytelling, as a patient talks about his/her trauma and the therapist listens, that the public and the private begin to intersect. Something that is most private, namely, a set of recollected scenes, especially traumatic ones, is exposed to the eyes and ears of a representative of the power structure of the clinic. The doctors are the chosen people to whom a story is told, in the hope that through their act of listening they should help the patients transform the fragments of their trauma into a narrative – a process of *working through* their

---

[4] In the preface to her long essay "Playing in the Dark" (1992), Toni Morrison also makes use of this pun and explains that "[w]riting and reading mean being aware of the writer's notions of risk and safety, the serene achievement of, or sweaty fight for, meaning and response-ability" (xi). Furthermore, the idea that the subject is responsible for his/her response to the various "texts" life confronts him/her with also (roughly) corresponds to Bakhtin's idea of "answerability" (cf. Holquist 167).

memories. For Laurence J. Kirmayer, storytelling is of paramount importance for psychiatric treatment, given that "one effective ingredient in narrating previously suppressed memories is the structuring or reorganizing effects of narration" (594). However, communication in the Parkin Institute is anomalous in this respect as well as in others – not least in that there is not exactly an excess of exchange among the doctors, nor among the patients. Put briefly, the community of the Institute, much as it seems spatially coherent, is disjointed and characterized by a sense of isolation and alienation. This stands in contrast to the second community created by the text: As opposed to the strict spatial boundaries of the Parkin Institute, the seemingly scattered individual readers still form a more coherent (albeit abstract) community that is predicated on their shared literary knowledge and understanding.

The psychological gain which should result from a successful kind of narration, namely "heal[ing] by allowing symbolic closure, bringing a sense of completeness or coherent emplotment to the fragmented and chaotic elements of illness experience" (Kirmayer 595), is diametrically opposed to what Findley's Dr. Kurtz achieves (or even aims for); he rather uses the information imparted to him by his patients to raise money for his institution and thereby to increase his own power. According to Michel Foucault, power relations

> are not in a position of exteriority with respect to other types of relationships (economic processes, knowledge relationships, sexual relations), but are immanent in the latter; they are the immediate effects of the divisions, inequalities, and disequilibriums which occur in the latter, and conversely they are the internal conditions of these differentiations; relations of power are not in a superstructural position, with merely a role of prohibition or accompaniment; they have a directly productive role, wherever they come into play. (94)

All these "other types of relationships" are present in *Headhunter*. The economic processes are foregrounded in that Kurtz is always looking for investors for the Parkin Institute (107); knowledge relationships are illustrated by all the files stored in the clinic, to which Kurtz has access and which include all the secrets that make people vulnerable and blackmailable (348); and, finally, the sexual relations also play a vital role here, both in the form of romantic involvement and instances of rape which trouble hierarchical boundaries (Marlow's feelings for a patient [186]; adult patients "recruiting" boys for abuse [128f.]). It is important to note, however, that all these relationships are negotiated through acts and moments of storytelling.

Kurtz functions as the figure of an irresponsible reader, who *is able* to process the information, but abuses it in a breach of confidentiality. He is thus a threat to the transmission of stories and hence to the community of readers, in abstract terms. His abusiveness is summed up by the key pun of the novel. We read of a patient who walks through the clinic with her mother; she suddenly stops in her tracks and stares at one of the doors. "'That sign,' said Peggy. 'THERAPIST,' said Eloise, reading. – 'Yes, I can see that now, Mother. But when I saw it first, I thought it said THE RAPIST'" (370-71).[5] As the accompanying nurse comments, Peggy is not the first patient to commit this misreading, and what these misreaders have in common is a specific type of trauma. They illustrate the trope of readers who always understand a text along the lines of what they already know, or what Barthes calls the "déjà lu," the "already-read" (82). The survival of a traumatic event determines Peggy's misreading of the door sign, because the framework she thinks in establishes a highly revealing connection between the rapist who caused her trauma and the doctor who is supposed to help her cope with this trauma – but who might be equally abusive when it comes to power relations.

This creative misreading reveals a well-hidden kernel of truth. Yet unlike a competent reader, who might have recognized the warning inherent in the name of Kurtz, Peggy is obviously ignorant of *Heart of Darkness* – much in opposition to Lilah, who is an avid and passionate reader and anticipates what the appearance of Kurtz will bring along. As soon as Lilah's new neighbor, Dr. Marlow, moves in, she puts her faith in his abilities to overthrow Kurtz, and ultimately, she is shown to be right in doing so. Such examples abound, and Lilah functions as focalizer for many of the key scenes. This may be taken as a metareflection on the importance of reading, as those characters who *do* read widely are able to make important associations. At the same time, the choice of intertexts in *Headhunter* needs to be critically assessed with a view to what is considered the "Western Canon" (cf. Rippl and Straub; Morrison, "Unspeakable"); it raises questions of cultural imperialism (cf. Brydon). The central role of Conrad's reflection on colonialism, as well as other elements – such as Findley's mentioning of Susanna Moodie (49), a historical settler figure who would later also appear as a character in Margaret Atwood's *The Journals of Susanna Moodie* (1970) – all introduce the

---

[5] This pun is also employed in Nabokov's *Lolita*, when Humbert reflects upon his role vis-à-vis Lolita: "The rapist was Charlie Holmes; I am the therapist – a matter of nice spacing in the way of distinction" (150). Thus, *Lolita* serves as yet another intertext, especially given that the topic of pedophilia comes up in *Headhunter* as well.

idea of voices from the peripheries: Colonial subjects and women are given a voice, and, again, it is crucial for Findley's characters to take their accounts into consideration as they deal with "colonizers" such as Dr. Kurtz who attempt to keep them silent/silenced.

Analogously to other activities that involve hermeneutic processes, reading depends on previous instances of reading; in other words, having a broad knowledge of literature will help any reader categorize and handle new impressions. If the responses of different readers are then similar, we can observe the formation of what Stanley Fish calls an "interpretive community" (171) – and, as discussed above, in this case it is the ideal community of empathetic and responsible readers. However, readers' relations to the knowledge of others cannot be separated from power. The key power network (as defined by Foucault) linking all elements of *Headhunter* is a web of intertextual references, but associated with the ability to read are the dangers of subtle exclusion (as in cases of elitism) and of blatant abuse (as with Kurtz). Yet *Headhunter* is quintessentially dystopian in that another danger, namely, that of declaring obsolete the act of reading, or prohibiting it altogether, is equally present. Its world is one in which people do not read, and where the ones who *do* have a clear connection to literature are considered insane and put on medication that limits or eliminates their imagination. Although some books are still found in a wealthy character's house, these turn out to be abridged versions of classics "uniformly bound in green leather" (306) to fit into the design of the apartment; they were never read, most likely (307). In other words, art is only treasured as status symbol; it has lost its aesthetic or instructive value and has been reduced to a mere commodity. As a result, these books can be seen as failed transmission of information (across generations).

As we have seen, the novel presents instances of failed storytelling as the origins / causes of Findley's dystopia. So far, we have been mainly concerned with the failures on the part of the recipients of a story and less so with those of the speaker / writer. It is equally difficult to establish a working community based on stories if the stories needed are never told in the first place. In a novel concerned with many traumatic events and the patients who have witnessed those events, the idea of bearing witness is of great importance. Giving testimony of what happened is all too often impossible (if the patients do not survive what is done to them), very difficult (if the therapist does not respond in the way he / she should), or simply forbidden by the more powerful in the hierarchical system of the Parkin Institute. This last case is again closely related to our initial question of who has a voice and who is silenced. In the microcosm of the clinic, silencing also happens on a very literal level: The doctors working in the laboratories of the clinic cut the vocal cords of the rats used for tests because "their voices get in the way of human sensibilities" (290). In the macrocosm of the diegetic characters, there are cases whose accounts are presented solely through vivid descriptions by the third person narrator and where the reader is compelled to witness their trauma. The questions raised by this form of presentation (as opposed to allowing them to have a voice of their own in direct speech) is, ultimately, how big the community of silenced witnesses might be, or in other words, the question who, in such settings, is entirely denied the chance to verbalize their story and to testify to the horrors they have experienced.[6]

Another set of voices that is silenced radically in this dystopian world is that of starlings. As these birds are suspected of transmitting to human beings a mysterious, fatal, and highly contagious disease called Sturnusemia, special forces called D-Squads drive their tanks to streets with trees and spray gas at the birds in order to eradicate them. In addition to the actual animals, references to birds abound in *Headhunter*, generally loaded with symbolism. This is most visibly the case in relation to one patient at the Parkin Institute. A young poet named Amy is obsessed with saving the birds and does not believe that they need to be killed to save human lives, which is considered as yet another symptom of her madness. In the course of her treatment, Dr. Marlow has a PET scan done of her brain and the resulting image "looks like a Rorschach test" that can be read as "a bird in flight" (466). The open wings of the birds are used to visualize the flights of the imagination, and Amy's insistence that the birds be saved dovetails with her refusal of taking any further medication; she wants to remain a poet and be able to foster her creativity.[7] As Marlow explains, putting her on drugs would mean that

---

[6] An example are the children treated by Dr. Eleanor Farjeon at the Parkin Institute: Throughout the text, they never speak a word (and it is implied that they never speak at all – and that this is not an omission on the part of the narrator), but through the background information provided by the narrator which is partly presented as Eleanor's research, the reader learns about the trauma that resulted in their muted state (180).

[7] In staying true to herself and her originality, Amy manages to avoid what the feminist theologian Mary Daly describes as the detrimental effects of religious views on women and psychotherapy: "a woman's initial surrender of her private Self to the [therapist] is the condition for his cleansing of her original sin, that is, of her original Self-moving Self. This Self-Denial places her in a state of therapeutic grace, purified of Originality" (251-52). Daly is highly critical of the relationship between any male doctor and female "patient / penitent" (252) and, just like Findley, describes the doctor as "the/rapist" (255).

"[she] would have no poems, no birds, [. . .] no other world but the dead world out there now – and she would be *incapable of responding* to it" (466; my emphasis). Without her medication, on the other hand, "she could go home to her house – and be with her birds [. . .]. There is every chance this Amy would continue to produce poetry" (467). Here again, the explicit connection is made between having access to literature and being able to respond to the world around oneself.

If we thus accept that, in this novel, birds are used as symbols for (art and) literature, then violently and systematically getting rid of birds by means of D-Squad interventions stands for a radical attempt at eliminating (artwork and) literature, an objective that seems implicit in many of the proceedings of those in power at the Parkin Institute. Limiting access to books is then connected to one of the openly mentioned intertexts of *Headhunter* (49), namely, Ray Bradbury's *Fahrenheit 451* (first published in 1953), in which books are burned as an extreme form of censorship. Obviously, the gassing of the birds also recalls the Shoah. The novel even compares the two scenarios openly, but immediately points out this dystopian Toronto's devious attitude towards history. What happens is that, after one of the D-Squad missions is witnessed by different people in the street,

> some – mostly senior citizens with extended memories – said prayers. Others – mostly children – applauded. It *depended on what one knew about the past* – and the young, for some time, had been sheltered from all history containing episodes of chemical warfare. (Findley 217; my emphasis)

The narrating voice thus highlights the importance of memories and the transmission of the memory of warfare with tremendous atrocities to future generations, as well as the fatal consequences of any discontinuation of this form of storytelling. It is as if the author made the case that literature is a key way of maintaining knowledge once the last survivors of historical events are gone and that "shelter[ing]" people from this knowledge may lead to the repetition of terrible historical events.

What further becomes clear is that historical events for Findley often function as a multitude of stories, serving as yet another form of intertexts. The fact that people are no longer familiar with their history is yet another act of misreading which has its roots in a fundamental lack of knowledge, which in turn makes it possible for terrible things to happen again due to people's failure to recognize the similarities or references to previous moments in history / stories. As Brydon puts it, "if the world is also a text, it demands attentive reading" (57), and a novel like *Headhunter* with its clear self-reflexive thrust certainly highlights the textuality of the world and the vital importance of being attentive, empathetic and responsible readers.

Another historical connection evoked by Findley's discussion of Sturnusemia is alluded to with the propaganda of the D-Squads, who come in to spray the trees with chemicals: It takes on the form of the slogan "Kill a starling – save a life!" (422) and thus evokes the residential schools in Canada, which served the purpose of a systematic elimination of First Nation cultures from the mid-nineteenth to the late twentieth century.[8] Under the motto "Kill the Indian and Save the Man" (Child 78), First Nation children were taken away from their families to be so-called "westernized," ideally losing any last trace of their native cultures. This often resulted in horrible physical treatment, with a high number of children who did not survive their stays in those institutions (Child 80). These children are thus another implicit community of silenced witnesses who never had a voice and could not even respond to history. With this, the reader figures are called upon to recognize the allusion and to respond to or provide a voice for the telling of their untold stories. Findley's narrator, when restating the slogan "Kill a starling – save a life," merely adds the afterthought "life, presumably, was a human possession only" (422). But indirectly, the question remains whether what in the eyes of North American settlers was worth saving was a white/Western possession only.

As another historical intertext, psychiatric experiments must not go unmentioned. In *Headhunter*, Kurtz cooperates with a female doctor named Shelley, "whose vision of re-created lives was almost *literary* in its *imaginative* applications of science" (135; my emphasis), which reveals her very favourable attitude towards extreme and dangerous experiments. The reference to Mary Shelley and her novel *Frankenstein*, and hence to the idea that scientific progress can have disastrous outcomes, is almost impossible to miss. For a Canadian audience, however, the topic of medical experiments would certainly also recall the public scandal surrounding the experiments conducted by Dr. Donald Ewen Cameron in Montreal in the 1960s (cf. *McGill Daily*) which are even mentioned in passing in the novel (134). From what is known about these real-life experiments, similar to the "The White Mind Theory" (134) Findley's Kurtz employs, scientists at McGill University, headed by Cameron, tried to delete the memories of patients and to "re-pattern" their brains with new impressions (cf. McCoy 42-45; Krishnan 24).

---

[8] Findley did not live to see Prime Minister Stephen Harper's official apology for those schools in 2008 – after the last school had been closed only in 1996.

Cameron was a highly ambitious psychiatrist, and at the time the highest-ranking doctor at the Allan Memorial Institute in Montreal. There are thus clear parallels between this real-life person and the Kurtz character Findley draws in *Headhunter*. Given that the CIA was allegedly involved in the experiments, there is very little official information on these proceedings, and the information available is often dangerously close to conspiracy theories. Furthermore, it was not until many years later that survivor testimonies began to surface (cf. Collins; Weinstein; both published in 1988, i.e., several decades after the events – and only a few years before *Headhunter* was first published). Due to the traumatic effects of the experiments and the time elapsed between the event and its telling, the reliability of these testimonies is uncertain. This, in combination with the secrecy surrounding the events, amounts to a radical form of censorship, which again resonates in the silencing of entire groups of witnesses – rats, birds, patients on medication to name but a few – in Findley's text.

As mentioned earlier, the importance of intertextuality in *Headhunter* reaches far beyond Kurtz and Marlow, and also beyond hints toward chapters in mainstream Canadian history. Some allusions to other famous literary texts are straightforward and prominent, but in the majority they are brief and playful: Books are read and treasured by characters, for example *Wuthering Heights* (11) and *Peter Rabbit* (29) for Lilah; a pet dog's name is Grendel (174), and one character's name is Mr. Gatz (185). The allusion to *The Great Gatsby* seems to bring together several aspects discussed above: Not only does Fitzgerald's novel prominently touch upon "reading the signs" and "being attentive," it also evokes questions of privilege – and it pokes fun at a society that fetishizes a form of book-related habitus (cf. the famous pages in Gatsby's library that he "didn't cut," [Fitzgerald 46-47]), an idea *Headhunter* seems to take up in the form of the abridged classics bound in green leather.

Scenes that deal with reading – clichéd or not – are never innocent, particularly given the opening of *Headhunter* discussed above, and given that the metalepsis does not stop there. Metalepsis is here understood in Genette's sense, namely, as

> that deliberate transgression of the threshold of embedding [. . .]: when an author (or his reader) introduces himself into the fictive action of the narrative or when a character in that fiction intrudes into the extradiegetic existence of the author or reader, such intrusions disturb, to say the least, the distinction between levels. (Genette 88)

In *Headhunter*, there are several instances where characters from one diegetic level suddenly appear on a different one. The Kurtz who physically escapes out of the book *Heart of Darkness*, and "arrives" on the diegetic level of Lilah and the Torontonian clinic is later mirrored by the reverse case, when the author of the novel, Timothy Findley, writes himself into the plot and is mentioned as a character. Although he is far less central to the plot than Kurtz, and only mentioned in passing, it is relevant to note the function of this character. When Marlow arrives as a new doctor at the clinic, he receives a set of patients from his predecessor Dr. Rain, and the first is "this fellow Findley" (162). As he reads his file to prepare himself for Findley's appointment, Marlow finds a note that Findley "has threatened to sue [the] Parkin Institute," and goes on to reflect, "ah, yes. *A ranter.* And *a writer. Novels. Stories. Plays"* (162). Whilst the biographical information is correct – the real-life Findley had indeed written novels, short stories, and plays – the character Findley seems to use language not only for art, but also to stir up unrest. The next item in Marlow's folder is a transcript, and he reads,

> Findley was saying: *you know, Rain, we do the same thing, you and I. We're both trying to figure out what makes the human race tick. And the way we do that – both of us – is by climbing down inside other people's lives to see if they're telling the truth or not. Most of us are lying.* (162)

In the context of our argument, it is crucial to note that the real-life author's fictional double has the role of a patient. Both Findleys are creative thinkers, and it is due to this attribute that the intradiegetic one is considered unstable and problematic by the predominant regimen at the Parkin. Similar to Amy, Findley the character does not neatly fit into the categories of either "sane" or "mentally ill" and causes trouble for the Parkin community. The lawsuit against the clinic he has allegedly threatened is presented as one way in which language could be employed to counter corrupt power structures, just as literature is shown to be the more effective way of doing so in the long run, which is – thus goes the implication – what Findley the real-life author pursues. Lastly, if the writer figure takes the position of the patient, i.e., the one who is telling his own story, this reinforces my previous claim that the implied reader is modelled to have the function of both reader and therapist, i.e., as the one who receives the story and is asked to respond to it. Just like Marlow, the implied reader of the novel is asked to put the bits and pieces together to form a coherent narrative. With reference to Kirmayer's stance about the importance of narrativizing trauma testimony, this might be read as follows: Findley's novel brings up the topic of how an individual responsible reader can lend an ear to society's collective trauma.

With the reading experience of one character, Lilah, as its frame, the novel positions itself clearly on the side of the intradiegetic community of readers, and paints a bleak picture of what could happen in a dystopian future if literature were lost. Literature hence takes on a connecting function not only between people, but also between the past and the present. It also blurs the boundaries between the communities of the "sane" and the "mentally ill," as defined by the institution in this novel. It is exactly some of the characters who are diagnosed as mentally ill (e.g., Lilah or Amy) that we end up relying on and identifying with, given that they embody the literary knowledge and readerly competence that seems necessary to navigate through the near-apocalyptic world of this novel. In putting the implied reader in a therapist's position, the novel further challenges us to make sense of a maze of stories, in short, to be responsible readers – readers who, beyond recognizing intertextual clues, can reflect on the multitude of communicative levels established in the act of reading.

Intradiegetically, Marlow, who even employs literature in his treatments (149), is shown as a responsible reader, and, just like the Marlow in *Heart of Darkness*, he survives – unlike Kurtz. The plot of *Headhunter* ends with Kurtz's death – by Sturnusemia, ironically – but without rendering Conrad's Kurtz's famous last words "The horror! The horror!" (Conrad 178).[9] In both Conrad's and Findley's text, Marlow witnesses Kurtz's death. Yet while it is spelt out that Conrad's Marlow hears Kurtz's final utterance – "revealed" to the reader in the form of direct speech – and then keeps it to himself (Conrad 186), Findley's text immediately shifts to a different sub-plot and leaves Kurtz's death uncommented. This takes away Kurtz's voice and authority in the very final instance, while at the same time highlighting a crucial topic of the entire novel, namely, that of filling gaps and piecing together disjointed parts. Furthermore, not repeating Conrad's Kurtz's famous words at this point seems to imply that there are plenty of other characters in this dystopian world who had to witness their own horrors, and the reader has received their narration through their own voices, which renders any

---

[9] One of Findley's earlier novels is called *Famous Last Words* (1981). In that text, he focuses on the importance of written testimony for future generations and for the transmission of historical knowledge in the context and aftermath of the Second World War.

mediation through Kurtz unnecessary.[10] Finally, the ghostly presence of this intertextual quote raises the question of which horrors are alluded to in this novel, and what heart of darkness these characters have encountered. The almost clichéd "abyss" of the human psyche that is exposed at the Parkin Institute (less so in mental illnesses than in abusive power games) accounts for many of the horrors, but the dystopian world in which people no longer recognize when the horrors of history repeat themselves – this seems to be the true darkness, the one cloaked in the name of progress, analogous to the colonial endeavours described by Conrad.

On the very last pages, we return to the key reader figure, Lilah, who notices that Kurtz, after his death in her world, has returned into her copy of *Heart of Darkness*. As she goes back to her medication, the novel ends with her solitary reflection, "*who would believe it?* – no one. [. . .] *It's only a book*, they would say. *That's all it is. A story. Just a story*" (510). As Lilah closes her book, we notice that we, too, are on the final page of our book, and the mise-en-abyme of the two paralleled acts of reading makes us reflect upon Lilah's questions on a second level. Brydon reads this as unmistakably a final call to us readers: "The novel's ending challenges its readers to move beyond the frame, connecting the text we have just read back to the world in which we live" (57). These connections between the novel(s) and our real world are often established and made visible via intertextual links, and engaging with them is important to avoid repeating the horrors of history. Yet what it takes is the willingness to perceive the value of literature beyond entertainment and cultural capital, and to foster empathy and response-ability, to enter the realm where literature can make voices heard. Therefore, *Headhunter*, if it manages to create a community of responsible listeners and responders, is far more than "just a story."

---

[10] To be precise, the words are not entirely suppressed, but can be found throughout *Headhunter*. As demonstrated above, the opening of the novel already shows us a "horror-stricken" Lilah (3), and Kurtz is introduced as the "horror-meister" (6).

References

Barthes, Roland. *S/Z*. Trans. Richard Miller. Oxford: Blackwell, 1996.
"bounty-hunter, *n.*" *OED Online*. Oxford University Press. Accessed on 6 January 2017.
Bradbury, Ray. *Fahrenheit 451*. London: Harper Voyager, 2008.
Brydon, Diana. "Intertextuality in Timothy Findley's *Headhunter*." *Journal of Canadian Studies* 33.4 (1998/99): 53-62.
Child, Brenda J. "Boarding Schools." *Encyclopedia of North American Indians*. Ed. Frederick E. Hoxie. New York: Houghton Mifflin, 1996. 78-80.
Collins, Anne. *In the Sleep Room: The Story of the CIA Brainwashing Experiments in Canada*. Toronto: Lester and Orpen Dennys, 1988.
Conrad, Joseph. *Heart of Darkness and Other Tales*. Oxford: Oxford University Press, 2002.
Culler, Jonathan. *The Pursuit of Signs: Semiotics, Literature, Deconstruction*. London: Routledge and Kegan Paul, 1981.
Daly, Mary. *Gyn/Ecology: The Metaethics of Radical Feminism*. London: The Women's Press, 1979.
Findley, Timothy. *Headhunter*. Toronto: Harper Perennial, 1999.
Fish, Stanley. *Is There a Text in This Class? The Authority of Interpretive Communities*. Cambridge: Harvard University Press, 1980.
Fitzgerald, F. Scott. *The Great Gatsby*. Introd. Tony Tanner. London: Penguin, 1990.
Foucault, Michel. *The Will to Knowledge. The History of Sexuality Vol. 1*. 1976. Trans. Robert Hurley. London: Penguin Books, 1998.
Genette, Gérard. *Narrative Discourse Revisited*. Trans. Jane E. Lewin. New York: Cornell University Press, 1988.
"headhunter, *n.*" *OED Online*. Oxford University Press. Accessed on 6 January 2017.
"headhunting, *n.*" *OED Online*. Oxford University Press. Accessed on 6 January 2017.
Herman, Judith Lewis. *Trauma and Recovery*. New York: Basic Books, 1997.
Holquist, Michael. *Dialogism: Bakhtin and his World*. London: Routledge, 1990.
Iser, Wolfgang. *The Act of Reading: A Theory of Aesthetic Response*. Baltimore: Johns Hopkins University Press, 1978.
Keen, Suzanne. *Empathy and the Novel*. Oxford: Oxford University Press, 2007.

Kirmayer, Laurence J. "Toward a Medicine of the Imagination." *New Literary History* 37.3 (2006): 583-605.

Krishnan, Armin. *Military Neuroscience and the Coming Age of Neurowarfare.* New York: Routledge, 2017.

Lupton, Deborah. *Medicine as Culture: Illness, Disease and the Body.* London: Sage Publications, 2012.

May, Carl. "Individual Care? Power and Subjectivity in Therapeutic Relationships." *Sociology* 26.4 (1992): 589-602.

McCoy, Alfred. *A Question of Torture: CIA Interrogation, from the Cold War to the War on Terror.* New York: Owl Books, 2006.

McGill Daily. "MK-ULTRAViolence: Or, how McGill pioneered psychological torture." 6 September 2012. <http://www.mcgilldaily.com/2012/09/mk-ultraviolence/>. Accessed on 7 January 2017.

Morrison, Toni. "Unspeakable Things Unspoken: The Afro-American Presence in American Literature." *Michigan Quarterly Review* 28.1 (1989) 1-34.

———. *Playing in the Dark: Whiteness and the Literary Imagination.* New York: Vintage, 1993.

Nabokov, Vladimir. *Lolita.* New York: Vintage International, 1997.

Rippl, Gabriele and Julia Straub. "Zentrum und Peripherie: Kanon und Macht (Gender, Race, Postcolonialism)." *Handbuch Kanon und Wertung.* Ed. Gabriele Rippl and Simone Winko. Stuttgart: J. B. Metzler, 2013. 110-19.

Shelley, Mary. *Frankenstein.* Second Norton Critical Edition. Ed. J. Paul Hunter. New York: Norton, 2012.

Weinstein, Harvey. *Father, Son, and CIA.* Toronto: James Lorimer, 1988.

"We're not fighting for *the people* anymore... We're just *fighting*." US-American Superhero Comics Between Criticisms of Community and Critical Communities

Thomas Nehrlich and Joanna Nowotny

From its creation in the late 1930s onwards, the figure of the superhero has become increasingly ambiguous and problematic. Especially in two crucial periods of recent history – the height of the Cold War in the 1980s as well as after 9/11 – superheroes are presented as precarious, dubious characters that have lost the ability to fulfill traditional heroic functions such as conveying social norms and moral values, and regulating the use of violence. To reinforce their social relevance and to reestablish their bond with the (usually US-American) community, modern superhero narratives focus on the very relationships between superheroes and the population. Seminal publications of the genre such as Alan Moore's *Watchmen* (1986/87), Frank Miller's *The Dark Knight Returns* (1986) and Mark Millar's *Civil War* (2006/07) open up a discussion of what heroism means and how it relates to "ordinary" people. In them, the question arises if superheroes are even capable of speaking for their communities. Analyzing the relationship between superheroes and their communities contributes to understanding how superhero narratives have become a hugely influential medium of social debate.

The popularity of the figure of the superhero has reached new heights with the success of Marvel's and DC's movie and TV franchises in recent years. This success bears testimony to the ongoing attempts of the comics industry to make their products as relatable as possible for as many people as possible. Originally, superhero comics sought to address younger readers,[1] as evidenced by the frequent presence of a young sidekick that served as a figure of identification for the intended audiences in many of the famous early stories – Batman and Robin would be the most known example. Early stories often presented a rather simplistic moral tale and plain power fantasies to their young readers. At the genre's inception during the 1930s through the 1950s, female characters,[2] non-white ethnicities, and members of the lower class were marginalized or appeared mostly in the roles of antagonists.[3]

In order to diversify their stories' appeal and to address different communities, the publishers have taken a number of measures: Since the 1960s and 1970s, the comics' ethnic diversity has been increased by the presence of black and Native American superheroes like The Falcon (first appearance in 1969) and Thunderbird (first appearance in 1975). More recently, religious diversity has been promoted, for example, through the inclusion of Muslim characters: Since 2013, Pakistani-American Kamala Khan has been appearing as Miss Marvel, wearing a modified burkini as her costume. Also in more recent years, LGBT themes have been addressed for example through same-sex superhero couples.[4] Such measures have made the diegetic communities more diverse, and, accordingly, superhero comics have gathered a large and rather pluralistic audience of committed aficionados.[5] Superhero fandom is characterized by a strong dedication to the source material and a

---

[1] Dittmer remarks that apart from having a readership mostly made up of "preadolescent male[s]," superhero comics, during World War II, were also sent overseas as entertainment for the troops. But "as the medium has aged, so has its readership," with older fans and collectors gaining prominence at the latest in the 1980s (Dittmer 4-5).

[2] The exception would be Wonder Woman (introduced in 1941), a character that was used specifically to target female audiences and encourage emancipation (Daniels 22-23 et passim).

[3] For the racial aspects, cf. e.g., Munson; C. Scott.

[4] This list does not imply that all diversity in comic books is necessarily "progressive," when studied in detail. To give an example: LGBT themes have also been addressed in a problematic manner, e.g., when DC comics introduced the superhero Extraño ("the strange one") in *New Guardians* 1988, a homosexual Peruvian mage in brightly-colored robes who often referred to himself as a "witch" and was HIV-positive, a perpetuation of several of the most common prejudices against gay men. Extraño has been revived recently in an obvious attempt to reinvent the character in a manner less damaging to the LGBT cause (*Midnighter and Apollo* 1, 2016).

[5] As evidenced, for example, by online communities such as worldofblackheroes.com, carol-corps.wikia.org and gayleague.com.

collectivizing cohesion within the fan community, as evidenced by numerous fanzines, wikis, comic conferences, and cosplay practices.

With those real-world communities and the issue of representation in mind, the question arises what kinds of communities are relevant within the genre and how exactly those communities and the superheroes' interactions with them are depicted. As Miczo along with others has noted, an essential characteristic of superheroism is the capacity of the heroes to act in concert with one another (Miczo 1 et passim). These types of superhero communities are evident in a number of successful superhero teams, such as The Justice League (DC) or The Avengers (Marvel). However, the superheroes also interact with another kind of community, namely, the (often US-American) ordinary population. This interaction takes place in what Miczo calls "the public sphere" (ibid. xi et passim). Here, the superhero acts as a special kind of public servant, serving the "common good."[6] Naturally, however, there are "rival definitions of this good that, from time to time, cause friction within the superhero community" (ibid. 22). We would argue that such frictions, rather than being limited to the superhero community, also extend to the "public sphere": When superheroes and ordinary people disagree about their mutual rights and duties, their relationship, too, becomes problematic.

Our essay traces these two types of precarious relationships in seminal examples of the genre. By doing so, we aim to show that through notions of superheroism, communal values such as civil rights, security, and personal liberties are debated. Superheroes can be construed as representatives of ideological positions within this ethical debate about how human society should be organized.[7] However, in the provocative examples of the genre we have chosen for analysis, it becomes less than clear-cut how such ideological positions relate to real-world politics and ethics, and whether their representatives, the superheroes, in fact speak on behalf, or even to the benefit, of the ordinary people – within the narratives and beyond.

---

[6] This is not necessarily a specificity of superheroism but rather a common trait of heroic narratives, such as the so-called American monomyth (cf. Dittmer 11).
[7] Cf. Pellitteri.

The Early Days: Superheroes as Protectors and Crime Fighters

Ever since Superman's first appearance in a comic book in 1938, superheroes have challenged society's relationship with them. By their sheer extraordinariness, they are their readers' opposite by definition. Their superpowers make them outsiders, yet they often defend the social status quo. Simultaneously embodying and transgressing the law, they clash with the official institutions of the USA, for example, while still representing truly "American" values. This ambiguity has led to superheroes being used for nationalistic purposes such as fighting Hitler and advocating American military mobilization during World War II. For example, they were used to advertise war stamps and bonds, using slogans such as "Wonder Woman says – do your duty for Uncle Sam by buying U.S [sic] savings stamps and bonds!" (*Sensation Comics* 8, 1942).

Ditschke and Anhut argue that, essentially, there are two classical models of superheroes with slightly different approaches towards society (150-56). On the one hand, superheroes act as protectors of the innocents, save lives, and defend good against evil, as do the classical versions of Superman, Captain America, and the Flash. On the other hand, they act as crime fighters, targeting criminals and villains, which is true for many iterations of Batman and Daredevil. These different intentions can be seen, for instance, in the visual rhetoric of the superheroes' costume design, with Superman's bright colors and unmasked face likening him to a police officer while Batman's dark and gadget-rigged suit resembles the gear of counterterrorism units (e.g., in Christopher Nolan's recent movie adaptations). Aside from their differing methods, both models convey the same view of the relationship between superheroes and society, namely, a stable, affirmative, and unquestioned bond. This is what Peter Coogan, in his famous definition of the superhero, refers to as the "selfless, pro-social mission" (21) that is a crucial quality of superheroes. As a reward, the superhero is venerated by the community. In other words, altruism, solidarity, and communality as well as admiration and gratitude are the ideological foundations of the classical superhero in the so-called Golden Age of the genre, from the late 1930s until after World War II.

However, this positive depiction of the relationship between superhero and society has not remained uncontested. Since the 1950s, as the immediate military justification for their existence had faded away, superheroes have been criticized from political, legal, religious, educational, and psychological points of view. For instance, superhero comics have been accused of weakening the authority of the government and disrespecting the government's monopoly on violence and the use of force. The 1954 anti-comics study *Seduction of the Innocent* by the psychiatrist Fredric Wertham is the best-known example of such critique, claiming that different comic genres such as horror and superhero comics propagate sexual deviance and cause juvenile delinquency. As a result, the comics industry established the Comics Code Authority, a system of self-censorship designed to avoid controversial content.

Such tensions that question the beneficial role of superheroes have fueled stories within the genre itself that focus on the relationship between superheroes, the people, and the government. The question these comics ask is how the bond between superhero and the community of ordinary people is affected and regulated by the state. As a matter of fact, some of the most acclaimed superhero comics since the 1960s have featured a government's attempt to limit the powers of the superheroes, forcing them to cooperate or to become outlaws, excluded from their communities. Essentially, these are stories about the conflict between control, registration, and bureaucracy on the one hand, and freedom, nonconformity, privacy on the other; they deal with the tensions between the individual's, the community's, and the state's interests.[8] This turns superhero comics into an inherently political genre: What is at stake is nothing less than how US-America, the country in which the majority of superhero comics are set, defines itself and the rights of its citizens.

The Problematization of the Superhero: Frank Miller and Alan Moore

In the 1980s, two works of great influence were published that were particularly self-reflective with regard to the problematic triad of superhero, community and state: Frank Miller's *The Dark Knight Returns* (1986) and Alan Moore's *Watchmen* (1986/87). They contributed to what was widely seen as a corruption of the figure of the superhero, a tendency – adopted in many other comics of the era – towards presenting the characters as borderline psychopathic vigilantes or power-hungry narcissists. This destruction of innocence has led to the 1980s being considered the "dark and gritty" age of superhero comics.

---

[8] For a Derridean reading of the political implications of superhero comics see Curtis 212-15.

Miller's comic presents us with an aged Batman who retired ten years before the beginning of the story, deliberately disrupting his bond with the community. His "return to duty" is provoked by a brutal criminal organization that he then manages to defeat. Instead of securing and repacifying the city, however, his renewed presence as a masked vigilante becomes itself the cause of intensified criminal activity.[9] Villains such as his archenemy, the Joker, who had long been dormant, resurface and terrorize the population. The fact that the resurgence of crime coincides with the return of the hero implies that superheroes might not be a solution, but rather part of the problem. What legitimates the presence of superheroes if their very existence causes the threats they claim to fight in the name of the community?

Later in the story, during a nuclear crisis between the USA and the Soviet Union, Batman, by acting as a local peacekeeper, comes into conflict with the US government. The president himself, easily identifiable as a caricature of Ronald Reagan, sees his authority challenged and sends the police after Batman, declaring him an outlaw and forcing him to fight the police and the very people he tried to protect. Ultimately, the president orders Superman, who acts as a state official and as a pawn of the government, to dispose of Batman. In the final fight, Batman, through the use of kryptonite, seems to have the upper hand against Superman, but is suddenly stopped and nearly killed by a heart attack. In one of the last panels, the picture of a beaten up Superman comforting an agonizing Batman demonstrates the senselessness and absurdity of superheroes forced to fight each other for political purposes. *The Dark Knight Returns* was one of the first comics to drastically depict violent conflicts between fellow superheroes instead of showing how their ability to set aside differences is a major factor in their heroism. In so doing, it calls into question the superheroes' beneficial role and their value for the community of ordinary people.

Moore's *Watchmen* raises similarly provocative questions: Do extraordinary individuals have the right to elevate themselves above the law and supposedly defend the US-American communities? Or should superheroes be state-supervised because the population needs to be protected from them? Who watches the watchmen?[10] To problematize the legal, ethical, political, and ideological foundation of our community with superheroes, *Watchmen* confronts us with a number of superheroes

---

[9] For a discussion of the intricate politics and ethics of Batman's vigilantism in *The Dark Knight Returns* see DuBose 919-23.

[10] Cf. Hughes 546-48, 556.

who challenge the classical patterns of superheroism.[11] Rorschach is the only member of a former superhero group who, once the government has banned vigilantism, keeps on with his activities in secret. His stubbornness is mixed with pessimism and cruelty. In his view, mankind is, in essence, evil. Dr. Manhattan, who has gained god-like powers in a nuclear accident, prefers to live on Mars and distances himself from earthly matters and almost all human beings. Night Owl tries to remedy his impotence by engaging in a superhero costume fetish; his superheroic identity becomes the outlet of a crisis of masculinity instead of a sign of altruism. And Ozymandias kills millions in his attempt to fake an alien invasion and to unite the world against an external enemy.

The common denominator of all these characters, who can be construed as perversions or escalations of classical superheroes, is their antisocial behavior. At the height of the Cold War, Alan Moore uses them as a means to deconstruct the image of the shining superhero and to demonstrate the detrimental effects of both state control and unrestrained heroic politics.

It is part of Moore's astute irony that he eventually has Ozymandias's plan work, despite, or precisely because of, its immorality and inhumanity. Rorschach, the only superhero to oppose Ozymandias, is silenced and killed by Dr. Manhattan. Faced with an allegedly extraterrestrial threat, the USA and the Soviet Union manage to overcome their antagonism; the Cold War ends. At the very end of the story, however, Rorschach's notebook, the only proof of the superhero conspiracy, falls into the hands of an inexperienced civilian journalist. The ultimate moral decision lies with a character that is not part of the community of superheroes. It remains unclear whether the journalist grasps the significance of the notebook and will make its contents public. Thus, instead of presenting them with a ready-made morality, *Watchmen* opens a dialogue with the readers and requests them to make up their own minds. It asks them whether they would want the superheroes to be exposed and potentially punished, or whether they would want the greater good – world peace – and the bond between the superheroes and the people to be preserved at all costs. If they were in the shoes of that ordinary journalist, what would they do?

---

[11] Pellitteri explains in great detail which superhero in *Watchmen* represents which ideology (cf. Pellitteri 85-88).

Real-life Heroism and Corrective Communities: Superheroes after 9/11

Some 15 years later, after the terrorist attacks of 9/11, superheroes were again used to directly comment on political developments. As in the 1980s, the depiction and symbolic value of superheroes remain profoundly ambivalent. On the one hand, they are assimilated to the "ordinary man" in positive terms, representing the heroic in all Americans and thereby reinforcing the community's bond with them. On the other hand, they are used to illustrate the dangerous clash between the individual and the state in an age of increasing surveillance and preemptive strikes against perceived threats to the nation.

The attacks on the World Trade Center saw a kind of "real-life American heroism" celebrated across the media. Both Marvel and DC produced comic books featuring the "heroes" of 9/11, for example by showing the Avengers standing alongside the firefighters and other first responders and rescue workers that were on duty on Ground Zero.[12] Marvel published two comic books in immediate reaction to the attack; both were benefit products and financially very successful.[13] The first one was called *Heroes* and was published in December 2001 with *The world's greatest superhero creators honor the world's greatest heroes* printed on the cover as a subtitle; the second one followed in February 2002 and was entitled *A Moment of Silence*. The first volume especially featured contributions from a multitude of creators, some of whom had a reputation of being rebellious and of taking an ironic or subversive stance towards comic books, like Alan Moore. Others, like Neal Adams, had not even primarily been associated with Marvel previously, which bears testimony to the unifying quality the events of 9/11 had within the comics industry.

A prominent figure in *Heroes* is Captain America, who represents the USA unlike any other Marvel character. He is frequently shown alongside and somewhat on par with the rescue personnel, the NYPD and the FDNY. In an artwork by Rob Haynes, Tim Townsend, and David Self, a policeman and a fireman are shown giving comfort to a weeping, overwhelmed Captain America and encouraging him to go on. As this scene shows, *Heroes* has a simple premise, as does *A Moment of Silence*. Both books try to establish that heroes akin to or even superior to the super-

---

[12] C. Scott (336-37) compared the propaganda in comic books after 9/11 with that during World War II and discussed the DC and Marvel tributes.

[13] Furthermore, *Amazing Spider-Man* 2:36 (2001), with its entirely black cover, also dealt with the events of 9/11.

heroes exist in the real world, thereby inverting the classical roles of the superhero and the community. This assertion comes with the idea that it is necessary to transition from adolescence to adulthood, a phase in which one comes to realize what responsibility in the real world entails (Diekmann). Paradoxically, growing up seems to require one to leave the superheroes of fiction behind, to overcome them, a point which seems rather out of place in a superhero comic, of all things. Marvel's 9/11 comics seem to advocate the superfluousness of fictional heroes for adults by selling them a comic book featuring those very fictional heroes.

However, the real-life heroism that is celebrated both in *A Moment of Silence* and in *Heroes* is not that different from what is advocated in many superhero comics. It is a concept of heroism that relies on the immediate deed, on action in the face of calamity and in the name of a community that gets attacked from without. In *A Moment of Silence*, this notion is put into practice through the almost complete absence of text.[14] This comic book thereby becomes a manifesto against the inaction of people that are more concerned with medially spreading their experiences than with actively taking part in them, as Bill Jemas writes. Action takes precedence to speech, which is framed as escapist and "meaningless":

> When hell hit the World Trade Center, most of us stood around talking – making phone calls, writing e-mails and, generally, filling in that hole in our bellies with meaningless chatter. But in the face of extreme danger, thousands of New York firefighters, police officers and rescue workers burst onto the scene. These men and women saved thousands of lives and many sacrificed their own. "Judge people by what they do, not by what they say". That's what I learned from my mother and my father; that is what I teach my children, but I did not truly know what that meant until this past September. (Jemas, Bagley, and Hanna n. pag.)

While many 9/11 comic books dealt with this new kind of American heroism and focused on the solidarity of the US-American community across ethnicities and religions, with the characters often calling "for tolerance of ethnic groups that lived in the United States, especially Arab-Americans" (C. Scott 336), the other side of the coin was just as present in superhero comics. The "War on Terror" slipped into super-

---

[14] Some scholars, like Robert C. Harvey, would go as far as to hold that images *and* text are essential in order for a cultural artefact to be classified as a "comic." Such a definition would make the lack of text in a publication within the superhero comic genre even more striking. For an overview of the debate around the definition of comics as a medium, see Meskin.

hero stories almost as soon as it was declared.[15] A prime example of comics partaking in and thereby also shaping this political discourse is *Civil War*, the 7-issue comic event Marvel published in 2006/2007, written by Mark Millar and penciled by Steve McNiven.[16] It implicitly deals with the political situation in the USA post 9/11 and specifically with the *USA PATRIOT ACT* that was passed immediately after the terrorist attacks and that aimed to enhance "domestic security against terrorism," to "deter and punish terrorist acts in the United States and around the world," and to remove "obstacles to investigating terrorism."[17] Naturally, the debate about this act dealt with questions of civil rights and privacy (Veloso and Bateman 428-29).

Civil War reflects on this debate. It poses some fundamental political and philosophical questions by making the issue personal for its two protagonists, Captain America and Iron Man. A "Superhero Registration Act" (SHRA) gets approved by Congress after a catastrophe caused by a young, untrained superhero claims the life of many innocents, mainly children. Iron Man aka Tony Stark decides to support the Act, obliging the costumed heroes to expose their identities to the government. His argumentation in favor of the Act centers on the responsibilities superheroes have for their communities – just like policemen, they should not be allowed to operate outside of jurisdiction. Iron Man's decision in favor of accountability pits him against Captain America aka Steve Rogers, who insists on the freedom of the individual and criticizes the infringement of privacy. A gulf opens up between the 'real' American values that the patriotically named Captain America upholds and potentially corrupt institutions betraying them. In his opinion, the state institutions do not properly represent the American communities anymore; instead, the superheroes do, protecting all Americans to the best of their abilities even if they have to go against official US-American law. After a clash with some government officials, the Captain goes underground and proceeds to fight the Act illegally.

Both known and respected figures in the superhero community, Iron Man and Captain America quickly gather a number of followers, respectively. The split in the superhero community becomes bigger as both fractions resort to increasingly dubious, even evil methods, such as

---

[15] For a reading of the superhero movies *Batman Begins* and *V for Vendetta* as implicitly participating in a post-9/11 discourse, see Hassler-Forest.

[16] A whole edited volume dealing with the event from a critical perspective has just been published: Scott, *Marvel Comics' Civil War and the Age of Terror*.

[17] Cf. USA PATRIOT ACT.

enlisting known villains to fight in their ranks. When the fight escalates into a full-blown war in the middle of New York, Rogers gets the opportunity to deliver a killing blow to a defeated Stark, who asks his friend-turned-enemy to *"finish* it." However, a group of civilians holds him back, which prompts the Captain to question his actions and vocalize the tensions inherent in the relationship between the superheroes and their community: "We're not fighting for *the people* anymore . . . We're just *fighting*" (*Civil War* 7, 2007). In stark contrast to the image found in *Heroes* of Captain America receiving comfort from rescue workers, the panels from *Civil War*, published a mere few years later, feature policemen and firefighters confronting Captain America. The group of citizens is obviously intended to represent modern US-American society as a whole, as it is, for instance, racially diverse, featuring white persons, African Americans, and a man who seems to be of Asian ancestry. Accordingly, the US-American community here clearly stands in opposition to the superhero named after his nation.[18] The very rescue workers that were shown to represent a higher brand of heroism for their community in the comics explicitly dealing with 9/11 step in to stop the superhero from making a grave mistake. Thus, the heroism of the superhero is called into question: Not only are 'normal' citizens shown to be potentially equally heroic, as in the immediate post-9/11 comics, but in addition they act as a moral corrective to the superheroes in the *Civil War* event. Hence the classical roles of superhero narratives are inverted, the superheroes cease to be the morally superior guides and protectors of an admiring society; rather, the "people" emancipate themselves from the superheroes. The superheroes themselves are endangering their own communities by "just fighting," fighting each other rather than criminals and villains. Hence, superheroes fail at fulfilling their social function, which includes representing moral values and advocating the rights of their communities.

The conflict in *Civil War*, while political, is also elevated to a level of moral philosophy. Formulated in such a way, two outlooks on life and ethical behavior clash, Captain America's deontology insisting on the intrinsic moral value of certain acts, and Iron Man's utilitarianism, holding that in a climate of fear and distrust people have a right to expect accountability.[19] This philosophical underpinning waters down the po-

---

[18] This choice of side characters is explicitly noted in the script to the series; see *Civil War: Script Book* 7, 19: "rescue workers [medics, firefighters, cops, etc.] all grabbing Cap and pulling him back off Tony."

[19] In tie-ins to the main series, the fact that Stark is choosing the "lesser evil" is driven home in particularly obvious terms, as it is revealed that he was aware of alternative

litical thrust of the series, as it masks a concrete political issue in general terms where no "right" or "wrong" can be determined. In fact, the tag used for the event all along – "Whose side are you on?" – implies that there is no "right" side to choose. Befitting the emotional tone of the advertisements and the story itself, the event was hotly debated among readers, reviewers, and, apparently, the creators themselves.[20]

Civil War follows the typical structure of newer Marvel event books, a structure consisting of a main series written by one writer, tie-ins into other series of the Marvelverse, and some one-shots or mini-series only published as part of the event. All in all, it consists of more than 100 comic books. If one were to analyze in detail the ways the narrative is built and framed in the entire event, it would become obvious that even basic tenets such as what the Superhero Registration Act precisely entails are not consistently depicted – in fact, not even the name of the Act remains the same throughout.[21] In some comics the Act requires the heroes to give up their identities to the government and undergo frequent testing or training of their superpowers, while in others it is implied that they actually have to make their identities public. In some comics, the refusal to sign the Act would lead to legal persecution, while in others the heroes in question would be locked away without a trial or any regular legal procedure until they agree to sign, becoming "legal nonentities" at the mercy of the state (cf. *Amazing Spider-Man* 535).[22] Such inconsistencies[23] lead to a different image of each side depending on what parts of the event one has read. Both certain parts of the read-

---

plans for the superhero community which would have involved locking up its members to experiment on their augmented biologies (*Civil War: Casualties of War*).

[20] For example, several remarks by Millar and others in the *Civil War: Script Book* insinuate such conflicts, see e.g., editor Tom Brevoort's quote about the depiction of Stark in tie-in issues (No. 4, page 6) or Millar's quote about issue 6, page 11, where he contends that the writers of the tie-in books "demonized" some characters.

[21] See e.g., the "Superhero Registration Act" in *New Avengers: Illuminati* 0. The name changes to the "Superhuman Registration Act" in *New Avengers* 1:22 although both are written by the same writer, Brian Michael Bendis – a point also made by Davidson (12-13).

[22] Miczo deals with the Spider-Man tie-ins that describe *prison 42* – designated holding place for heroes convicted under the SHRA – as non-American soil. In Stark's words: "American laws don't touch here. [. . .] Once non-registrants come here, they're legal nonentities." In Miczo's eyes, those issues show the "critical mistake of the pro-registration side" that "forfeit[s] the moral high ground" they would otherwise possess (Miczo 32-33).

[23] These and other problems with the depiction of the SHRA are also highlighted by Davidson, who holds that such inconsistencies, along with the legal illogic of the proposed act, contributed to the very mixed reception of the event; cf. Davidson 11-25.

ership[24] as well as some of the creators seem to have responded very negatively to Iron Man's side in the conflict,[25] which in real-life terms would be a poorly disguised stand-in for the much debated Bush administration and its USA PATRIOT ACT infringing on the privacy of the ordinary citizens. Such readings construe the pro-registration side as the "evil" that needs to be vanquished in the series and, to put it in extreme terms, by extension qualify the actions of the US government after 9/11 as villainous.

Veloso and Bateman have analyzed the main series of *Civil War*, the seven issues written by Mark Millar and drawn by Steve McNiven, and come to a very different conclusion. While they do emphasize that there seems to be no clear separation of right and wrong at the beginning of the story, they hold that this changes as the series progresses. They argue that the beginning of the story allows both sides to have valid arguments, presumably a strategy to augment the potential economic success of the book: presenting both points of view as valid means ensuring a larger audience. Furthermore, in Veloso's and Bateman's eyes, refraining from moral judgments at the outset of *Civil War* allows the writers to potentially change people's minds by the end of the story (Veloso and Bateman 434). But by the end, Veloso and Bateman claim that the event does present a clear "right" after all, and it lies with the winner of the war. According to the researchers, the end is entirely positive: Captain America has surrendered and Tony Stark is shown at sunset, looking directly at the reader, a smile on his lips as he says: "the best is yet to come" (*Civil War* 7, 2007). They claim:

> What is discursively constructed here, therefore, is that when different groups oppose each other against the Registration Act (as the allegory of the PATRIOT Act), they lose their focus on what is the most important thing: fighting against terrorism. [. . .] The system is not perfect, there are collateral damages, to use the military term, but it is necessary and the system is to be trusted. Thus, criticism is offered only to, in the end, save the Government, which then emerges from the narrative stronger and clearly necessary for maintaining order and public safety. (Veloso and Bateman 439)

---

[24] Of course, such things are difficult to measure, but Tony Stark seems to have been seen as the villain in the story by many readers. This certainly contributed to the fact that Marvel tried to "redeem" him in the years after the event, finally having him wipe the memories of his actions during *Civil War* from his mind to start anew.

[25] See also Miczo (34), who, however, does not establish a connection between those reactions and the clear political subtext of the event at the time of its publication.

To capture the essence of the argument: According to Veloso and Bateman, the event ends up favoring Iron Man's side and, by extension, presenting the Bush administration as justified and as capable of meeting the needs of the US-American people.

While Veloso and Bateman's analysis of the multimodal construction of meaning in the *Civil War* series is very thorough and also impressive in its attention to the formal aspects of the comic, this conclusion could be called into question. The last panels of the comic can for example just as well be construed as ironic, especially in the light of Iron Man's questionable actions in the preceding war. "The best is yet to come," then, might not be a comforting final chord but a disharmonious announcement of ever more conflict or ever more dubious actions on the part of the superheroes elevating themselves above their communities.
Furthermore, Veloso and Bateman deliberately only focus on the 7 issues of the main series, leaving out both the tie-ins and one-shots linked to the event and the wider macro-narrative at play in the Marvel universe. For over a decade, the serial storytelling in Marvel comics has been characterized by a very developed macro structure, where events tie together and often have consequences for the world state. Taking into account both the tie-ins, in which Iron Man's side is at times presented in exceedingly negative terms,[26] and above all the wider narrative context in which the *Civil War* event stands, the "message" and with it the identification of what side is wrong becomes much less clear-cut than Veloso and Bateman ultimately claim.

At the end of *Civil War*, Stark becomes head of the global peacekeeping organization S.H.I.E.L.D., which leads Veloso and Bateman to conclude that 'all is well' in government (despite the fact that it is, by the way, not entirely clear what S.H.I.E.L.D.'s legal status is – as an international organization, it is not supposed to be directly linked to the US government).[27] However, the next few events Marvel has published radically destroy this notion of the "good" political leaders or the trustworthy government. First, there is *World War Hulk*, which is partly caused by Stark and other pro-registration advocates like Reed Richards and wreaks havoc in New York. This catastrophe is followed by *Secret Invasion* (2008). If *Civil War* depicts an inner instead of an outer enemy

---

[26] For example in the Spider-Man tie-ins (*Amazing Spider-Man* 1:529-38) or the *War Crimes* one-shot.

[27] The exact status of the "global peacekeeping organization" S.H.I.E.L.D. is unclear (or rather contradictory) in the comics, but in *Civil War* the Director, Maria Hill, clearly speaks on behalf of "the American people" (*Civil War* 1, 2006). See also Davidson 13-14.

that seeds unrest in the country, *Secret Invasion* deals with this topic even more explicitly by having aliens in disguise – the so-called Skrulls – invade the USA and its governmental institutions, destroying the nation from within. Naturally, humanity manages to prevail, but at a high price, with countless casualties and damages all over the world. Norman Osborn, the known supervillain Green Goblin, rises to power in Stark's stead, dismantles S.H.I.E.L.D., and ushers in a reign of terror known as *Dark Reign* that lasts for several years both within the fictional Marvelverse and in Marvel's actual comics output during the late 2000s, forcing most of the known heroes into hiding.

Taking the wider narrative context of the *Civil War* event into account is one way of dismantling a reading of the event as a straightforward defense of the political status quo in the USA post 9/11. Another interpretative strategy relies on questioning how seamlessly and clearly the political metaphor of the USA PATRIOT ACT can be applied to the comic book(s). As noted, most political readings of the *Civil War* event identify the Iron Man's pro-registration side with the Bush administration and presume that the readers would identify with the anti-registration heroes as stand-ins for the members of the US-American communities whose civil liberties are threatened. However, such readings completely ignore the third party involved in the argument the narrative presents: the ordinary citizens threatened by the unregulated use of violence by the superheroes and antagonized by their refusal to be held accountable. These citizens come to the forefront in the final battle; they interject before Captain America can deal the final blow to a defeated Stark, and ostensibly defend the figurehead of the pro-registration heroes (*"Get the hell away from him!"*, *Civil War* 7, 2007).

Dittmer has rightfully noted how Captain America "discursively frames the Superhero Registration Act in terms of government control and individual liberty – the same terms that the US government uses to describe its own need to escape the bounds of international society" in the "War on Terror," disregarding international law (Dittmer 13-14). Hence, it is just as plausible to read Captain America and the anti-registration heroes as analogues for the Bush administration, if one so desires, as they break the law ostensibly to protect the ordinary citizens. This reveals how paradoxical the set-up of the *Civil War* comic books is from the very beginning with regards to the political metaphors at play: Captain America violently defends the right of other *superheroes* to stand above the law. Still, his position is usually read as a metaphor for the ordinary citizens who defend their civil liberties against an overreaching government. Simultaneously, Iron Man pledges to hold superheroes responsible for their actions, to comply with the "will of the people," and to make sure that a group of enhanced individuals does not have a monopoly of force.[28] And still, his side is usually identified with the hegemonic use of power by a government stripping its citizens of their democratic rights.

Why the sympathies of readers and critics alike seem to have been so clearly with the anti-registration heroes (a fact also noted by Dittmer 13) is hard to say. Using the "nationalist superhero" (Dittmer) Captain America as the leader of the rebellious superheroes certainly contributed to an exceedingly apologetic view of their actions and ideals. Furthermore, the often unnamed members of the US-American communities that Iron Man's side purports to speak for do not typically seem to invite the readers' sympathies within the conventions of the superhero comic genre (see also Dittmer 13). The prime figures of identification within the comics genre are usually the superheroes themselves, with "ordinary people" relegated to the roles of bystanders and side characters. However, *Civil War* does give those communities a voice and above all a visual and narrative presence:

> CAPTAIN AMERICA: Let me *go*! Please, I don't want to *hurt* you ...
> UNNAMED CITIZEN 1: Don't want to *hurt* us? Are you trying to be *funny*?
> UNNAMED CITIZEN 2: It's a little late for that, man!
> [...]
> CAPTAIN AMERICA: Oh my God.
> FALCON: What's wrong?
> CAPTAIN AMERICA: They're *right*. We're not fighting for *the people* anymore, Falcon ... *Look* at us. We're just *fighting*.
> (*Civil War* 7, 2007)

Civil War shows a community of superheroes at odds with one another, which disrupts the relationship between the superheroes, the state, and the ordinary "people." When superheroes assume stately power, like Iron Man after *Civil War*, catastrophe ensues; the same goes for situations in which the state tries to interfere with the relationship between the superheroes and their communities, as seen in *Watchmen* and *The Dark Knight Returns*. In such cases, only the community of ordinary people seems to be able to act as a moral corrective to the superheroes gone

---

[28] Accordingly, Iron Man's position could be seen as more democratic according to Miczo, who holds that Civil War mirrors a debate from the early days of the US-American republic. Iron Man would stand on the side of "actual representation," while Captain America propagates "virtual representation" (Miczo 28-29).

wild. However, this radically calls into question the superheroes' ability to act as representatives for their communities. Hence, modern superhero comics discuss the benefits and limits of heroism, and the social relevance of the values it conveys. They engage in a dialogue with their readers, not least of all by representing real-world communities within the narratives. And they confront them with debatable concepts of communal representation, government, civil rights, and individualism, and even with the question of why they read superhero comics in the first place. In doing so, superhero comics truly do link the popular with the political.

References

Coogan, Peter. "The Definition of the Superhero." *Super/Heroes: From Hercules to Superman*. Ed. Wendy Haslem, Angela Ndalianis, and Chris Mackie. Washington: New Academia 2007. 21-36.

Curtis, Neal. "Superheroes and the contradiction of sovereignty." *Journal of Graphic Novels and Comics* 4.2 (2013): 209-22.

Daniels, Les: *Wonder Woman: The Complete History*. San Francisco: Chronicle Books, 2000.

Davidson, Ryan M. "The Superhuman Registration Act, the Constitution, and the Patient Protection and Affordable Care Act." *Marvel Comics' Civil War and the Age of Terror: Critical Essays on the Comic Saga*. Ed. Kevin Michael Scott. Jefferson: McFarland, 2015. 11-25.

Diekmann, Stefanie. "Hero and Superhero." *The Guardian*. 24 April 2004. <https://www.theguardian.com/culture/2004/apr/24/guesteditors3>. Accessed 30 November 2016.

Ditschke, Stephan and Anjin Anhut. "Menschliches, Übermenschliches. Zur narrativen Struktur von Superheldencomics." *Comics: Zur Geschichte und Theorie eines populärkulturellen Mediums*. Ed. Stephan Ditschke, Katerina Kroucheva, and Daniel Stein. Bielefeld: transcript, 2009. 131-78.

Dittmer, Jason. *Captain America and the Nationalist Superhero: Metaphors, Narratives, and Geopolitics*. Philadelphia: Temple University Press, 2013.

DuBose, Mike S. "Holding Out for a Hero: Reaganism, Comic Book Vigilantes, and Captain America." *The Journal of Popular Culture* 40.6 (2007): 915-35.

Hassler-Forest, Dan A. "From Trauma Victim to Terrorist: Redefining Superheroes in Post-9/11 Hollywood." *Comics as a Nexus of Cultures*. Ed. Mark Berninger, Jochen Ecke, and Guido Haberkorn. Jefferson: McFarland, 2010. 33-44.

Hughes, Jamie A. "'Who Watches the Watchmen?': Ideology and 'Real World' Superheroes." *The Journal of Popular Culture* 39.4 (2006): 546-57.

Jemas, Bill, Mark Bagley, and Scott Hanna. "Moment of Truth." *A Moment of Silence* 1.1 (2002).

Meskin, Aaron. "Defining Comics?" *The Journal of Aesthetics and Art Criticism* 65.4 (2007) 369-79.

Miczo, Nathan. *How Superheroes Model Community: Philosophically, Communicatively, Relationally*. Lanham: Lexington, 2016.

Munson, Todd S. "'Superman Says You Can Slap a Jap!' The Man of Steel and Race Hatred in World War II." *The Ages of Superman: Essays on the Man of Steel in Changing Times*. Ed. Joseph Darowski. Jefferson: McFarland, 2012. 5-15.

Pellitteri, Marco. "Alan Moore, *Watchmen* and Some Notes on the Ideology of Superhero Comics." *Studies in Comics* 2.1 (2011): 81-91.

Scott, Cord. "Written in Red, White, and Blue: A Comparison of Comic Book Propaganda from World War II and September 11." *The Journal of Popular Culture* 40.2 (2007): 325-43.

Scott, Kevin Michael, ed. *Marvel Comics'* Civil War *and the Age of Terror: Critical Essays on the Comic Saga*. Jefferson: McFarland, 2015.

USA PATRIOT ACT. <https://www.gpo.gov/fdsys/pkg/BILLS-107hr3162enr/pdf/BILLS-107hr3162enr.pdf>. Accessed 28 March 2017.

Veloso, Francisco and John Bateman. "The Multimodal Construction of Acceptability: Marvel's Civil War Comic Books and the PATRIOT Act." *Critical Discourse Studies* 10.4 (2013): 427-43.

Notes on Contributors

CHRISTIAN ARNSPERGER is professor for sustainability and economic anthropology at the University of Lausanne. His teaching and research focus on sustainable lifestyles, existential economics, the sociopolitics of transition (including monetary reform), the critique of contemporary economic growth as well as the unsustainable aspects of North American culture and their roots in English and Scottish history. His most recent books are *Money and Sustainability: The Missing Link* (with B. Lietaer, Triarchy Press, 2012) and *Pour une économie permacirculaire* (with D. Bourg, Presses Universitaires de France, 2017).

SOFIE BEHLULI is assistant to Chair of Literatures in English at the University of Bern and will start her PhD thesis at the University of Oxford in September 2017. Her doctoral project focuses on ekphrastic practices in the contemporary US-American novel. Other research interests include intermediality, post-postmodernism, the history of the novel, fiction in the digital age, aura, and issues of originality and reproduction.

DUSTIN BREITENWISCHER is Assistant Professor for American Studies and postdoctoral researcher at the Graduiertenkolleg "Faktuales und fiktionales Erzählen" at Albert-Ludwigs-Universität, Freiburg im Breisgau. His current research project is entitled "The Force Field of Creativity in the Antebellum Culture of Letters." He is the author of the monograph *Dazwischen: Über Wesen und Wirken ästhetischer Erfahrung* (Fink Verlag, forthcoming) and co-editor of *Die neue amerikanische Fernsehserie* (Fink Verlag, 2014).

LUKAS ETTER completed a PhD project (*Auteurgraphy: Distinctiveness of Styles in Alternative Graphic Narratives*) at the University of Bern in 2014. Apart from revising the manuscript for a monograph on style in graphic narratives, Lukas Etter also has an ongoing research project called "*Word*

Problems": Popular and Educational Discourses on School Mathematics in the Antebellum United States (University of Siegen).

ROXANE HUGHES is a PhD candidate at the University of Lausanne specializing in Ethnic American literature. Her research interest includes immigration and diaspora studies, world literatures, short fiction, and cultural studies. Her dissertation thesis focuses on the ambivalent Orientalism of footbinding representations and tropes in Chinese American literature and culture. She is currently working on a side project exploring the use of water imageries in Luso-American literature.

SABIN JEANMAIRE is a PhD student at the English Department of the University of Zurich, working on her project on the Representation and Representability of Trauma in a selection of novels by the Canadian author Timothy Findley. She is a member of the current *Leitungsteam* of the GKS Nachwuchsforum (Young Scholars in Canadian Studies). Her research interests include Canadian literature, metafiction, and psychoanalysis.

AGNIESZKA SOLTYSIK MONNET is Professor of American Literature and Culture at the University of Lausanne, and co-director of the MA Specialization Program in American Studies at Lausanne. She is the author of *The Poetics and Politics of the American Gothic: Gender and Slavery in Nineteenth Century American Literature* (Ashgate, 2010) and the co-editor of several collections of essays, including *The Gothic in Contemporary Literature and Popular Culture* (with Justin Edwards, Routledge, 2012), *War Gothic* (with Steffen Hantke, Routledge, 2016), *Neoliberal Gothic: International Gothic in the Neoliberal Age* (with Linnie Blake, Manchester University Press, 2017), and a special issue of *Gothic Studies* (with Marie Lienard-Yeterian, published by Manchester University Press) on "The Gothic in an Age of Terror(ism)."

PIERRE-HÉLI MONOT is a German Research Foundation Postdoctoral Fellow in Comparative Literature at the Ludwig Maximilian University of Munich. He received his PhD from the Humboldt University of Berlin in 2014 and was a Visiting Fellow at Harvard in 2012-2013. His study of abolitionism and Romantic hermeneutics, entitled *Mensch als Methode:*

Allgemeine Hermeneutik und partielle Demokratie, was published by Winter (Heidelberg) in 2016.

THOMAS NEHRLICH holds a BA and MA in Comparative Literature from Freie Universität Berlin and is currently teaching in the German Department of the University of Bern. In 2015, he was a visiting lecturer at the California State University, Long Beach. His PhD project focuses on rebels in literature after 1945. He is also involved in the critical edition of Alexander von Humboldt's complete essays. His publications include books and articles on E. A. Poe, Heinrich von Kleist as well as the history and theory of superheroes.

JOANNA NOWOTNY holds an MA in German Studies from the University of Bern and is currently a PhD student working on her thesis on *The German-Jewish reception of Sören Kierkegaard* at the Federal Institute of Technology, Zurich (project funded by the Swiss National Science Foundation, SNSF). She studied German language and literature, art history, and philosophy and worked in the art business during her studies. Her academic fields of interest include German-Jewish literature and culture, contemporary German literature, game and comics studies.

A. ELISABETH REICHEL is PhD candidate in Anglophone Literary and Cultural Studies at the University of Basel. Her thesis is entitled "Sounding Primitives, Writing Anthropologists: The Poetry and Scholarship of Edward Sapir, Margaret Mead, and Ruth Benedict." She has published and presented on Sapir, Mead, and Benedict as well as on the functions of music in twentieth-century theory and the novels of Richard Powers.

PHILIPP REISNER teaches as a lecturer at the American Studies Department of Heinrich Heine University, Düsseldorf. His approach to research is multidisciplinary. His dissertation on the theological role that the New English theologian Cotton Mather (1663-1728) played in the context of early modern society appeared in 2012. He is currently working on his habilitation project, which is a structural study of Genesis motifs in contemporary Anglo-American poetry.

PHILIPP SCHWEIGHAUSER is Associate Professor and Head of American and General Literatures at the University of Basel. He is the author of *The Noises of American Literature, 1890-1985: Toward a History of Literary Acoustics* (University Press of Florida, 2006) and *Beautiful Deceptions: European Aesthetics, the Early American Novel, and Illusionist Art* (University of Virginia Press, 2016).

JULIA STRAUB is a senior lecturer in North American Literature at the University of Bern. She is the author of *A Victorian Muse: The Afterlife of Dante's Beatrice in Nineteenth-Century Literature* (Continuum, 2009) and *The Rise of New Media, 1750-1850: Transatlantic Discourse and American Memory* (Palgrave Macmillan, 2017) and editor of the *Handbook of Transatlantic North American Studies* (De Gruyter, 2016).

EVA-SABINE ZEHELEIN is currently Adjunct Professor of American Studies at Goethe University, Frankfurt and a 2017/18 Visiting Research Associate at the Women's Studies Research Center, Brandeis University (supported by the Fritz Thyssen Stiftung). She has published broadly in North American literatures and popular cultures, mostly of the twentieth and twenty-first century, with monographs on John Updike and science-in-theater as well as articles e.g. on Joan Didion, Johnny Cash, Alison Bechdel, Starbucks, and 55+ communities.

Index of Names

Aberley, Doug, 151n2, 156, 160n3
Adams, Neal, 230
Adjmi, David, 16, 188, 190-200
Ahmed, Sara, 2
Alexander, Christopher, 150
Anderson, Benedict, 12
Anderson, Sherwood, 66
Anhut, Anjin, 226
Aristotle, 86, 98
Aronoff, Eric, 75
Arsić, Branka, 112, 116
Austin, Mary, 65
Atwood, Margaret, 212
Balibar, Étienne, 46
Barbeau, Marius, 61, 63, 64n5, 68-71, 76-77
Barthes, Roland, 48, 212
Bataille, George, 46
Bateman, John, 235, 236
Bauman, Zygmunt, 28, 33
Bhabha, Homi, 12
Beckett, Samuel, 45
Bellah, Robert N., 24
Benedict, Ruth Fulton, 62n1, 64, 65n6
Bercovitch, Sacvan, 108n7
Berg, Peter, 146, 152, 156
Berry, Thomas, 154, 157, 158
Birkle, Carmen, 49
Blanchot, Maurice, 46
Blechmann, Andrew, 32
Böger, Astrid, 52
Bouchard, Larry D., 194

Bourne, Randolph, 67
Boxall, Peter, 46, 47n5
Bradbury, Ray, 215
Brisbane, Albert, 129
Brooks, Neil, 46
Bruck, Peter, 189
Brydon, Diana, 215, 220
Bullins, Ed, 189
Butler, Judith, 50
Byatt, A. S., 48
Cabet, Etienne, 128
Callenbach, Ernest, 160
Carlyle, Thomas, 106
Carson, Rachel, 135
Cavell, Stanley, 105n3, 107n5, 111
Channing, William Ellery, 95
Claviez, Thomas, 45
Conrad, Joseph, 205-08, 212, 219, 220
Coogan, Peter, 226
Crane, Stephen, 66
Croce, Benedetto, 72-75
Cronyn, George W., 66
Daly, Mary, 214n7
Dasmann, Raymond, 152-55, 159
Davis, Rocío, 170
Dawson, Jonathan, 124
De Andrade Tosta, Antonio Luciano, 171
De Saint-Simon, Henri, 128
Derrida, Jacques, 45, 56, 96, 96n14

Dewey, John, 112n18
Didion, Joan, 152
Ditschke, Stephan, 226
Dittmer, Jason, 224n1, 237
Dunbar, Paul Laurence, 66
Dunn, Maggie, 168n3
Durkheim, Emile, 65n7, 140
Eisenhower, Dwight, 134
Eitzen, D. Stanley, 29
Eliot, T. S., 62, 70
Ellison, Julie, 115n22
Emerson, Ralph Waldo, 14, 15, 85, 88, 90n7, 91-96, 103-19
Engberg, Maria, 47n7
Esposito, Roberto, 141
Eugenides, Jeffrey, 48
Figal, Günter, 110n12, 117n25
Findley, Timothy, 16, 205-19
Fish, Stanley, 213
Fitzgerald, F. Scott, 217
Fjellestad, Danuta, 47n7
Foucault, Michel, 209n3, 211, 213
Fourier, Charles, 106n4, 128, 130
Franzen, Jonathan, 48
Friedl, Herwig, 104n1, 105n3, 111
Frost, Robert, 62
Gadamer, Hans-Georg, 96, 110n11, 112n18
Gardley, Marcus, 16, 188, 194, 195, 198-200
Geis, Deborah R., 197
Genette, Gérard, 217
Ginsberg, Allen, 133
Gordon, Frank S., 65
Gottlieb, Lou, 135
Handler, Richard, 65n6
Harper, Stephen, 216n8
Harris, Joel Chandler, 66

Harte, Bret, 66
Hassan, Ihab, 46, 56
Haugeland, John, 109n10
Hawthorne, Nathaniel, 105n4, 130, 141
Hay, John, 66
Haynes, Rob, 230
Heidegger, Martin, 107n5, 109, 109n8, n10
Heine, Heinrich, 74-77
Hemingway, Ernest, 21
Henderson, Alice Corbin, 65, 67, 77
Herder, Johann Gottfried, 14, 85, 92-94
Herman, Judith, 210
Herz, Henriette, 89
Hickman, Larry A., 46n3
Huber, Irmtraud, 45
Hustvedt, Siri, 13, 14, 43-57
Hutcheon, Linda, 45
Huyssen, Andreas, 21
Ingram, Forrest L., 167, 168
Iser, Wolfgang, 110n14
Jackson, Wes, 156
Jacobs, Jane, 29
Jameson, Frederic, 46
Jemas, Bill, 231
Joseph, Miranda, 12, 131, 132, 141
Junger, Sebastian, 148, 149
Kant, Immanuel, 85, 91, 110n11
Kateb, George, 105, 113
Keen, Suzanne, 206n1
Kelleter, Frank, 12
Kennedy, David, 51
Kerouac, Jack, 133
Kirmayer, Laurence J., 211, 218
Lee, Ann, 125-127

Index of Names

Lee, Young Jean, 16, 188, 190, 195-200
Letourneau, Joey, 166
Leypoldt, Günter, 188
Lindsay, Vachel, 66
Locke, John, 26
Lowell, Amy, 62, 63
Lowell, James Russell, 66
Luhmann, Niklas, 144n19
Lundén, Rolf, 168
Lundin, Roger, 89
Luscher, Robert, 168n3
Lyotard, Jean-François, 48
Lysaker, John, 113
Marks, Christine, 52
Marsh, James, 93, 94
Marx, Karl, 65n7, 71, 86
McKenzie, Evan, 26
McNeill, William H., 126
McNiven, Steve, 232
Merleau-Ponty, Maurice, 52
Miczo, Nathan, 225, 234n22, 235n25, 238n28
Millar, Mark, 223, 232, 234n20, 235
Miller, Frank, 223-228
Miller, Timothy, 124, 134-36
Milner, Jean-Claude, 86
Mitchell, David, 48
Monroe, Harriet, 65, 66, 77, 78
Moore, Alan, 223, 227-30
Morris, Ann R., 168n3
Morrison, Toni, 210 n4
Moser, Robert Henry, 171
Nabokov, Vladimir, 212n5
Nancy, Jean-Luc, 14, 46, 85, 97-99
Newfield, Christopher, 113
Nietzsche, Friedrich, 56, 109n8
Nixon, Rob, 147
Nolan, Christopher, 226

Noyes, John Humphrey, 126
Ostwalt, Conrad Jr., 188
Owen, David, 29
Owen, Robert, 128
Page, Jake, 149
Page, Susanne, 149
Patea, Viorica, 168
Picasso, Pablo, 67
Plater-Zyberk, Elizabeth, 29
Posnock, Ross, 105n3, 111, 118
Pound, Ezra, 61, 62
Reagan, Ronald, 228
Renan, Ernest, 95, 96, 96n13
Ripley, George, 105n4, 130, 131
Rippl, Gabriele, 51, 62n1
Rohan, Ethel, 172, 181
Rosenthal, Caroline, 48
Sandburg, Carl, 66
Sapir, Edward, 14, 61, 78
Schirmeister, Pamela, 107, 108
Schlegel, Friedrich, 88, 89, 97
Schleiermacher, Friedrich, 87, 88, 91, 95, 96
Shakespeare, William, 74, 77
Shelley, Mary, 216
Simpson, David, 156
Skinner, Constance Lindsay, 65
Sousa, Brian, 15, 165-75, 179, 182
Spingarn, Joel, 75
Spivak, Gayatri Chakravorty, 12
Stevens, Wallace, 62
Snyder, Gary, 146, 148, 150, 153, 190
Thiemann, Anna, 49n8
Thomashow, Mitchell, 156
Tiebout, Charles, 27
Timmer, Nicoline, 43, 46-49, 51, 55, 56
Tocqueville, Alexis de, 87, 88
Trombly, Albert Edmund, 64

Tzara, Tristan, 67
Udvardy, Miklos, 155
Uhl, Christopher, 156
Veit, Dorothea, 89
Veloso, Franciso, 235, 236
Voelz, Johannes, 105n2, 108, 110, 115n20
Von Hayek, Friedrich, 150, 151
Webb, Del, 30
Wertham, Fredric, 227
Whorf, Benjamin Lee, 71
Williams, William Carlos, 62
Winthrop, John, 125